I0024239

Felix Fontaine

The Golden Wheel Dream-Book and Fortune-Teller

Being the most complete work on fortune-telling and interpreting dreams ever

printed, containing an alphabetical list of dreams, with their interpretation, and the

lucky numbers they signify

Felix Fontaine

The Golden Wheel Dream-Book and Fortune-Teller
*Being the most complete work on fortune-telling and interpreting dreams ever printed,
containing an alphabetical list of dreams, with their interpretation, and the lucky numbers
they signify*

ISBN/EAN: 9783337370626

Printed in Europe, USA, Canada, Australia, Japan

Cover: Foto ©Thomas Meinert / pixelio.de

More available books at **www.hansebooks.com**

THE

GOLDEN WHEEL DREAM-BOOK,

AND

FORTUNE-TELLER,

BEING THE MOST COMPLETE WORK ON FORTUNE-TELLING AND INTERPRETING DREAMS
EVER PRINTED, CONTAINING AN

ALPHABETICAL LIST OF DREAMS, WITH THEIR INTERPRETATION,

AND THE LUCKY NUMBERS THEY SIGNIFY.

ALSO EXPLAINING HOW TO TELL FORTUNES BY THE MYSTERIOUS GOLDEN WHEEL,
WITH CARDS, DICE, AND DOMINOES. HOW TO TELL FUTURE EVENTS BY
THE LINES OF THE HANDS, BY MOLES ON THE BODY, BY THE FACE,
NAILS OF THE FINGERS, HAIR AND SHAPE OF THE HEAD.
HOW TO FIND WHERE TO DIG FOR WATER, COAL,
AND ALL KINDS OF METALS, BY MEANS OF

THE CELEBRATED DIVINING OR LUCK ROD.

HOW TO TELL THE TEMPER AND DISPOSITION OF ANYBODY, HOW TO TELL FORTUNES
WITH TEA LEAVES AND COFFEE GROUNDS, SIGNS OF THE MOON'S AGE, LUCKY
AND UNLUCKY DAYS, TOGETHER WITH CHARMS TO MAKE YOUR
SWEETHEART LOVE YOU, AND TO MAKE A LOVER POP THE
QUESTION, WITH TWENTY WAYS OF TELLING FOR-
TUNES ON NEW YEAR'S EVE, AND A COM-
PLETE LANGUAGE AND SIGNIFI-
CATION OF THE FLOWERS.

BY FELIX FONTAINE,

Professor of Astrology, and Lecturer on Astronomy and Spiritual Philosophy.

ILLUSTRATED WITH NUMEROUS ENGRAVINGS.

NEW YORK:
DICK & FITZGERALD, PUBLISHERS,
18 ANN STREET.

CONTENTS.

	PAGE.		PAGE.
Bride's Omen	129	Means to compel Love	123
Bridge Omen	132	Moles, Telling Fortunes by	114
Candle Spell	132	Nail Token	133
" Token	129	New Moon	126
Card Charm	127	New Year's Eve, How to tell For-	
Cards, Fortune-telling with	94	tunes on	13,
Cat Portent	126	Nutshell Witchery	132
Charm against Nightmare	130		
Charms and Magic Prognostications	124	Omen of Riches	128
Cricket	128		
Crow Sign	129	Palmistry	109
		Phrenology and Physiognomy	111
Death-tick	128		
Dice, How to find Lucky Numbers		Rabbit Augury	130
with	92	Rye Charm	130
Dice, How to tell Fortunes with	106		
Dominoes, How to tell Fortunes		Saucer Charm	131
with	101	Scissor or Knife Prognostic	126
Dreams, about the Interpretation		Sheep and Swine Token	130
of	7	Shift Charm	93
Dreams, Alphabetical List of	10–92	Signs from the Moon's age	137
" What are	7	Sign of a Sneeze	123
		Sign of Visitors	126
Easter-water	130	Sign when your Ear tingles	128
		" " " Nose itches	128
Finger-nails, Signification of the	120	" " you wet your Apron	133
Frog Prognostic	129	Spider Omen	127
		Star Augury	129
Golden Wheel, How to tell For-		Strange Bed	128
tunes by the	3	Straw Sign	126
Golden Wheel of Fortune, The	3	String Token	128
Hair Spell	133	Table to find Lucky Numbers	9
Hair, To choose a Husband by the	119	Tea or Coffee-Grounds, Fortune-tel-	
Hand, Telling Fortunes by the		ling by	121
Lines of the	109	Telling Fortunes by Dominoes and	
How a Girl may ascertain if she will		Dice	100
ever marry	125	The Divining-rod, to tell where to	
How to be sure of a Partner at a		dig for Water and Metals	134
Dance	129	Thirty Physiological Significations	142
How to discover if your Wish will		To find out whom one is to have for	
be Fulfilled	100	a Husband	99
How to get a Sweetheart	130	To know if a Woman with Child	
How to tell the first letter of your		will have a Girl or a Boy	129
future Wife's or Husband's name	131	To know the Temper and Disposi-	
Key and Book Charm	126	tion of every one	135
		To prepare a Love Potion	124
Language of Flowers	139	What a Prick in the Finger signi-	
Lead and Wax Spell	131	fies	130
Lucky and Unlucky Days	133	What a Spider-web foretells	130

Entered according to Act of Congress, in the year 1862,

BY DICK & FITZGERALD,

In the Clerk's Office of the District Court of the United States for the Southern District of New York.

FONTAINE'S

GOLDEN WHEEL DREAM-BOOK,

AND

FORTUNE-TELLER.

THE GOLDEN WHEEL OF FORTUNE.

THIS singular wheel was much consulted in the middle ages, and is said to have been used by Cagliostro to aid him in his divinations. I have selected it from an old Latin manuscript on Astrology, and translated it into English for the benefit of those of my readers who cannot read the former language. SEE FRONTISPIECE.

THE GOLDEN WHEEL OF FORTUNE SHOWS:

    I. *Whether you shall obtain the favor of the person you desire?*
    II. *If the querent shall meet with the preferment he wisheth for?*
    III. *Whether a sick person will recover?*
    IV. *If the said sickness will be long or short?*
    V. *Shall your expectation or wish succeed?*
    VI. *If it is good for you to marry, or otherwise?*
    VII. *Whether the friendship of a certain person will prove advantageous or not?*
    VIII. *Whether a person shall be rich or poor? etc., etc.*

HOW TO TELL FORTUNES BY THE GOLDEN WHEEL.

The person whose fortune is to be told, must place the wheel of Fortune face downward, prick into a number (it is better to do it with their eyes shut), then refer for an explanation, which stands at the corresponding number as that you pricked into. (See Frontispiece.)

The following observations answer for either sex, the party, therefore, trying this wheel, must alter wife for husband, or just as the answers may suit either party.

1. If this number is fixed upon, it assures the person that you will marry an homely person, but rich.

2. Whatever your intentions are, for the present, decline them. Those absent will return.

3. Shows loss of friends; bad success at law; loss of money; unfaithfulness in love.

4. If your desires are extravagant, they will not be granted; but mind how you make use of your fortune.

5. Very good fortune; sudden prosperity ; great respect from high personages ; a letter bringing important news.

6. Look well to those who owe you money, if ever so little, a letter of abuse may be expected.

7. Your lover will act constant and true toward you.

8. A friend has crossed the sea, and will bring home riches, by which you will be much benefited.

9. A loving partner; success in your undertakings; a large and prosperous family.

10. Your husband will not have a great fortune, but with your assistance he is likely to live in middling circumstances.

11. A very sudden journey, with a pleasant fellow-traveller, and the result of the journey will be generally beneficial to your family.

12. You may regain that which you have lost with great perseverance and trouble.

13. A letter of importance will arrive, announcing the death of a relative for whom you have no very great respect, but who has left you a legacy.

14. By venturing carefully, you will gain doubly, though you will suffer great privation.

15. You will meet with many crosses before you are comfortably settled.

16. Too sudden acquaintance with the opposite sex; but which will be opposed; notwithstanding the party should persevere, as it will be to his or her advantage.

17. An agreeable partner, a good temper, and a large family of children.

18. Let the chooser of this number persevere; for your schemes are good, and must succeed.

19. You will marry young, and have dutiful children.

20. Your lover may be low in circumstances, but affectionate.

21. Your marriage will add to your welfare, and you will be very happy.

22. A drunken partner, bad success in trade, but the party will never be very poor, though always unhappy.

23. Do not neglect your lover; let your conduct command respect.

24. You have many friends, and will probably have a large and virtuous family.

25. Your travels will be prosperous, if you are prudent.

26. You have many enemies, who will endeavor to make you unhappy.

27. The luck that is ordained for you, will be coveted by others.

28. Be very prudent in your conduct, as this number is very precarious, and much depends upon yourself; it is generally good.

29. Beware, or you will be deceived by the person you are paying your attentions to.

30. You love one who is affectionate and true, and deserves respect.

31. You too fantastically refuse offers. Be prudent when you accept, or you will be sorry.

32. You will be very unfortunate for a short time, but be careful, and your situation will very soon alter.

33. A fortune will be yours, but be not over anxious.

34. Alter you intentions, or you will be sorry when it is too late.

35. You will have a rich, but jealous partner, and will live very uncomfortably.

36. You will have a sober, steady, and affectionate partner, but poor.

37. A very good fortune, sudden prosperity, and a large family.

38. The persons who choose this unlucky number, must look well to their conduct; or justice will overtake them.

39. Remain among your friends, then you will escape misfortune.

40. You will have an affectionate partner, but no family; and a large fortune.

41. If you have a fortune, be charitable; if but little, be frugal.

42. You will have a quarrel with your lover, through jealousy.

43. You must bear your losses with fortitude.

44. You will get a handsome, young, and wealthy partner.

45. When your conduct changes, your fortune will mend, by marrying a rich partner.

46. You have mixed with bad company, and you may depend on it, that you will be brought to disgrace.

47. A large family of healthy children, give them learning, and they will honor their father and mother.

48. You will be very unfortunate at first, but persevere, and your schemes will be successful.

49. You have a number of secret enemies, who will try to do you an injury; be on your guard and you will prosper.

50. Your happiness will consist in doing good: they are pleasing spots in the memory, which vexations cannot erase.

51. You will die an old maid, you have been too whimsical in choosing for yourself a partner.

52. Your lover will travel in Europe, and will be very successful.

53. You will marry a person with whom you will have but little comfort.

54. This is a very lucky number; whatever you do, will always prove successful.

55. After much misfortune, you will be pretty comfortable and happy.

56. Good conduct will produce much luck and happiness.

57. Through affection you will marry unfortunately; but you must make one another happy.

58. You have many lovers, but mind how you choose, or else you will suffer for it.

59. Your lover is on his return home, but he has met with severe losses.

60. A letter announcing the loss of money.

61. You have a secret enemy, mind or he will do you some harm.

62. Warns you against the evil consequences of idleness, either in yourself or partner.

63. Your partner will be very rich, but very neglectful.

64. You will be very poor and miserable, with one child.

65. Sincere love from an upright heart will be rewarded.

66. You will marry an old person with whom you will be very unhappy.

67. Plenty of offers will happen before one is worthy of acceptance, be cautious how you make your choice.

68. You will play with the mouse till you lose it.

69. Take heed, you are being deceived by your lover.

70. You will meet with great trouble, you should have consulted your friends.

71. Beware, the person you love, does not love you, he seeks your ruin.

72. If you marry in haste, you will be deceived, wait patiently, and you will be happy.

73. Hard work, hard fare, little joy, and much care.

74. A scolding wife, but rich.

75. Your partner will be very rich, but will have no children.

76. You have a rival, be not deceived; depend on our tablets, and you will better your condition.

77. You will have many children, but will be very poor.

78. Do not delay, hasten your marriage, or you will lose your virtue.

79. Your wife will have no children, and will be addicted to drinking liquors.

80. Be honest and industrious, and you will triumph over your enemies.

81. You will have children, who, if you give them a good education, will make you happy.

82. You will fall into great difficulties, you will lose your partner, and marry a drunkard.

83. Hasten your marriage; the person is faithful, and you will be happy.

84. You must break off the connection you have formed, or you will come to absolute want.

85. Your lover is jealous of you, and will break off the connection.

86. You will travel in Europe, and be married there, but will have no children.

87. You will get married, but not till you begin to get old.

88. Beware, you have a secret enemy who will try and do you some injury.

89. You will die an old maid.

90. You will marry three different times, and still be very poor and miserable.

91. The person you are paying your attentions to, is deceitful.

92. If you marry, you will have great trouble, and many children; be persuaded, and live single, then you will be happy.

93. You will live to a great age and be happy.

94. There is a young man dying in love for you, but mind you are not led astray.

95. You will marry poor, but in the end be rich.

96. You are too whimsical and deceitful ever to be happy.

97. Be not flattered, for you have an amorous sweetheart.

98. A shocking accident will happen to you, or to your children, which will cause great trouble.

99. You will discover your false lover.

100. You will have a very handsome, but artful partner.

WHAT ARE DREAMS?

I OFFER you in this work, my dear reader, all that can be collected in reference to dreams. Notwithstanding the proverbial saying, " All dreams are lies," we frequently see the realization of them, and by them we are informed of more or less interesting events which afterward happen to us. A prudent and enlightened man will therefore examine carefully his dreams to know which he ought to interpret, neglecting those which are extravagant because of too exalted an imagination or of a disturbed digestion.

In consulting this book with attention, in seeking in it for the explanation of your dreams, and calculating the causes which have produced them, you will rarely depart from the truth, because you will be following the rules of a wise combination, which will prevent you from falling into an illusory if not fatal error.

FOREKNOWLEDGE, OR INTERPRETATION OF DREAMS.

In the Holy Scriptures God says, that he " will pour his Spirit on all flesh, that the young men and maidens shall prophesy, the old men shall see visions, and the young men dream dreams." Both sacred and profane history are full of so many examples of the fulfilment of dreams, that he must be very skeptical and but little versed in natural science who would refuse to have faith in them.

Hippocrates says that when the body is asleep the soul is awake, and transports itself everywhere, where the body would be able to go, that it knows and sees all that the body could know or see were it awake; that it touches all the body could touch, in a word, that it performs all the actions that the body of a sleeping man could do were he awake.

There are five kinds of dreams, differently named according to their different qualities. The first is dream, the second vision, the third oracle, the fourth revery, and the fifth apparition.

A dream is that which, while we are asleep, shows us the truth hidden under certain figures, as when Joseph interpreted to king Pharaoh the dream concerning the seven lean kine that devoured the seven fat ones; the dream of the seven full ears of corn, etc.

A vision is simply a dream happening when the body is awake instead of sleeping, as Vespasian when he saw the surgeon who had extracted Nero's tooth.

The oracle is a revelation, or information given us by some angel or other celestial spirit who does God's bidding. The angel appearing to Joseph the husband of the Virgin, and to the wise men, are examples of this.

Revery occurs when the passions are so vehement that they destroy the mental equilibrium for a time. Then what one thinks of during the day he will dream of at night, as a lover who has been thinking during the day of his beloved one will continue to do so at night while he is sleeping. Sometimes when one fears to meet a person, he will dream at night that he has met him; having fasted during the day, he will dream of eating, or, having been thirsty, of drinking. Avarice will make the miser dream of his gold, and speak of it when sleeping, as he would not do when awake.

Apparition is named Phantom by the Greeks, and is only that nocturnal vision sometimes presented to children and weak-minded persons, who imagine they see objects presented to intimidate or pain them.

Of these five kinds of dreams, the three first have an appearance of truth, but the last two are absolutely false.

It is to be remarked, with regard to all dreams, that those of which only parts are remembered, signify nothing at all; that those that memory retains are good and true; that they ought to occur about day-break, or at least after midnight, because until that time the senses and the body are occupied in the labor of digestion, and the mind disturbed by the remembrance of dinner, can dream of nothing reasonable. Nevertheless Artemidorus says, that a sober, temperate, and tranquil man can dream at any hour of the night, or even during the day, and that the fulfilment of such dreams will be certain.

Some authors divide dreams into three kinds, namely, dreams of natural objects, of animals, and of celestial objects. The natural things are those by which physicians judge of the temperament; dreams of animals show the passions and cares that the mind has felt during the day; those of celestial objects are the intimations of divine things, as for example, the statue that the king of Babylon saw when asleep, which is so well explained by the prophet Daniel.

There are few persons who have the gift of dreaming that which will be fulfilled, fewer still who know how to interpret them, because it is necessary to observe many things not generally known.

There are two principal kinds of dreams, the speculative or contemplative, and the allegorical or significative. To these one ought to pay attention, the speculative happening in the fulfilment as it occurred in dreams, for example: A prisoner in a small prison at Paris dreamed that a cord was being attached to his neck to hang him, that after it was done a stranger appeared with a sword who severed the cord and delivered him from death; this was fulfilled the next day, for the judge having pronounced his sentence, and given him to the hangman. he was delivered by unknown persons employed by his friends. Allegorical dreams on the contrary never happen as one has dreamed. Thus, to dream of an angel, signifies revelation or good news, but to see a serpent which tries to bite one signifies troubles arising from the envy of others.

Speculative dreams are soon fulfilled, allegorical ones not so quickly; a day or two often intervening between the dream and its completion.

ABOUT THE INTERPRETATION OF DREAMS.

"Dreams? Nonsense!" I hear some grave-faced person cry. Indeed! And where did this grave-faced person learn his wisdom? Not from experience, I will engage. No, experience teaches us the reverse of this. Dreams are *by no means* nonsense. This I maintain openly in the face of all the world.

I maintain even that *every dream has its signification*. Not that it always discloses the future, I am far from asserting that. I say only it *has its signification*. Commonly a dream permits us to cast a glance into the soul or into the heart of man. The thoughts which dwell in the former, and the feelings which sway the latter, shape themselves in sleep into various images, which throw a strong light upon the character. There have no doubt been many extravagant fictions palmed off as facts relative to dreams, but yet enough credible evidence exists of their importance to make any strange dream the subject of reflection and examination on the part of the dreamer; and it cannot be denied that many things in our dreams are actually ominous,

A List of Dreams, with their True Interpretation, together with the Lucky Numbers of the Lottery which they signify.

ABOVE. To dream you see any thing hanging *above* you signifies you will improve in your worldly prospects, and soon be in a better situation than you were before you had the dream.   76, 62, 14.

ABSENCE. To dream of absent persons, signifies that they will soon return.   It also denotes success in business.   4, 22.

ABSCESS. If you dream you have an abscess, or running sore on your person, it fortells good fortune and good health, to be preceded by sickness.   3, 27.

ABUSE. To dream that you are abused and insulted, is a sign that some dispute will happen between you and some person with whom you have business; if you are in love, be assured that some one has attempted to injure you with the object of your affections, and that they have in a great measure succeeded.   6, 38, 44.

ABUNDANCE. If you dream you have an over-abundance of any thing, it goes by contrary, and is a sign of a scarcity; as if a farmer should dream that he had a great crop, it would predict a scarcity— not perhaps of that particular article of which he dreamed, but of something that would be important to him.   15.

ABYSS. To see an abyss, or deep hole, is a warning; avoid, after such a dream, taking a journey by land, or a voyage by sea, for eight-and forty hours, because it forebodes accidents by travelling. 62, 19.

ACCIDENT. To dream that an accident has happened to you, or to any one of your household, or with whom you live, foretells that you will see some one whom you little expect to see.   72, 3, 11.

ACCOUNTS. Dreams that relate to making up accounts are good omens.   If you dream you found an error in your money account, it foretells that you will have a piece of good luck.   Accounts blotted with ink is a sign of sickness.   14.

ACCUSE. To dream a person accuses you of any thing, is favorable to the dreamer.   66, 4.

ACORN. (*See Oak.*) To dream you see swine eating acorns denotes that you will have reverses in business, and lose if you are not very careful; to dream of picking acorns signifies that a rich relative will leave you a fortune.   65.

ACQUAINTANCE. To dream you quarrel or fight with an acquaintance, forbodes divisions in your own family; in love, unfaithfulness; and losses in business.   42, 6.

ACTRESS. If you dream you love her, it is a sign you will meet with adversities.   If you dream you see her on the stage you will be successful in all your undertakings.   68, 5, 18.

ADDER. To dream of this reptile is a sign that some one whom you think friendly to you will injure you in some way.   19, 2.

ADULTERY. It is in most cases a bad omen to dream that you have perpetrated this act.   If the person you dreamed about is married, or is a prostitute, you may almost be sure that some misfortune will overtake you. If she is a virgin, it merely predicts that you will shortly have an invitation to a wedding. For a married woman to dream of adultery is a sign she will soon conceive and have a girl. To an unmarried woman such a dream is a sign of misfortune. 51, 7, 3.

AGUE. To dream that you have one, warns you against an inclination to strong drink; to dream your sweetheart has an ague, denotes affection and happiness. 39, 6, 1.

AIR. To dream that you see it clear and serene, shows that you shall be beloved and esteemed by most people; if at law, success. In short, all good is denoted by clear and serene air. But to dream that the air is thick, cloudy, dark, and troubled, denotes to the dreamer, grief, sickness, loss of good, hindrance of business, and crosses in love. 12, 9.

ALMONDS. Signify riches and happiness; to eat them shows you will have good luck in love matters. 73, 18, 10.

ALLIGATOR. (*See Reptile.*)

ALMS. To dream they are begged of you, and you refuse them, shows want and misery to the dreamer; but to dream you give them freely, is a sign of joy and long life. 11, 13, 4.

ALTAR. To dream of an altar, betokens gladness, and affection in love. Of an *Ark*, the same. 71, 63, 4.

ANCHOR. To dream you see one, signifies unexpected success in love; but in business, it shows the success to be distant, and only obtainable with care. 47, 36.

ANGEL. To dream you see angels in your sleep, is a sign some are near you, and that the rest of your dream will come to pass. To see many angels, is a sign of many children, and much prosperity. 16, 8, 24.

ANGER. (*See Rage.*) To dream that you have been provoked to anger, shows that you have powerful enemies; and warns you to be careful that all you do should be strictly honorable; but it also signifies you will hear good news, and be in a good humor. 44, 16.

ANGLING. (*See Fish.*)

ANTS. To dream of ants, is unlucky; and to dream too often of them, shows the dreamer not to be long lived. 7, 49, 20.

APES. (*See Monkey.*) To dream you have seen or had any thing to do with them, signifies malicious, though secret enemies; and warns you against carrying on law-suits. 17, 6.

APPARITION. To dream you see an apparition or spirit, clothed in white, signifies deceit, temptation to sin, and disappointment in love. 57.

The following is an old prediction in verse:

To dream of seeing strange apparitions,
As devils, hobgoblins, and such visions,
Does show thy love, or thy sweetheart,
Hath a fair face, but devil's heart.

APPAREL. (*See Silks and Stain.*) To dream that your clothes are

good, denotes prosperity and happiness; of white apparel, is good
only for clergymen; to others it is a sign of trouble; to mechanics,
decline of business; to the sick, death. If of black, however, it is of
their recovery; of rich scarlet apparel, is good for rich men, signify-
ing honor; but is death to the sick, and loss or captivity to the poor;
to dream of women's apparel, is good for the unmarried; but to a
married man loss of his wife or sickness. 17, 20.

APPLES, or APPLE-TREES. (*See Orchard.*) If sweet, denote joy
and pleasure, especially to women and maids. Sour apples signify
contention and sedition. 4, 11, 44.

APRICOTS. Content, health, and pleasure, if in season; if otherwise, vain hopes, bad fortune. 22, 5, 64.

ARMS. To dream your arms are withered or lean, denotes affliction, sickness and poverty; and if a woman, she is in danger of being
a widow. If any person dream his arms are hairy it denotes increase
of riches. 7.

ARMED MEN. (*See Zouave.*)

ASHES. Great misfortune is at hand; to a lover or sweetheart,
such a dream forebodes that he or she will be jealous because of seeing some one in company with their intended. 70.

ASP. To dream of the asp or adder, is a sign of designing enemies;
but it is good, if they do not bite you. 17, 4.

ASS. To dream you hear an ass bray, shows you will meet with
some loss; to see an ass run, signifies misfortune. 62, 18, 20.

ATTORNEYS. (*See Lawyer.*) To dream you are speaking with
them, shows hindrance of business, and that it requires much circumspection to insure success in your affairs. It also denotes loss of
property. 16.

AWAKING. To dream you awake yourself is a happy end to all
sorrow. To awake another is a sign you will inspire with love the
one you wish. 61, 4.

BACK. To dream that your back is broken, hurt, or scabby, shows
that your enemies will get the better of you. To dream of the back-
bone, signifies health and much joy. To see your back denotes misfortune. 2, 19, 42.

BACKGAMMON. (*See Dice.*)

BACON. To dream of bacon or pork, denotes the death of some
friend or relation, and that enemies will endeavor to do you a mischief; in love, it denotes a disappointment of some kind. 74.

BAGPIPES. To dream of bagpipes, signifies trouble, contention,
and loss of a lawsuit. 20, 1.

BAKING. (*See Oven.*) For a woman to dream she is baking bread,
foretells thrift. If she is a farmer's wife, it is a sign of good crops.
If she burns her bread it is a sign that she will have a miscarriage.
18, 54.

BALL. (*See Dancing.*) If you dream you are at a ball, and are
dancing with a lady, it is a sign you will marry her; if you dream
that she is gone, and you are looking round to find her and cannot, it foretells that she will not live long after marriage. Dream-

ing of playing ball, or seeing it played, foretells the speedy receipt of money; to see the ball roll about, signifies delay in its reception. 54, 11, 55.

BALLOON. Signifies you will undertake many visionary things in business, and success will not attend you. 46.

BANANA. To dream of this delicious fruit is a good omen; if you dream you are eating a banana, it is a sign you will be rich and happy. To dream you see bananas growing denotes success in love matters. If a girl dreams that her lover presents her with a ripe banana it foretells she will soon be married, or ought to be. 4, 11, 44.

BANK. If you dream you go to a large bank, and have money there, it is a sign that you will be poor at some future period of your life. 5, 78.

BANK-BILLS. (See Money.)

BANKRUPT. A bad dream, your business is in a dangerous position, and without great care you will be forced to stop. 17, 60, 46.

BARBER. To dream of a barber, denotes losses. 55.

BARN. If you dream that you are in a barn that is well stored with hay and grain, it predicts that you will marry rich, or else inherit land. If the barn be empty, it will be the reverse of this, or else you will meet with a loss. 4, 75.

BARKING DOGS. Is a sign you have enemies who will detract, and insult you. 17, 61

BARRELS. Signify wealth if they appear full; if empty, poverty. 14, 1, 7.

BASIN. If you dream that it is full r oney; if empty, you will make many debts. 2, 13, 69.

BATH, or BATHING. To dream you are at a bath where you see people bathing, is a sign you will have good luck in some undertaking. If you are in, bathing yourself, it predicts that you will confer a benefit on some person who will be very grateful. This dream also foretells a change of residence. 20, 31.

BAT. To dream of a bat, or bats, is a sign you will go on a bootless journey, or one that is not satisfactory. 42.

BATTLE. If you dream you are engaged in a battle, or see a battle, it is a sign that you will soon undertake some new enterprise, and will leave off the business or calling in which you are then engaged; it also predicts to a girl that she will meet a young man in whom she is much interested; to a soldier it foretells that he will be advanced in rank. 14.

BAYONET. To dream of a bayonet indicates that you have vindictive enemies. 64, 7.

BEAM. This signifies you will attain a high position in life. 9.

BEANS. To dream of eating beans is a sign of trouble. If you are picking beans, it denotes poverty. 72, 18, 11.

BEAR. To dream of seeing a bear, or bears, is a sign you have one or more enemies; if a bear attacks you, it predicts that you will overcome your enemy. 68.

BEARD. To dream you have a very little beard, signifies suits at law; if it is a long thick beard, the dream is a good one, for it shows success; for a person to dream of his beard falling out, he will lose some near relative, or will come to disgrace. 47, 3.

BEATING. For married people to dream of beating some one, shows that they will live a peaceful life; to bachelors, good fortune in their amours; if a lover beats his mistress, or a lady her suitor, it shows that the match will be broken off. 5.

BED. To dream that you are lying in bed, signifies that you are in danger; being in bed and not able to sleep, sickness; to see a stranger in your bed, brings quarrels in married life; a well-made bed, shows that you will become established in life. 63, 9.

BED-BUGS. Denote strife, and quarrels. 2, 10.

BEER. To dream you are drinking beer, is a sure sign of domestic troubles. 6, 8.

BEES. (*See Sting.*) It is good and lucky to dream of bees; to a farmer it predicts good crops; to a lover, excellent success with his sweetheart; to a maid it promises a good and wealthy husband. 17, 62, 4.

BEGGARS. To dream that a beggar annoys you, is a sign of misfortune, or some piece of bad luck. To a young girl who has a suitor, it predicts that if she marries him she will be poor. 26.

BEHEADING. To dream that you see a person that is going to be beheaded, or if you see one beheaded, it is an excellent sign; in love you will be successful; in prison you will be released; and any trouble you have will soon vanish; it is also a sign you will soon meet a long absent friend who will be glad to see you. 74, 19, 10.

BELLS. To dream that you hear bells ringing merrily is a sign of a wedding, or else that you will soon hear some good news. If the bell tolls solemnly, it foretells a funeral or bad news. To a girl, the tolling of a bell predicts that some one will deceive her. 16.

BELLY. To dream one's belly is bigger and fuller than ordinary, shows his family and estate will increase; if one dreams his belly is grown lean and shrunk up, he will be joyfully delivered of some bad accident; if any one dreams that his belly is swelled, and yet notwithstanding be empty, he will become poor; if a girl dreams of a big belly, it is a sign of marriage. 24, 77.

BET. To dream that you bet with any one, shows that you will suffer from your own imprudence. 66, 12, 72.

BIRDS. To dream of birds is much better for the rich than the poor; to dream of little birds, the contrary; to dream that you hear birds chirp is a good sign; to see birds fighting, signifies adversity: to see birds fly over you head, signifies prejudice by enemies. 14, 77.

BIRDS' NESTS. To dream that you find one is a good sign; to dream that you find one without either eggs or birds, shows you will meet with great disappointment. 64.

BIRTH. (*See Still-born.*) To dream of a birth is good for a poor man; to the sick it denotes death. 18, 42.

BITE. To dream that you are bitten, foretells much jealousy and sorrow. 15, 19.

BLASPHEMY. If you dream that you are cursing, it foretells bad fortune; if you are cursed, all your expectations will be fulfilled. 4, 72.

BLEEDING. (*See Fingers.*) To dream of bleeding at the nose signifies loss of goods, and decay of riches; to a young girl it foretells the loss of her lover. 75, 19, 5.

BLIND. (*See Eye.*) To dream of being blind shows that you are deceived in a supposed friend; this dream also threatens the dreamer with want of money; to a lover, it predicts that his sweetheart is untrue to him; this dream also foretells death. 66.

BLOOD. To dream you vomit blood, is good for him that is poor, for he shall soon get a sum of money. It is also very good for him that has no children, and whose kindred are in a strange country; the first shall see a child of his own; the other will hear favorable news of his kindred, or see them returning home. 11, 19.

BLOSSOMS. If you dream you see trees or plants in blossom, it predicts that you will get some money, or some article that you little expected. It also signifies that you will be pleased at something that will soon happen. 43, 14, 7.

BOAT. (*See Oar, and Rudder.*) To dream you are sailing in a boat in pleasant weather, and enjoying yourself, denotes good success in business; to lovers it foretells happiness; if the weather is boisterous, it predicts quarrels, which will be speedily settled; dreams of sailing smoothly in boats are emphatically good ones to all kinds of people. 71, 10.

> To dream of being in a boat,
> Does show that maidens' fancies float;
> And whether sink or swim they do,
> To try love's sport their skill they'll show.

BOOKS. To be reading serious books, shows honor and station in life; to read lascivious books, shame and disgrace. 4.

BOOTS. (*See Shoes.*) To dream of new boots and shoes, indicates sweethearts to the single, and friends to the married; old shoes or boots show separation, and dirty or old ones are a sign of poverty and sorrow. 33.

BOTTLES. To dream of bottles is a good sign; to a man, success in business; to a maid, speedy marriage; if they are broken, they signify sorrow. 56, 34.

BOUQUET. To receive one, much pleasure; to give one, signifies that your lover is constant. 43, 7.

BOY. If a lady dreams that she is delivered of a boy, her life will be a pleasant one. 52.

BREAD. (*See Thick.*) To dream of bread is an excellent sign. If you see a good deal, the better the dream. It foretells good fortune to either man or woman. To lovers it predicts that they will make a good match and be well off, if not rich. To farmers it promises full and abundant crops. 1, 15.

BREAKFAST. To dream that you are eating breakfast shows you will do something of which you will be sorry. 21, 4.

BRASS. (*See Metals.*)

BREAST. (*See Milk.*) To dream of breasts, denotes great gain and profit to men; but to a woman, losses. If a young woman dreams that her breasts are full of milk, it signifies she is near her marriage. 76, 1, 10.

BREWING. To dream of brewing is a sign you should be up and doing; in love, it denotes idleness in your sweetheart; if in trade, you will sustain losses. 31.

> To dream of brewing and of baking,
> Does signify a match is making,
> Between a maiden and some other,
> Both by her father and her mother.

BRIDGE. To dream you are crossing over a bridge, denotes prosperity in life, and success in love; but to dream you are passing under a bridge, indicates difficulties in life, both in love and business; if you meet with obstructions, either on or under the bridge, it foretells illness. To dream a bridge breaks down with you, denotes sudden death. 56, 2.

BRIARS. To dream that you are among briars and get pricked, foretells that you will have an angry dispute with somebody. If a young girl who has a lover dreams it, she will probably get vexed at him. 39, 78.

BROTH. To dream of eating broths, or soups, is a good sign, and denotes profit and gain. 32, 9.

BROTHERS. To dream you see your brothers and sisters, signifies long life to the dreamer, but it portends a death in your family. 24, 8.

BUILDING. To dream of seeing a large building is a sign that you will be introduced to some one with whom you will afterward become intimate. To a young lady it predicts that she will have a new admirer. 17, 25, 1.

BULL. To dream that you have been gored, or received some hurt from a bull, shows you are likely to receive some harm from a great man. To dream you are pursued by a bull, denotes loss of friends and ill reports; if in love, your sweetheart will be in danger, and you will narrowly escape some misfortune. 64, 7.

BURNING. (*See Fire.*) To see, in your dream, one or more houses burning, but not wholly destroyed, signifies, for the poor, that they will become rich; and for the rich man, that his riches will be augmented; but if the fire is furious, and the houses fall down, the dreamer may expect losses, disappointments, shame, and death. To dream you burn yourself is a sign the malice of a stupid enemy will be foiled. Play your age first.

BURIED ALIVE. To dream that you are buried alive denotes that you will be rich and powerful. To wealthy people it is a sign of addition to their wealth. 11, 14.

BUSINESS. To dream of being full of business, is significant of some unexpected good fortune; to finish it, marriage; if the business appears to be bad, it is a good sign. 41.

BUTCHER. If, in your dream, you see a butcher killing any animal, it is a sign of the death of a friend or near relative. If a farmer dreams of seeing sheep killed, he will probably have a prolific flock. 73, 33, 16.

BUTTER. If you eat it, you will be surprised by some good fortune, but mixed with sadness. 11, 7.

BUTTERMILK. Losses from an extension of business. To the sick it is a sign of speedy convalescence. 71.

BUTTERFLIES. To dream you see gaudy butterflies, portends much happiness and luxury. 46, 18.

BUYING. To dream you buy all sorts of things that one uses, is good; to buy that which is only for victuals and relief, is good for the poor; but to the rich it signifies expenses and great charges. 19, 2, 69.

CABBAGE. To dream of cabbage, signifies very bad news from abroad. 16.

CAGE. To dream of letting birds out of a cage, is a sign that you will lose something. If a young girl dreams this, it predicts a loss of her chastity. 36, 5.

CAKES. (*See Thick.*) If a housewife dreams of making round cakes, it predicts that her husband will have a good store of luck, and will make her a present. To dream of eating cakes, is also a favorable dream. 18, 78.

CALF. To dream of a calf, is a sign of good luck. 14, 7.

CALIFORNIA. If you dream of going there, it predicts to you a misfortune; but if, in your dream, you imagine you are in California, and that it is a pleasant country, it foretells that you will receive a valuable present, or a legacy, or else that you will draw a prize in the lottery. 71, 10, 6.

CANDLES. To dream of lighted candles, is a sign that you will become religious, or will be soon visited by a minister who will tell you good news. To see a candle extinguished, is a sign of a funeral. To light a candle, success in what you undertake. 21, 67, 46.

CANNON. Beware of treacherous friends. To dream you hear a cannon, is a sign of sickness or death. 57.

CANNON BALL. To see a cannon ball, denotes misfortune. 6, 2.

CANDY. To dream of candy, is a sign of domestic tranquillity. 47, 8.

CANCER. (*See Abscess.*)

CANE. To dream of a cane, is considered a most inauspicious dream; and some authors forbid the dreamer to undertake any business on that day. 24, 2.

CAP. To put one on, be careful in your love affairs; to take one down, shows that that which you wish to hide will be discovered; if you receive a cap you will soon be married. 64, 38.

CARDS. Playing at cards, dice, or any other game in a dream, shows the party will be fortunate in love affairs; for the tables and cards allude to love. 76, 17.

2

CARROTS. To dream of carrots, or parsnips, signifies profit and strength to those who are at law for an inheritance. 10, 35.

CARRIAGE. To dream you ride in a carriage, is a sign of success in business and love. If the carriage breaks down, it is a sign you will meet with sudden losses. 31, 67, 3.

CARRYING. To dream that one is carrying another, is better than to dream one is carried; to be carried by a woman, a child. or a poor person, means profit and success; by a rich person, the contrary. 4, 44, 1.

CART. To dream of being tied to a cart to draw like a horse, denotes servitude and pain; but to dream that you are carried in a cart, the contrary, 6, 5, 17.

CASH. (See *Money*.)

CATS. To see cats is hidden enmity; to be bitten by them, denotes misfortune; to be scratched, care and trouble; to caress them, false friends; to kill one is triumph over your enemies; to dream of cats is also a sign of loss by thieves. 54, 42, 16.

CATERPILLARS. To dream you see caterpillars, denotes misfortune by secret enemies. 71, 77.

CATTLE. (See *Pasture, Pound, and Yoke*.) To dream you see cattle feeding, denotes great prosperity, and unexpected success; to a lover, it foretells a happy marriage, with many children; and to a married man, it shows that his wife will receive some unexpected legacy; to dream you are driving cattle, denotes that you will become rich by industry; if you see fat cattle, it denotes a plentiful year; if you see lean and hungry cattle in your dream, it denotes scarcity and famine. 6, 11, 66.

CAVERN, OR CAVE. (See *Grotto*.)

CELLAR. To dream you are in a cellar, is a sign of sickness and an unlucky law suit. 75, 2.

CELLERY. To dream of cellery is a good omen, it portends success in business and love. 48, 1.

CHAIN. If you dream of gold chains it is a sign of a wedding; if a girl dreams she is presented with one, it is a sure sign of a speedy marriage. Such a dream to a man in business predicts that he will be prevented from doing something that he specially desires to do. 15, 11.

CHAIR. To dream you are sitting on a chair, is a sign you will soon have an increase in your family; if a maiden has this dream it is a sign she soon will be married. To dream you are sitting in a rocking chair, denotes you will very soon better your condition. 25.

CHARITY. For a rich person to dream that he is charitable, signifies loss of fortune; if a lady dreams it, she will bestow her affections on an unworthy person. 17, 42, 5.

CHEESE. To dream you eat cheese, signifies profit and gain in trade; in love, deceit. 65, 3.

CHEMISE. (See *Smock and Shifts*.)

CHESS. To play at, denotes gain by lying and deceit; to see another play, loss by craftiness. Anselmus Julianus regarded this dream as indicative of the success which would attend the dreamer in his undertaking, according to his fancied success in his dream. 8, 78.

CHESTNUTS. To dream you are eating raw chestnuts, shows you will be fortunate in love affairs. Boiled chestnuts, signifies you will be fortunate in business. To dream you prick your hand with a chestnut burr, is a sign your confidence will be abused by a pretended friend. 7, 18.

CHERRIES. To dream of ripe cherries foretells that you will hear good news, or that some one will do you a favor. After such a dream you can easily borrow money if you wish to. If the cherries are green or mixed, your news will be a mixture of good and bad. 14, 54.

CHICKEN. To dream of a hen, or chicken, signifies losses in trade, and deceit in love. 19.

CHILD. (*See Boy.*) Dreaming of children is a good omen. If a woman dreams she is about to have a child, it foretells a rich legacy or other good fortune: if she is a maid that has this dream, she must be on her guard, or she will lose her virtue. 5, 56.

CHIMNEY. To dream of sitting in the chimney corner, to a maid, shows speedy marriage; if there is a fire burning brightly, you will become heir to some money. 61.

CHOCOLATE. To dream of chocolate, signifies trouble, brought about by gossiping. 47, 15.

CHRISTENING. To dream that you are present at a christening, is a good sign, you will get what you hope for; to a maid, it signifies that she will soon be married. 70, 50, 1.

CHURCH. To dream one is at church, and praying there, signifies joy and comfort. To dream of singing in church, is a dream of bad consequence. 13, 6.

CHURCHYARD. To dream of a churchyard, is a sign you will have a long and happy life. 76.

CLAMS. To a lover, this dream is a sign he will be successful with his sweetheart; if the clams are large, it signifies he will get through the world easy, but if they are small he may get into difficulties, and be caught in a tight place. 49, 24.

CLIMB. If you dream of climbing, it is a sign you will have some dignity conferred upon you, or that your circumstances in life will improve. To unmarried people it predicts that they will marry above their station. 4, 19.

CLOCK. To dream you hear the clock strike, denotes speedy marriage; if you dream the clock falls or breaks, it denotes danger. To dream of counting the hours of the forenoon, is lucky; the afternoon, unlucky. 72, 3, 12.

CLOUDS. To dream of white clouds, signifies prosperity; clouds mounting high from the earth, denotes voyages, the return of the absent, and revealing of secrets; clouds red and inflamed, show an ill-issue of affairs; dark and obscure clouds, obstructions in love. 47, 8.

CLOTHING. (*See Apparel.*)

COAL. To dream you see dead coal, signifies expedition in business; but to dream you see burning coal, threatens you with shame and reproach. 12.

COACH. (*See Carriage.*)

COCK. (*See Rooster.*) To dream you see a cock in the house, is a good sign to those who would marry; to hear a cock crow denotes great prosperity. 19, 10.

COFFEE. To dream of coffee, signifies loss of reputation. For a young girl to have such a dream, predicts the loss of her virtue. 39, 17.

COFFIN. To dream of one, denotes the death of a friend, or some near relation. 74, 6.

COMEDY. To dream you see a comedy, or farce, is a good omen. To the business man it betokens success, and to the maiden a speedy marriage to the one she loves. 22.

CONCERT. To dream of being at a concert, foretells the enjoyment of good health; to the sick, recovery. 12, 22.

COMMAND. To dream you command any one, shows trouble; to dream you see one command, signifies anger and authority. 14, 62, 7.

COOK. To dream you see a cook in the house, is good to those who would marry, and to the poor; but it is also the revealing of secrets; to dream of cooking, is also a sign of a wedding. 6, 34.

COPPER. (*See Metals.*)

CORN. To dream that you see corn eared, and gather it, signifies profit and riches; to dream that you see stacks of corn, signifies wealth and abundance to the dreamer; and on the contrary, to see a small quantity, denotes poverty. 69.

CORNS. For a man to dream his flesh is full of corns, shows he will grow rich proportionably to his corns. 70, 12.

CORPSE. (*See Shroud.*) To dream you see a corpse, is a sign of long life. 39, 11.

> Dreams of rivers, ships and horses,
> Of snow and frost, and of dead corpses,
> Are signs by which it may be read,
> Your sweetheart's love is cold or dead.

COWS. If you dream of seeing large herds of cows, it predicts prosperity and wealth. To see one cow in your dream is a sign of a good piece of luck of some kind. If a young girl dreams of cows, it is a sign she will marry a rich man, and have numerous children. 4, 26, 1.

CRABS, signify you will quarrel with a friend. To the married, this dream is a sign of separation. 49, 19.

CRIMINAL. (*See Reprieve.*) To dream that you are a criminal, shows that disgrace and danger are in store for you. 9, 61.

CRADLE. To dream you are rocking a cradle, is a good omen, and signifies a long and prosperous life. To the married, it is a sign of domestic happiness, and to the single a sign of speedy marriage with the object of their affection. To dream you upset a cradle, portends sickness or a loss in business. 46, 5.

CROCODILE. (*See Reptile.*) To dream of a crocodile, signifies pirates or robbers by sea, or deceitful persons, and troubles. 18, 2.

CROSS. To dream you see a cross, signifies sadness. 68.

CROW. A crow indicates expedition in business, adultery, or a thief; if croaking, an ill omen; if it flies on to the head of a child, the child will be in great danger of a misfortune. 74, 6.

CROWN. To dream a golden crown is placed upon your head, foretells that success and great honor await you; if the crown be silver, you will enjoy good health; if crowned with green leaves, friends and fortune will forsake you. 52, 6, 13.

CRYING. (*See Weeping.*)

CRUTCHES. If you dream you use them, your love will forsake you; if you only see them, some infirmity will press upon you; if you break them, you will recover from sickness. 46, 19.

CUCUMBERS. To dream of these vegetables, signifies that your business will not be very prosperous; for a sick person to dream of them, foretells a speedy recovery. 16, 8.

CURRANTS. Red currants denote happiness in life, and success in love. White currants portend that your partner will fall into difficulties, and will have a long illness. 12, 5, 60.

DAGGER. To dream of a dagger, you may expect news of absent persons, and your dearest hope will be fulfilled. 9.

DAHLIA. To dream of these flowers, is a sign of thrift. If a lady dreams of them, it foretells that her husband will make money rapidly. To a young girl, it predicts the same of her lover. 19, 20, 12.

DAIRY. To dream you are in a dairy, busy at work, is a very favorable omen; to the maid it indicates that her lover will be of an industrious turn and will rise to honor. To the farmer, it denotes that his crops will be abundant; to the tradesman, good news. 11, 2.

DANCING. (*See Ball.*) To dream you are dancing at a ball or entertainment, foretells that you will shortly receive joyful news; it also foretells success and happiness in love. To see others dance there, signifies pleasure and an inheritance. 55, 27.

DANGER. To dream of being in danger, shows success in life; to shun it, misfortune. (*See Difficulty.*) 27, 17.

DARKNESS. To dream you are in a dark place, is an unfavorable omen; to the lovers it denotes, loss of sweethearts, to the trader, loss of goods; but to dream of getting out of darkness into light, is good; if you are in poverty, it foretells riches; if in love, a happy marriage. 4, 16.

DATES. Dates denote many enemies, and you will receive much injury by a person you little expect. 6, 44.

DAY. To dream of a clear, sunshiny day, portends long life and happiness, but to dream of a dark, cloudy, and stormy day, is an unlucky omen. 3, 33, 9.

DAYBREAK. Good fortune in every thing you undertake. 64, 7.

DEATH. To dream you see death, denotes happiness and long life;

that you will be either speedily married yourself, or assist at a wedding. To dream you see another person dead, denotes hasty news from friends. 61, 4.

DEBT. To dream of paying a debt with money, foretells that you will soon receive some. If you imagine that you owe a debt, and are worrying to get the money to pay, it is a sign of sickness. 18, 64.

DEEDS. To sign your name to deeds, is a bad sign; to a man, loss in business; to a woman, the inconstancy of her lover. 7, 8.

DEER. If you see these animals in your dream, it shows that you will hear some unexpected news—no matter what—perhaps a marriage, a death, an accident, or a legacy has been left to you; or that some one is in love with you. 12.

DEVIL. To dream of this enemy to the human race, denotes that many dangers threaten you, all of which you will overcome if you carefully withstand all temptations to do evil; in love it forebodes loss of the affections; in trade, opposition; to dream you are pursued by an evil spirit, is also a bad omen. 61, 18.

DIAMONDS. To dream you wear a diamond, denotes that you will be crossed in love, and that your lover is unfaithful. For a man of business to dream that he is dealing in diamonds, is good, it is a sure thing with him, that he will become wealthy, and retire to private life much respected. 33, 3.

DICE. To dream you are playing at dice, backgammon, or draughts, denotes much good to the dreamer, in either love, marriage, or business. To a young girl, engaged to be married, dreaming of dice foretells that her lover will be wild and not of much account. 54.

DIFFICULTY. If you imagine in your dream that you are in great difficulty, or in personal danger of any kind, it is a favorable sign, as such dreams always go by contrary. 17, 27.

DIGGING. To dream of digging in clean and healthy ground, is a sign of thrift, and good luck generally: if the ground be dirty or wet, it shows trouble: if you are digging for gold, and find large and rich lumps, it shows you'll have some good luck, but if the product is meagre, or if you don't find any, it foretells disappointment. If you lose any of your tools it is a sign of a quarrel. 14, 71.

DINNER. If you dream of sitting down to dinner with a large company, it is a sign you will either go a journey, or change the present location either of your dwelling or business. 76, 11.

DIRT. To dream of dirty dirt or mud, signifies that some one will speak ill of you. If it is clean sand or soil, and you do not get befouled with it, it is a sign of thrift and good fortune. If some one throws dirt on you, it foretells that you will be abused. 22, 41.

DISEASE. If you dream you have any contagious or foul disease on you, it foretells luck and benefit, as such a dream goes by contrary. 18, 2.

DITCHES. To dream of ditches, steep mountains, rocks, and other eminences, foretells danger and misfortune: expect thieves to rob your dwelling, or that your children will be undutiful, and bring you into trouble: if you are in love, it foretells unhappiness if you marry your present sweetheart: if you are in trade, it denotes loss of goods, and other trouble: to farmers, it foretells accidents to their live stock, loss of sheep, &c. 73, 8.

DOGS. (*See Mad Dog.*) To dream of those animals, has very different significations; if they fawn and fondle upon you, it is a lucky omen; if you are in love, it portends marriage and happiness; but if they bark and snarl at you, it denotes that enemies are endeavoring to destroy your reputation and happiness; if in love, crosses. 17, 61.

DOLL. If a girl dreams she has a new doll with which she is greatly pleased, it foretells a disappointment. 61.

DOLPHINS. To dream of seeing these beautiful fishes playing in the water, denotes the death of some dear friend or relative. 5, 4.

DOMESTICS. (*See Servants.*) To dream of having a great number of servants, is illness. 71, 11.

DOORS. To dream you knock at a door, and gain admittance, shows success in your undertakings; if you cannot obtain entrance, it shows disappointment. 16, 9.

DOVE. To dream you see these emblems of love, denotes good fortune to the dreamer. 36.

DROWNING. (*See Water and Resuscitate.*) To dream you are drowning, or that you see another drowned, portends good to the dreamer; to the lover, good-tempered sweethearts and marriage; but to a girl it is a sign she should keep an eye on her lover. 54, 18, 1.

DREAMS. (*See Sleep.*) To dream you relate your dreams to any one, shows something unlooked for will take place. 41, 18.

DROUGHT. For a farmer or planter to dream of seeing his grass or crops drying up for want of rain, denotes that an accident will happen to him or his property during a storm, or that some of his live stock will die or meet an accident. 12.

DRINK. To dream you drink cold water, is good to all; hot, sickness and hinderance; wine, is good; sweet wine, success in love; oil, sickness; from vessels of gold, or silver, or earthenware, intends tranquillity; of horn, implies good; glass, evil. 67.

> If maids do dream of drawing drink
> In cellars, they may waking think,
> That their sweethearts without delay,
> Will leave them, and soon run away.

DRUM. To dream you hear the rolling of a drum signifies that you will be called away from your home or business unexpectedly. If you see soldiers marching when you hear the drum, it shows that though you may not have to leave, yet you will receive an unexpected message that will cause you trouble or excitement. 49.

DRUNKENNESS. To dream you are drunk, is loss in business; but success in love; to a woman, it denotes she will be beloved by a stranger; and to a man that he will be married to a rich young widow. To the married it denotes domestic bliss. To see a drunken man, shows that you will be guilty of some foolish action. 18, 20.

DUCK. To hear ducks quacking, or to see these fowls in your dream, denotes that somebody is coming to see you who is hungry, or that you will shortly have a visitor in your family who will stop to dinner. 73, 1.

DUET. To dream you sing a duet with a lady shows that you can win her if you desire. To dream you sing with a man shows you have a secret but powerful enemy, and is a sign you will never marry. To hear a duet denotes business troubles. 50, 51.

DUMB. If you dream that you are dumb, or that any of your speaking friends are so afflicted, it foretells sickness or misfortune. But should you dream that a deaf mute of your acquaintance speaks, it foretells joy and gladness at something that will happen. 14.

DUN. If you are troubled in your dreams by imagining that people are dunning you for money, it is a sure sign you will get some unexpectedly. 41.

DUST. If you dream you are in a room or in the road where the dust is flying so as to choke you, it shows that some one is plotting to injure you in some way or to make a speculation out of you. 64, 2.

DWARF. Should a single lady dream she sees a very small man or Dwarf, it indicates that her husband will be a very large man, or have a great intellect. If a single man has this dream it is a sign he will marry a scold. For married people to dream of dwarfs shows that their children will give them much trouble.

EAGLES. To dream you see an eagle soaring very high in the air, denotes prosperity, riches and honors: to the lover, it foretells success in love and marriage. 48.

EARS. To dream of boring many ears denotes obedience and readiness; to dream of cleansing them, good news; of having your ears boxed, ill news; of having large ears, prosperity and honor; of being hurt or slit, offence and treachery; of loss of ears, loss of friendship; of loss of hearing, betrayal of secrets; and to a woman, ruin. 3, 19.

EAR-RINGS. To dream of purchasing a pair of ear-rings is a good dream to the fair sex; to widows and maids they signify marriage; to those that have no children, that they shall have children; and to those that have husbands and children, purchases and riches; for as women are provided with these deckings, so shall they be stored with husbands, children, and goods. 32.

EARTHQUAKES. Change of estate, injuries, death; to see a town destroyed by, famine, war, and desolation. 17.

EATING. If you dream of eating a good meal with a relish, it foretells good crops to a farmer, and successful business to any one. 70, 14.

ECLIPSE. For one to dream he sees the sun in eclipse, signifies the loss of his father; if he sees the moon eclipsed, it denotes the death of his mother; but if he has neither father nor mother, then it denotes the death of a relation. 8.

EELS. To dream of catching or handling eels, denotes that you will have good fortune, but difficulty. If the eels slip through your hands and escape from you, it shows that you will experience a loss. 41, 6.

EGGS. (*See Rotten.*) If married people dream of eggs it is a sign they will be prolific of children. If a newly married lady dreams of finding a nest full of eggs, it foretells that her first born will be twins or triplets. If a young girl dreams such a dream, it is a sign that she will soon be married, or get in a condition that she ought to be a wife. 4, 47.

ELDERBERRIES. To dream of elderberries augurs content and riches: to a maiden they bespeak a speedy marriage; to a married woman, that she will shortly be with child; to the tradesman, success in business; to the farmer, good crops. 30, 33.

ELEPHANT. To dream of an elephant is a very fortunate dream, for it denotes an acquirement of riches: if you are in love, it foretells a speedy marriage with your sweetheart, and many children, chiefly boys, who will distinguish themselves by their learning. 33.

ELOPEMENT. For a young girl to dream she elopes with her beau, is a sign her parents will give their consent and she will soon be married to the one she loves. If a man dreams that he elopes with his sweetheart, it portends that he will be "*cut out*" by a stranger. 4, 44, 8.

ENEMY. If you dream that some one is trying to injure you, or that a person who you know is your enemy endeavors to work to your disadvantage, it foretells good fortune and success. Such dreams always go by contrary, and you may calculate a benefit just in proportion to the injury you dream you are about to sustain. 69, 78.

ENTRAILS. This is a good dream for the poor, but to the rich it portends loss of riches. To sweethearts and beaus it shows that they will be happy in their loves. 10, 20.

EMBRACE. To dream of embracing relatives is a warning of treachery; if friends, disappointments; if one unknown embrace you, you will travel; the embrace of a woman brings good luck. 3, 11, 33.

ERRAND. To dream that you are sent of an errand, signifies great loss to the married; to the lover it denotes success in his pursuits, and that he will shortly marry a very amiable and accomplished maiden. 39.

EXECUTION. (*See Hanged and Gallows.*) To dream of seeing a man hanged denotes that some friend or relative will shortly come to good fortune. If you dream that you yourself are going to be hanged, you may safely calculate on good luck for that year: if you are in business you will be successful. 7, 6, 10.

EYE. (*See Squinting and Blind.*) If you dream you see a person with a defective eye, it denotes disappointment: to see a glaring squint eye in your dream, shows that you will be defeated or crossed in some enterprise. To dream that your own eyes are defective, or squint, is a sure sign of bad luck: sore eyes denote sickness: blindness, death, or deception. 66, 49, 78.

EYE-BROWS. Thick eye-brows are a sign of friends; thin, ill-will and vexation; black, good luck. 18.

FACE. To dream that your face is swelled, indicates an augmentation of wealth and honor; but if it grows pale or emaciated, you will be severely disappointed. Of a fresh smiling face, friendship and joy; black face, long life; washing, repentance. 5, 11, 55.

FACTION OR SEDITION. Denotes health, and trouble, and shame. 16, 10.

FAINTING. To dream you see a person fainting indicates that you will soon hear of the death of a dear friend. 64.

FAIR. To dream you are at a fair, is a bad omen; it denotes that some pretended friend is about to do you an injury; if you are in trade, keep a keen look out, for some swindler will certainly attempt to defraud you. 31, 15.

FAIRY. If you dream of seeing a fairy, you will meet a woman, who will seduce you from the path of propriety, and make your life vexatious. 2, 22.

> To dream of blust'ring storms of wind,
> Does show inconstancy of mind;
> But if you dream of elves and fairies,
> Beware the girls and night-vagaries.

FALL. To dream you are falling from an eminence, shows you will have some dignity conferred upon you, or else will marry above your sphere. If a young girl dreams this, it is a sign she will marry a rich husband. 65, 70.

FAMILY. If a man or woman dreams that they have a large family, it is a sign of thrift and riches. Such a dream is a lucky one to anybody. 18, 41.

FAMINE. If a farmer dreams that his crops have failed, or of any scarcity of food, it shows that there will be a quarrel, which, though it may not be among his people, yet he will witness or hear about it, and it will worry him. 34, 8, 26.

FAN. To dream you see your sweetheart fanning herself, signifies that a stranger will step in some fine day and "cut you out." If a maid dreams that her beau presents her with a fan, or offers to fan her, it is a sign he will attempt to take improper liberties with her. 41, 18.

FAREWELL. To say farewell, or to hear another say it, is a bad sign, you will hear painful news. 45, 9.

FARM. (See Land.) If a man dreams he has a good farm, well enclosed, with pleasant pastures, bestowed upon him, he will have a handsome wife; but if the land seems spacious, and not enclosed, that denotes pleasure, joy, and riches. To dream you are working on a farm, denotes you will soon receive a legacy from a distant relative. 42.

FAST. (See Hungry.) To dream of fasting, or going without food until you are very hungry, is a sign of a quarrel; but it foretells success in love and business. 29, 7.

FAT. To dream you are growing fat, if you are a married woman, signifies you will soon have a son; to a maiden, it signifies she will soon be engaged; to men, it is a sign of success in business. To dream you are cutting or eating fat, portends sickness and misfortune. 66, 3.

FATHER. To dream you see your father, is fortunate; to see him die, is unlucky and portends sickness. 28.

FATIGUE. To dream you are very much fatigued, portends that you will be successful in business, but it is a sign of sickness. 4, 78.

FAULT. If you dream you commit a fault, be very careful in your conduct; if you see a fault in a lady who is very dear to you, should you trust her, she will be faithful to you in every thing. 22, 13, 27.

FAVOR. If you dream that you ask a favor of a friend, and he grants it, it foretells that he has been talking about you; but if he refuses it, it shows that some other person has spoken ill of you to him. 16, 71.

FEAR. To feel fear, signifies that you will be courageous in your waking moments; to dream of frightening others, shows that your courage is weak. 68.

FEAST. If you dream of feasting at a friend's house, or eating with him anywhere, it shows you will make a new acquaintance through his means. If a girl dreams this, it is a sign she will soon have a lover from that very house or place where she dreams of feasting. 76, 18.

FEET. (See Corns.) To dream of washing your feet, denotes trouble of some kind; of scratching or tickling the soles of your feet, shows that you will be flattered by some one to your disadvantage; dreaming of dirty feet predicts sickness or trouble; if, in your dream, you imagine your feet are covered with corns, you will have great riches. 51.

FESTER. Dreaming that you have a fester on your hand, or fingers, is a sign that you will give somebody a present; if on your feet, or legs, it shows you will go to see some one who will be glad to see you. 76, 14.

FIDDLE. If you dream that you are playing on a fiddle, or hearing the music of one, it is a sign you will soon attend a funeral. Such a dream is a bad omen to girls, as it points to the death of a lover, or of some dear friend. 61.

FIELDS. (See Meadow and Green.) To dream you are in a ploughed field, forebodes some severe disputes that will be brought upon you by some person who has no children; to dream you are in a meadow covered with flowers, is a very handsome wife, who will bring you lovely children and make you very happy; to a woman, it denotes that she will marry a handsome young fellow, by whom she will have beautiful children, that they will become rich and live to a good old age. 16, 72, 6.

FIFE. For a girl to dream she hears the shrill music of a fife, is a sign she will soon have a beau, and that he will be a smart and desirable young man. 77, 5.

FIGS. To dream of eating good figs, signifies joy and happiness; if the figs are mouldy or defective, your pleasure will be marred by some disagreeable event. 6, 29.

FIGHT. If you dream of being engaged in a fight, it foretells to a man of business that he will soon engage in some new enterprise that will be successful; to a laboring man, it predicts increased pay. 44, 78.

FIGURES. Any number above *one*, and below *seventy-eight*, is deemed to portend good fortune to the dreamer, but *forty-nine* is the most lucky. All numbers above *seventy-eight* are uncertain, except *three hundred and forty-three*, and that is a very lucky number. 49, 10, 13.

FINGERS. To dream that you cut your fingers, if they bleed, is a very good omen; you will be successful in love, and your sweetheart will prove kind and true. 1, 2.

FIRE. (*See Burning.*) If in your dream, you see a house on fire other than your own, it foretells that some event will happen to make you melancholy and sorrowful, such as the death or ruin of some esteemed friend. If you dream your own house or place of business is burning, it is an omen of good fortune. If you dream of playing with fire, it is a sign of a quarrel in bed. For this dream play your age first. 26.

> To dream of sitting by the fire,
> When it is late, doth show desire;
> But if you sit till the fire's out,
> Your love will prove false out of doubt.

FIRE-ARMS. (*See Gun, Pistol, and Cannon.*)

FISH. To dream of catching fish is a sign of excellent good for- tune, particularly if you haul up large ones; if the fish fall off your hook, it predicts troublesome fortune. If you dream of fishing with- out catching any, it shows that you will fail in some undertaking or speculation; and to a lover it is a sign that he will get the mitten. To dream that you see an abundance of fish, foretells the receipt of money, or success in collecting it. 14, 71.

FLAG. To dream you see a flag waving, betokens great danger from enemies, or sickness. To dream you carry a flag, signifies you will receive some mark of distinction from your fellow-citizens. If a maid dream she is making a flag, it is a sign she will marry a rich officer in the Army or Navy; but if a married woman has this dream, it foretells the birth of a son who will become a great general. 13, 35, 61.

FLEAS. To dream you are tormented with these little insects, is of an unfavorable kind; evil and malicious enemies will do you much injury; your sweetheart will prove false. 45.

FLIES. To dream of a swarm of flies, denotes that you have many enemies; it also denotes that your sweetheart is not sincere, and cares but little about you; to dream you kill them is a very good omen: it denotes success in love and trade. 21, 49.

FLOOD. (*See Overflow.*) To dream of a flood, generally denotes riches and plenty, particularly if the water is calm, it shows that though you may lose something, you will be fortunate in other ways sufficient to counterbalance it. 2, 66, 9.

FLOUR. (*See Mill.*) To dream that you buy flour is a bad omen, and portends sickness, or the death of a near friend. 41.

FLOWERS. (*See Blossom.*) To dream you are gathering flowers, is a very favorable omen: expect to thrive in every thing you undertake, and that you will be successful in love, marry happily, and have beautiful children; should the flowers wither under your hands, it foretells heavy losses in trade; that your sweetheart will die; or if you are married, that you will lose your husband or wife, or perhaps your favorite child. 14, 7, 43.

FLUTE. To dream you play or hear playing on a flute, signifies trouble and contention with your friends. 47, 8.

> If your kind fancy you present
> With playing on an instrument,
> Your sweetheart shall not you disdain,
> But yield true love for love again.

FLYING. To dream you are flying is a very excellent omen; if you are in love, your sweetheart will be true to you; and if you marry, you will have many children, who will all do very well and be happy. 35.

FORK. To dream of a fork indicates that a false friend will attempt your ruin by flattery. 69.

FORTUNE. If you dream that some one told your fortune, you may calculate every thing will go pretty nearly the reverse of what was assured to you: if you were promised money you will get poverty, and *vice versa*. To dream of making a sudden fortune is a sign of want. All dreams of this kind go by the rule of contrary. 76, 8, 4.

FOUNTAIN. To dream you are at a fountain, is a favorable omen; if the water is clear, it denotes riches and honors; and in love, it foretells happiness in marriage; but if muddy, it denotes vexation and trouble. 71, 20, 18.

FOX. A sign of thieves; to dream of fighting with them, shows that you will have to deal with some cunning enemy; to keep a tame fox, signifies that you will love a lewd woman, or have a bad servant, who will rob you. A number of foxes, false friends. 11, 17.

FREE MASON. To dream you are a free mason denotes you will soon make a number of new friends who will treat you on the square, it also foretells you will take a journey to the east. If you are already a member of that celebrated Order, and dream you attend a meeting of the lodge it portends sickness, and a heavy loss of property, to dream you are expelled from the Order shows you will attain a higher station in life. 2, 78.

FROG. If you dream of seeing a large frog, or a number of frogs, or of hearing frogs croak, it is a good omen as regards your health. To dream of catching frogs alive, without killing them, foretells some piece of good fortune; but if you kill them it is a sign some accident will befall you; 22, 3.

FRUIT. To dream of fruit which is ripe and fair to look upon is an excellent omen, as it foretells the most perfect success in all worldly matters: if the fruit is green or defective, it indicates trouble with your success. If you dream of eating fruit that proves to be sour or rotten, it shows disappointment: if a young girl dreams this, it is a sign that her lover will deceive her. 32.

FUNERAL. To dream of attending a funeral shows that you will probably be soon at a wedding or some gay party. If, in your dream, you see a funeral pass, it denotes a pleasure party out of doors, such as a pic-nic or excursion. 18, 1.

FUR. To dream of fur signifies much good; it denotes that your sweetheart is kind and true, and that if you marry, you will be very happy; it denotes to the merchant a good establishment in business, to the sailor a profitable voyage. 61, 78.

GAG. If you dream that your mouth is stopped by a gag, it denotes that you will soon thereafter be kissed by a pretty girl. To a young girl, such a dream predicts that she will see some gentleman who takes her fancy, and perhaps will fall in love with him. 13.

GAIN. If acquired justly, you may hope for wealth; if by injustice, you will lose your fortune. 33, 14.

GALLOWS. (*See Execution and Hanged.*) To dream of a gallows is a good omen, as it denotes that you will have a chance to make money, and if you are smart enough to avail yourself of the opportunity, it will be all right. To those embarking in new enterprises, such a dream foretells success. 10, 7, 6.

GAMBLING. (*See Raffling.*) To dream of gambling is a sign of poverty and disgrace. If, in your dream, you see others gamble, and do not engage in it yourself, it shows that some of your friends or relatives will have a reverse of fortune and become poor. 8, 44.

GARDEN. To see a beautiful and thrifty garden in your dream, denotes good luck and abundance: if the garden is run to weeds, you may still have luck, but much trouble and vexation will accompany it: if you see rats or pigs in the garden, it denotes thieves to annoy you. 31, 17.

GARLIC. For a man to dream he eats garlic, signifies he shall discover hidden secrets, and meet with some domestic jars; yet to dream he has it in the house is good. 6, 11, 66.

GARTER. This is a good dream to the lover, as it signifies he will soon be united to his sweetheart. To the married this dream portends much domestic trouble from jealousy. 4, 16.

GAS. If you dream of bright and pleasant gas-lights, it shows success in love matters. If the gas is dim and looks unnatural, your beau or sweetheart will either leave you, or die. 36.

GEESE. To dream of these birds is generally a good omen: if you see them quietly feeding it denotes success and pleasure in your undertakings; but if they are alarmed and cackling, it foretells trouble and annoyance, but yet nothing that will seriously affect you. 15, 69.

GHOST. (*See Apparition.*)

GIANT. If a lady dreams of seeing a very large man, or giant, and if she is pleased with his appearance, it shows that her future husband will be a small fellow, or else a man of small intellect: if she is disgusted with the giant, it is a sign that she will marry such a man herself, or else a man of great mind. For married people to dream of giants shows a prospect of smart children. · 31, 4.

GIFT. (*See Present.*) To dream that a friend presents you with a valuable gift, predicts that you will lose something. If a girl dreams that her lover gives her a present, it is a sign that she will allow him the husband's privilege before marriage. 64, 21.

GIG. To dream of riding alone in a gig, denotes delay, and that something you expected to happen will be put off: if you imagine you ride in a gig with your sweetheart, it foretells that your marriage day will be postponed, or will be far distant. 46, 1.

GIN. To dream of this liquor is a sign of poverty and disgrace: if you imagine you are drinking it, it foretells that you will lose money or property by some foolish act of your own. 74, 78.

GIPSY. If you dream of these wandering vagrants, it foretells that you will have trouble of some kind—either a vexatious loss, or else something will happen to worry you: to dream that a gipsy tells your fortune, shows that some one will rob you. 16, 57.

GLASS. To dream of receiving a glass of water, signifies that you will soon be married; if you break it, your lover will foresake you. 11, 64.

GLOBE. To dream you are looking at a globe, foretells much good, and that you will be a great traveller. 19.

GLOVES. To dream of wearing good gloves, brings happiness; if the gloves are torn, many disappointments. To the lover this dream is a sign he will get the mitten from his sweetheart. 25, 9.

GOAT. If you dream of seeing goats on a high place in a mountain, it shows that riches or honors await you: if the goats are merely on the road, or in a building, it predicts good luck. 64, 34.

GOGGLES. To dream that you are wearing these glasses to protect the eyes, is a sign that you will see something disagreeable. If a lover dreams such a dream, he will be apt to see some young fellow making love, or saying soft things, to his sweetheart. 45, 3.

GOLD. (*See Metals, also Money.*) To dream of receiving gold, is a very good omen: it denotes success in your present undertakings, after experiencing some little difficulties. If you pay gold, it betokens increase of friends and business. 49, 7.

GOLD-FISH. To dream of these beautiful fish is a sign of good fortune generally: if you dream of catching a large one, it foretells that you will soon get a large sum of money: any kind of a dream about these fish is lucky. 20, 6.

GOOSEBERRIES. To dream of gooseberries indicate many children, chiefly sons, and the accomplishment of your present pursuits. To the maiden they foretell a cheerful husband; they also denote happiness in marriage, and success in trade. 19, 8.

GOVERNOR. If you dream of seeing the Governor, or chief magistrate of a State, it foretells that something will soon happen to please you: if you shake hands with him, and he smiles upon you, the dream is all the better, as it predicts that you will have honors conferred upon you. 10, 11.

GRAIN. To dream of regular fields of ripe grain is a good omen, as it is a sign of thrift: if the grain is broken down or imperfect. it shows trouble with the thrift: if it is mouldy or mildewed, you will experience losses. An abundance of grain in bulk is likewise a sign of plenty; but scattered grain is the reverse of this. 69.

GRAPES. To dream of an abundance of grapes is a good omen, as is also a dream that you eat grapes of a pleasant flavor; but if the grapes are sour and broken, it shows that you will have sorrow. If a young girl dreams she has a present of beautiful grapes, she will marry well within the year, and be prolific of children. 70.

GRASS. Green grass, denotes long life; to cut grass, great trouble. 14, 6.

GRASSPLAT. Is a sign of a wedding. 16, 18, 46.

GRAZING. To see cattle grazing, denotes that you will be fortunate; to the lover it is a sign he will marry a rich wife, and to the merchant it foretells a great increase of business. 76, 10.

GRASSHOPPERS. This is an unfavorable dream to the sick, but to a healthy person it foretells long life. 17, 66.

GRAVE. To dream of a fresh made grave, is a sign of losses: a man of business will probably lose money that is owing to him. But to lovers, this sign is apt to be a "grave to their dearest hopes:" such a dream is decidedly a bad one for them. 21, 72.

GRAVEL. To see heaps of clean gravel, denotes that you will soon go a journey by land, which will be a pleasant or profitable one. 44, 19, 22, 1.

GREASE. If you dream of grease, it foretells that any undertaking you may then be engaged in will go right, and according to your mind: if the grease is dirty you will experience difficulties, but will get through them. Lovers who dream of grease, will be able to get married pretty easy, and have things go slick afterward. 4, 11, 44.

GREEN. If you see green things, such as fruit, grass, green fields, &c., in your dream, it is a sign of long life, but if the color has faded it is a sign of trouble. 2, 18.

GRIEF. Dreaming of grief is a sign of a jolly time, as such dreams go by the rule of contrary. Thus, if you dream you are in great grief at the death of a friend or relative, you may calculate that a happy wedding is soon to come off, at which you will be present. 24, 62.

GRIN. If you dream you see people grinning at you, it shows that you will do something of which you are ashamed: if you imagine that ladies are grinning at you, you will probably have some adventure with one that will make you appear ridiculous. 71, 6.

GRIP, or GRIPPE. To dream you have griping sensations in the bowels, denotes an accident causing a flesh wound: if you dream that a man takes you by the hand, or any part of your body, by a hard grip that hurts you, it is a sign that you will have a pressing invitation to go somewhere—perhaps a summons to court. 19, 16.

GROAN. To hear groans of agony in your dream, denotes that you

will soon go to a frolic, or to a place where you will be much entertained: if you see and recognize people groaning, it shows that they
will soon do something to amuse or please you. 41, 8.

GROG. To dream of drinking grog, foretells poverty, or disgrace,
or both. If you dream of drinking toddy that tastes very pleasant
and agreeable, it shows that something will occur which will make
you miserable. 55.

GROTTO. To dream of being in a grotto, or cavern in the earth,
shows that you will soon meet a near and dear relative: if you live
away from home, something will occur to cause your return: such a
dream always foretells meeting your absent friends. 49, 2.

GROVE. (*See Pic-Nic.*) To dream of pleasant and verdant groves
or woods, is an excellent sign, as it foretells happiness and success:
if the groves are barren of leaves, it is the reverse, and you will be
poor and unhappy. 65, 78.

> A maid who dreams of verdant groves,
> Will surely have the man she loves;
> But if the groves are nipped with frost,
> She'll be as sure in marriage crossed.

GROW. If you dream that a tree or shrub grows fast, it is a sign
that you will do something in a hurry that you will afterward be sorry
for: if it be your son, or daughter, or any near young relative that
you imagine to grow very rapidly, it foretells an accident to them.
1, 19.

GRUB. (*See Worm.*) To dream of clean-looking, white fat grubs, is
a sign of good crops to farmers, but to dream of black or dirty looking grubs is the reverse. For a girl to dream of grubs is a bad sign,
as it puts her in peril of losing her virtue; but to a married woman
it is a good sign, for the reason that she will soon be in the family
way. 49, 70, 65.

GRUEL. To dream of drinking gruel, is a good sign if you are
sick, as it shows a speedy recovery; but if you are well, it is a sign
that some one will overreach you in a bargain, or that you will do
some foolish act. 2, 11, 22.

GUITAR. This dream denotes luck in love affairs, if the dreamer
sings and plays on the instrument at the same time. 45, 24.

GUN. To dream of firing a gun, or hearing the report of a gun,
denotes strife: if you imagine some friend fires it, it shows that there
will be a difficulty with him. If you dream of killing a bird, squirrel,
or other animal, by shooting it, it foretells that you will act rashly in
some quarrel. For a lover to dream of firing a gun, is a sign he will
have trouble with his sweetheart. 21, 57, 16.

GUTS. (*See Entrails.*)

GUTTER. If you dream of lying in a gutter, or of seeing a man so
reclining, it foretells that some honor awaits you, or some one in
whose success you take an interest. If a girl dreams of a broken
gutter, she should be careful of allowing her lover to be too familiar
with her person, or some accident may happen. 27, 65.

HACK. (*See Carriage.*) If you see, in your dream, a row of hacks,

3

or carriages at a funeral, it shows that you'll soon attend a wedding or a jolly party. 32, 19.

HAIL. To dream of a hail-storm, is a sign that you will make a good bargain, or will be lucky in some undertaking, provided the hail is white or in crystals; black hail, denotes sorrow and death, therefore you should never dream of that kind of hail if you can help it o dream of seeing white hail lying on the ground intimates that ou'll soon get plenty of cash in some transaction. 21, 72.

HAIR. If you dream that your hair is thick and bushy, it shows that you'll grow rich or powerful; if you dream it is curly and kinky, when in fact it is not, it is a sign you'll do something that you will afterward be ashamed of; if, in your dream, you imagine that your hair has fallen off, or that it has become extremely thin, it is a bad omen, as it shadows forth sickness, and perhaps death. 42.

HAM. Dreaming of fine-looking hams is a good omen; but if they are wormy or in any way blemished, it spoils all the luck, and shows that you will be unfortunate. To dream of eating fine-tasting hams is a sign that you will do something noted that will create a talk, but all in your favor; if the ham that you eat is bad and wormy, the said talk will be a scandal against you. 30, 1.

HAMMER. To dream that you see or hear hammering, denotes thrift to some one of your friends; if you are using the hammer yourself, it shows that you will be fortunate. A hammer is a good article to dream about. 3.

HAND. If you dream that your right hand is injured, or any thing is the matter with it, it shows that you will soon be called upon to assist a friend in distress; if it is your left hand, assistance will be solicited from you for an unfortunate stranger. 22, 78.

HANGED. (See Execution.) To dream of being hanged is an excellent omen, as it foretells that you will become either rich or distinguished. If you dream you are going to be hanged, it is nearly as good, as it betokens success in all your undertakings; but should you imagine that you eluded the officers of the law and escaped, that is a bad omen, as it foretells disappointment and ill-luck. The theory of such dreams is, that they always work by contraries. 10, 7, 6.

HARP. To dream you play upon the harp, indicates that you have some envious enemies who seek to injure you with slander. To dream you hear any person play upon the harp, is a sign that if you have sick friends they will recover. In love affairs this dream is very lucky. 5, 11.

HARVEST. To dream of a harvest field is a good omen. If you dream you are working in one it indicates success in business. To lovers, this is one of the most fortunate signs; to a young man, it signifies he will wed a rich and beautiful bride; to a young maiden, it is a sign she will soon be engaged to the object of her affections; to the married, it signifies domestic bliss. 4, 11, 44.

HASTE. (See Running and Walking.)

HAT. For a man to dream he has got a new hat shadows forth

good luck and advancement; dreaming of an old or shabby hat is a sign he will soon fall in love; and if he dreams he is wearing such a hat, the omen is not so favorable, for he will probably endeavor to take improper liberties with his sweetheart and be successful. 21, 6.

HATCHING. To dream of hatching fowls of any kind is a sign of thrift; if you imagine, in your dream, that a hen comes off with a very large brood of chickens, it shadows forth so much cash to be made by you in some bargain. 24, 68.

HATRED. To dream that you hate any particular person is a sign that he or she has been talking bad about you. If a girl should ever be so silly as to dream such a dream about her lover, it shows that he meditates an attack upon her chastity; on the contrary, if she dreams that he hates her, it is a sign that she possesses his whole heart. 44.

HAWK. If you dream of seeing a very large hawk, it shows that you will soon begin a new enterprise; if the hawk darts down and takes a chicken, a bird, or a fish, you will probably be successful; if little birds attack the hawk and drive it away, you will have difficulties in your undertaking and may possibly fail in it. 5, 55.

HAY. (*See Raking and Harvest.*) To dream of making hay, signifies success in all your undertakings. This is a good omen to young lovers. To dream you are selling hay is a bad omen, and portends losses in business and dangerous accidents. 49, 11.

HEAD. To dream of heads in any way is a good omen: if you dream your own head is very large, it shows that you will probably become distinguished; if you see a large-headed person in your dream, it is a sign you will make the acquaintance of some one who will benefit you. 65, 9.

HEAL. If you dream of having a sore on your person that was healed up quick, it is a sign that some one will cut your acquaintance; if you have a sweetheart or lover, it is probable something will happen to break off the intimacy. 20.

HEART. To dream of a heart is a bad omen. If you lose your heart it signifies sickness and death. To the married it denotes infidelity of their marital vows. To dream you see a human heart shows you are sincerely beloved; but to dream you have a pain or palpitation in your heart shows you are doomed to suffer through treachery. 46, 11.

HEAT. If you dream of being in a place that is extremely hot, or if the weather is so hot that the heat affects you, it shows that some person is preparing either to attack you or give you a good scolding. 71, 6.

HEN. (*See Chicken.*)

HIDE, or HIDDEN. To dream of concealing anything by hiding it, or putting it in an out-of-the-way place, is a sign that some one will reveal a secret that you have told. It is a bad omen for lovers to dream of hiding things, as it predicts that their intimacy will be talked about as suspicious. 45, 78.

HILL. To dream of going up a hill is a sign you will rise in the world, and of going down hill the reverse; if, in your dream, you seem to be approaching a smooth high hill, it shows that you will shortly have a piece of good fortune; but if the hill be rugged and stony, it foretells difficulties in connection with the good fortune. 1, 46, 18.

> To dream of mountains, hills, or rocks,
> Does signify, slouts, scoffs, and mocks;
> Their pains in passing over shew,
> That she whom you love, loves not you.

· HISSING. To dream of hearing hissing noises, such as steam makes, or of geese hissing, is a sign of shame. If a girl dreams this, it foretells that she will do something she is ashamed of: to a man it is a sign he will do an undignified act, or one that will injure his prospects. 47.

HOG. To dream of well-kept and happy-looking hogs is a good omen, as it foretells luck and success: but if you see lean and hungry-looking hogs squealing, it shows that any speculation you may enter into about that time will not be of much account if it does not result in a loss. 64.

HOG'S-BRISTLES. This dream denotes great violence and danger. 21, 7.

HOLE. (*See Abyss.*)

HOMINY. To dream of eating hominy with a relish is a sign that you will marry below your station in life, or else you will entertain a new acquaintance who is much below you in position, who will eventually command your esteem. To an educated young girl such a dream predicts a runaway match. 2, 10.

HONEY. This dream denotes you will have a long and happy life. If you dream you are eating honey it denotes that something will happen that will give you great joy or pleasure. To a young girl it is a sign that she will soon have a lover that will please her. 49, 3, 1.

HOPS. To dream of seeing a large garden of hops in full leaf, denotes thrift and wealth: if you see dried hops, and smell their fragrance, it shows that you will shortly come into a good lump of money from a legacy or a successful speculation. 27, 9.

> To maid who dreams of fragrant hops,
> A lover soon the question pops!
> And marries, too, with quick dispatch—
> Nine children fair will bless that match!

HORNS. To see horns on the head of another person, danger to the dreamer on your own wealth and importance. To dream you are gored by a horned animal denotes unhappiness. To lovers it usually predicts that they will have difficulty in connection with their desires; if they think of marrying, some obstacle will be placed in the way of their union, though perhaps not prevent it in the end. 9, 18, 36.

HORSE. If you dream of riding well and easily on the back of this noble animal, your fortune is sure to advance in the world: but if you imagine you are thrown from a horse, it is a sign of disgrace. To dream of swapping horses shows that some one will cheat you in a bargain; of selling a horse, it is a sign of loss; but of buying one, predicts that you will make money by some speculation, or else by selling property. Horses are excellent animals to dream about. 2, 11, 22.

HOUSE. (*See Repairing.*) To dream you build a house denotes you will have a comfortable life: to burn your house signifies increased riches: to dream you spill water in a house is a sign of care and affliction: to dream you see a house fall denotes death. Dreaming of building houses, wearing fine clothes, and talking with ladies, is a sign that the parties will suddenly marry. 47, 66.

HOUSEHOLD UTENSILS. The pot denotes the life; the platter the actions of life; the candlestick intends the wife; the light, or lantern, the husband; the hearth the estate; vessels of wine are the servants; the stores cupboards, and cabinets mean the wife. 24, 7.

HUG. If a young girl dreams of being fondled and hugged by her lover, it is a sign he will soon get sick of her and want to be off: it is not half so bad to let him hug her in real earnest as it is to dream of it. The same sign holds good with the other sex. 2, 11.

HUNGRY. (*See Fast.*) To dream of being hungry foretells that you will soon engage in some new enterprise which will prove successful. Hungry dreams are excellent omens to lovers, as they denote energy and success. If a girl dreams that a gentleman comes to see her who is hungry, it is a sign that he will woo her in such an earnest and affectionate manner as to win her heart. 19, 37.

HUSBANDRY. To dream of implements in husbandry, has a variety of interpretations: to dream of a plough, denotes success in life, and a good marriage; to dream of a yoke, is unfavorable, unless it be broken; to dream of a team, death in a family; to dream of a scythe signifies sickness. 76, 44.

HUNTING. To dream of going a hunting brings an accusation of dishonesty: if you are returning from the chase, good fortune awaits you. 8, 10.

HUT. To dream that you live in a small hut is a sign that you will shortly have a house of your own. If, in your dream, you visit a little hut which is inhabited, it shows that you will be invited to partake of the hospitalities of some family. 29, 70.

ICE. (*See Skating and Sliding.*) To dream of walking on slippery ice in winter, is a sign that misfortune threatens you: if you slip down, it foreshadows bad luck: if you dream of gliding or skating easily over smooth ice, it shows that you will probably have a difficulty of some kind, but will overcome it and get through handsomely. For lovers to dream of going over ice is a bad omen. 4, 28.

ILLNESS. (*See Sickness.*) To dream that you are ill and confined to your bed is a sign that some one will overreach you in a bargain, or cheat you in some way. Such a dream is a bad omen to loves, as it predicts false vows. 16, 38.

ILLUMINATION. To dream of an illumination augurs success in life and much happiness; if the light begins to disappear, sorrow and many tears will be your portion. 24, 68.

IMPERTINENCE. If a girl dreams that she meets a gentleman

who is impertinent toward her in conversation, it is a sign she will make a new male acquaintance who will be very agreeable to her: if she gets angry at the said impertinence she will probably fall in love with her new friend and either marry him or be on improper intimate terms with him. 1, 11.

INDIGO. To dream of indigo, denotes to a female that she will cross the ocean. When she dreams of putting the indigo in water, and it gives no color, she may be assured she will arrive in India. But to embrace the water in the usual way, no such thing will come to pass. 27, 15.

INFANT. (*See Child.*) Dreaming of a young infant is an excellent omen, as it foretells joy and gladness, good luck, and success generally. Lovers who dream such a dream may be sure of a happy and thrifty marriage. To a business man this dream predicts a new and successful enterprise. 29, 76.

INK. To dream that you see splashes of ink on white paper, or on anything, is a sign of scandal: after such a dream, you may be sure that somebody will be talking pretty hard about you: the larger the splashes the bigger will be the stories that are told. 41.

INN. To dream of being at an inn, is very unfavorable; it denotes poverty and unsuccessfulness in business; to the lover, the unfaithfulness of his sweetheart; to the tradesman, loss of business and dishonest agents. 46, 33.

INQUEST. To dream that you are present at a coroner's inquest, is a bad sign; you will soon squander your fortune. 49, 16.

INSULT. (*See Abuse.*)

INUNDATION. (*See Overflow.*)

IRON. (*See Metals.*)

ITCH To dream that you have the itch, or that your body itches, shows that you will shortly receive money. 40, 9.

ISLAND. To dream that you are on a deserted island shows that you will commit some act to disgust your friends and make them cut your acquaintance; be careful how you behave after dreaming such a dream. 19, 65, 22.

IVORY. To dream of ivory, signifies that you will be very successful in business. To the single it is a sign they will soon fall in love and be fortunate in their courtship. To the married it denotes domestic happiness. 4, 75, 30.

IVY. To dream of seeing this vine running over and covering any house, is a sign of poverty, particularly if the ivy grows thick and abundant: if you dream that it covers your own house, the sign is still more sure: for a farmer to dream that he sees ivy covering a tree, denotes bad crops. A girl who dreams of being in a bower covered with ivy, will probably marry a poor and shiftless man. 2,

JAIL. (*See Prison.*) If a man dreams he is confined in a prison or jail, it shows that he will have honors or dignities conferred upon him, as such dreams go contrariwise: if his arrest and imprisonment worries him, it only shows that he will be the more delighted with his new dignities. 46.

JAR. To dream that a house is jarred or shook by an earthquake, an explosion, or anything that may occur outside, is a sign that the head of the family in that house will be sick. Jars of preserved fruit or jellies, seen in a dream, are good omens; if you dream you are presented with one or more of them, it shows you will be long lived and thrifty. 15, 39.

JEALOUSY. To dream you are jealous of your sweetheart, or wife, signifies that they will betray you; for a maiden to dream she is jealous of her sweetheart is a sign some particular friend will " *cu her out;*" for a wife to dream she is jealous of her husband, fortells the loss of his love. 28, 6.

JELLY. To dream of having pots of jelly given to you, or that you are eating jelly, and that plenty of it is around, is a sure sign of long life and good fortune generally; as many pots as are given to you, or as you may have, so many generations will you live to see. The same rule applies to preserved fruits. 65, 18, 78.

JEW. If you dream that a genuine Israelite comes along and annoys you in any way, it is a sign you will quarrel with your father; if you imagine that he cheats you in a bargain, it predicts that you will probably receive a present from some near relative; on the contrary, if he gives you an advantage in the bargain, it shows that your father, or some elderly relative, will ask a favor of you. 58, 21.

JEWELS. Chains, pearls, or precious stones, etc., and all adornings upon the heads and necks of women, are good dreams for the fair sex; to widows and maids they signify marriage; and to those that are married, riches. If a man dreams of possessing jewels, it is a sure sign he will lose something of great value. 46, 75.

JIG. To dream of dancing a jig with a lady is a sign she is in love with you, or is pleased with you; and if you like her you may go in at once for her favor with much confidence. The omen is the same to a girl who dreams of jigging with a young man. 1, 65, 14.

JOLLY. If you dream you are in company and feel particularly hilarious, or jolly, it is a sign of sorrow; mark well who it is that contributes most to your mirth, for he or she may cause you pain. If a girl dreams this of a young man, let her beware of him for a gay seducer. 20.

JOY. To dream that you are in the ecstasy of joy at anything that has happened, bodes pain and trouble; something will be sure to occur to make you unhappy. 46.

JUMPING. (*See Leaping.*)

JURY. If a man dreams he is serving on a jury, it is a sign some friend will ask a favor of him that he will hesitate to grant. 38, 3.

KALEIDOSCOPE. To dream you are looking through one of these curious instruments, and if you are delighted with the changes that present themselves, it is a sign that you will either travel in distant countries or be very discontented at home. 36, 75.

KEG. To dream of an empty one is a sign you will soon leave home; a keg of small fish, or oysters, denotes the receipt of money; a keg of spirits of any kind, promises poverty; a keg of powder foretells misfortune; a keg of paint predicts compliments to be paid you. 14.

KEY. If you dream of finding a key, or a bunch of keys, it is a sign that some one will tell you a secret; to dream of losing a key, or keys, is a bad omen, as it predicts that you will come to shame. Such a dream is particularly unfortunate to a young lady. 41, 8.

KID. To dream of a young and sportful kid, implies the birth of a child. A young girl who grants her lover too close intimacy before marriage should never dream of the innocent and harmless kid. It is a good dream for married people who desire children. 70.

KING. To dream of a king denotes that the dreamer is ambitious and will be disappointed. If you dream you speak to a king it is a happy omen, and is a sign of riches and honor. 4, 14.

KILL. If you dream of wantonly killing any animal, or insect, it predicts bad luck and poverty; but if the killing be done by accident, it shows that, though you may have a misfortune in consequence, it will not materially affect your interest. For butchers or farmers to dream of killing fat and healthy animals for food, is a sign of thrift and abundance; but if they dream of killing a hog that does not squeal, it shadows forth a death in the family. 41.

KISSING. (*See Stranger.*) Dreams of kissing work curiously: if a girl dreams that she is kissed by a young man in whom she takes no particular interest, it may be a good omen, and it may not; for if he happens to be a silly fellow who imagines that she is in love with him, it is a sign she will be slandered in a way that will make her unhappy; but if he has no such sentiment, then the sign is exactly the reverse—that is, some one will speak well of her to those whom she esteems highly—perhaps to her lover. If a girl dreams she is kissed by her lover, it predicts that he will say something unpleasant to her at their next meeting; if a lover dreams that his sweetheart kisses him the sign is similar. 1.

KITE. To dream of flying a kite is a sign that you will soon write a letter to some friend or acquaintance. For a girl to dream of seeing a kite in the air, predicts that she will receive a letter from a young man—whether a lover or not, is uncertain. 53, 62.

KNEE. To dream of falling on the knees, denotes misfortune in business. To see a woman's knees, good luck and marriage to the girl of your choice. For a woman to see a man's knee, shows that she will have many male children. 22, 37, 35.

KNIVES. To dream of knives is a bad omen; it betokens lawsuits, poverty, disgrace, and strife. In love, it shows quarrels and bad tempers. 33, 9.

LABOR. To dream you are hard at work, shows you will go a painful journey, unless you be very circumspect; but to see others at work, betokens good fortune. If a girl dreams she sees her lover at work, it signifies that he will try and seduce her. 27, 9.

LADDER. To dream of going up a ladder signifies that you will be a person of some consequence, yet poor: if you imagine you are in danger of falling, it shows that a person who envies your position will attempt to injure you; if you dream of going down a ladder it particularly denotes poverty, though it may allude to some misfortune that will overtake you. 14, 55.

LADIES. To see one, a sign of weakness; many ladies bring calumny and slander. To see a light-haired one, is a happy event to the dreamer; a brunette, sickness; a pregnant lady, brings good news; a naked lady, signifies the death of a relative. To hear a lady speak, without seeing her, foretells departure. 47, 51, 11.

LAKE. If you dream of sailing on a smooth and clear lake, it foreshadows success in all your undertakings; if the lake is rough, but yet has clear water, the sign still holds good, though you will encounter difficulties; if it is muddy water, it denotes sickness, and losses through dishonest people about you. 40, 17.

LAMBS. To see young lambs frisking around their mother, is an excellent omen, as it denotes thrift, and also happiness in your family ties; if you see them sucking, it is a sign of an increase in your family by the birth of a child. For lovers to dream of young lambs, foretells a speedy and happy marriage. 24, 60.

LAMP. To dream of dropping or breaking a lighted lamp, denotes disappointment. If, in your dream, you see the bright light of a lamp at a distance from you in the dark, and you approach it, it shows that you will either have good luck, or will be invited to visit somewhere and meet an agreeable person of the opposite sex. 19.

LAND. To dream of buying or inheriting land, is an excellent omen, as it foretells health and wealth; but to sell land in your dream, denotes sickness and poverty. If a young man dreams of buying land, it is a sign he will marry a rich wife. 34, 61, 18.

LANTERN. To dream of carrying a lantern in a dark night is a good sign, provided you have no difficulty in finding your way, for it shows that you will easily accomplish some fortunate object you may have in view; if you stumble, or have difficulty in finding your way with the lantern, it denotes trouble and vexation, though success will be achieved at last. 28, 10.

LARK. To dream of the lark, shows speedy increase of fortune. To lovers, this is a very favorable omen, and is a sign that the course of true love runs smooth. 47, 68.

LAUGHTER. This omen is unfavorable, and is a sign of tears; it also denotes that you will be worsted by your business engagements; if a lover dreams he sees his sweetheart laugh, it is a sign she will jilt him for a stranger; to the married it signifies domestic trouble. 40.

LAUREL or OLIVE. Denotes victory and pleasure; to the married, inheritance and children; to the single, marriage. 71, 13, 1.

LAW. To dream of instituting a suit at law, or entering a criminal complaint against any one, shows that some enemy will injure you pecuniarily, or that you will lose money by speculation or trade: if you dream you are sued, or prosecuted criminally, the sign is the reverse; you will probably receive money unexpectedly, or be uncommonly successful in your pursuits. 21, 8.

LAWYER. To dream of meeting a lawyer, brings bad tidings; if you speak to him, you will lose some property; if you hear some one speaking in his favor, you will meet with some misfortune. 16.

LAZY. To dream that you see lazy people lounging around, and that you are vexed with them, is a sign of bad luck to some of your relatives, who will depend upon you to assist them: if, in your dream, you imagine yourself to be lazy and sleepy over your work, it foretells either sickness or that you will meet with a loss. 62, 39, 69.

LEAD. (*See Metals.*)

LEAPING. To dream you are leaping over walls, doors or gates, is a sign that you will encounter many difficulties in your present pursuits and that your sweetheart will not marry you. 9, 31.

LEAVES. To dream you see leaves growing freshly on a tree or plant, is a good sign, and shows you will live long and be happy; but to see leaves wither and fall to the ground, is a sign of sickness and death. 47, 21.

LEGS. To dream of thick and fat legs is a bad omen, as it foreshadows sickness: thin, spindleshank legs are excellent ones to dream about, as they denote a successful race with fortune. It is not to be supposed that a lover will ever dream of his sweetheart's legs, but if he should do so, he will probably imagine them to be round, plump, and of an alabaster whiteness; this is a bad dream, and he should by all means avoid thinking of her legs when he goes to sleep: if a lady dreams that her lover's legs are thin, it foretells that he will be a rich man. 48, 5.

LEMONS. To dream of lemons denotes contentions in your family and uneasiness on account of children; they announce the death of some relation and disappointment in love. 22.

LEOPARD. To dream of this animal, signifies that you have many false friends, who are endeavoring to ruin you, it also betokens family quarrels and domestic unhappiness. 24, 76.

LETTERS. These paper missives are good to dream about: if you dream you receive a great number of letters, it foretells that honors await you: to receive one letter in your dream, denotes that some one is praising you behind your back. If a girl dreams that she receives a love-letter from her beau, it shows that he adores her: a gentleman who has a similar dream of a letter from his sweetheart, may rest satisfied that he only possesses her heart. 28, 54, 1.

LETTER CARRIER. To dream of a letter carrier, indicates you will hear from an absent one whom you love. 18, 50.

LETTUCE. To dream of eating lettuce, is a sign of health and happiness, provided that it looks green and nice, and tastes good; wilted or wormy lettuce shadows forth vexation and trouble. 47, 6.

LIAR. To dream that any one offends you by lying, or defaming your family by lies, is a sign you will receive a benefit at the hands of a stranger. 36.

LIBERTY. To dream of taking liberties with any one, bids you bo careful of them; if others take liberties with you, it shows they intend to cheat you. 39, 40.

LICE. To dream of lice denotes sickness and poverty. 3.

LIE. To dream of telling a lie about a woman, is a sign you will kiss a black one: to dream that you lie about your business, denotes that a colored man will rob you: lies generally, imagined in dreams, denote either injuries or caresses by colored people. 14, 64.

LIGHT. (*See Candles, Lamp and Torch.*) To dream you see a great light, is a happy presage; it denotes that you will attain honors, and become rich; in love it shows a sweetheart of an amiable disposition. 8, 70, 2.

LIGHTNING. To dream of bright and vivid white lightning, denotes that you will soon go on a pleasant trip or journey: blueish silver forked lightning foretells good crops and excellent success in business; red forked lightning the same, but attended with calamity, or the death of relatives by violence. 24.

LILIES. If you dream of an abundance of these beautiful flowers in your garden or door-yard, it foretells good luck in getting servants or people to work for you; it also denotes thrift generally about a farm. If a young girl dreams about lilies, it is a sign she will marry a smart and industrious man and live happily with him. 61.

LIMEKILN. To dream of burning lime in a kiln, or of seeing a kiln in full blast, is a sign of health and abundant crops; but to see a dilapidated and empty limekiln in your dream is the reverse of this, as far as the crops are concerned. 77, 5, 15.

LINEN. To dream you are arrayed in clean linen denotes that you will shortly receive some glad tidings; and that your sweetheart is faithful; if it is dirty, then it denotes poverty and disappointment in love. White linen, if dressed in it, presages death; colored linen, removal; shifts, a gay sweetheart; gowns, a gift. 24, 71.

LION. If you dream of seeing the king of beasts, and if he is mild and gentle looking, it shows that you will easily rise in the world to a better position than you now occupy: to dream of an angry and roaring lion, who tries to get at you, shows, that although you may rise in position, jealous people will annoy and try to injure you. 14.

> Dreams of lions, bears, bulls, bees,
> Nests of wasps or hornets, these
> Are emblems whereby are expressed
> Discord with those whom you love best.

LIPS. (*See Mouth.*)

LIQUOR. If you dream of seeing large quantities of liquor, or of buying brandy, rum, whisky, &c., it foretells poverty and disgrace: to dream of drinking it is the same, only worse if possible. 2.

LIZARD. To dream of lizards, is a sign you have secret enemies who will injure you if they can. If a girl dreams this, it shows that some one will question her virtue. 3.

LOG. To dream of seeing large logs around, is a sign that you will soon move into a new house; but if you imagine that you are splitting the logs, it will spoil all this, for it shows that you will want a house badly without being able to get one to your mind. 21, 78.

LOOKING-GLASS. To dream of a looking-glass, is a bad omen, and signifies that you will be surrounded with false friends, who will rob you until your property dwindles to a shadow. To dream you see your face in a looking-glass is a sign of sickness. To break a looking-glass portends death. If a girl dreams she sees her lover in a looking-glass, it is a sign he will desert or seduce her.   18, 61.

LOSSES. To dream of losing your hat is a sign you will entertain a large company, either by making a speech, or otherwise attracting their attention: dreaming of the loss of money, a watch, or any valuables of that kind, predicts that you will gain as much and perhaps more than your loss amounts to: if a girl dreams of losing her shoe-strings, she will be kissed by an agreeable young man; any article of clothing that you may dream of having lost, shows that you will rig yourself out in a new suit.   47, 6.

LOTTERY. (*See Prize.*)

LOVE. To dream you are in love is a sign you will make a fool of yourself and do something silly, of which you may afterwards be ashamed—thus showing that the dream works contrariwise—for love is anything but a silly sentiment unless indulged in by fools. For a young girl to dream of falling in love foretells that she will be laughed at and ridiculed for some folly.   64, 52, 1.

LUCK. To imagine in your dream that you have had excellent luck, in any enterprise, predicts a misfortune: if a man has had a quarrel with his sweetheart, and dreams that it is all made up, he may be sure that the quarrel will continue a great deal longer than is agreeable to him: to a young lady, the sign is the same relative to her beau.   18.

MAD DOG. To dream of seeing such an animal frothing at the mouth and running, is a sign you will be wrongfully accused of a dishonorable action or crime.   4, 12, 61.

MAGGOTS. To dream of seeing anything putrid and covered with maggots, is a sign of death; but the death may be that of your favorite dog, cat, or bird, though such a dream often foretells the death of a relative or friend.   5.

MAID. (*See Virgin.*) If you dream you are pleased with a pretty chambermaid, milkmaid, or any nice-looking young girl, whose occupation carries with it the title of maid, it is a good omen, for it predicts an excellent match, and plenty of children: it also foretells, in many cases, that the dreamer will marry a rich wife.   75, 39.

MAN. To dream of a man dressed in black is lucky; in white, a bad omen: to dream of a murdered man, is a sign of long life. To dream you meet a strange man, is a sign you have a vindictive enemy. For a girl to dream she sees her lover by her bedside, is a sign he will attempt some very improper things.   74, 60, 7.

MANNERS. To dream of ill-mannered people, who annoy you by their awkwardness and selfish conduct, shows that you will shortly go on a journey, and be introduced to a fool.   6, 65.

MAP. To dream of looking over a map, is a sign of an agreeable surprise by the arrival of some dear friend from a distance. If a girl dreams this when her lover is away, he will return unexpectedly. 24, 17.

MARKET. To dream you are in a large market, where all kinds of meats and vegetables are sold, is a sign you will want money that it will be difficult and perhaps impossible to raise; it is a bad sign for tradesmen and others who have notes to pay. 31, 9.

MARRIAGE. (*See Wedding.*) If any one should be so unfortunate as to dream that he or she was present at a happy and jolly wedding, it denotes that they will attend a funeral; it will not necessarily be at the burial of either of the persons you dreamed you saw married, but you will undoubtedly be called to mourn some friend or relative. To dream of being married yourself, foretells your death. 2, 78, 42.

MASK. To dream you see a person wearing a mask, is a sign of hypocrisy; to the lover, it shows that his sweetheart loves some one better than himself; to a girl, it signifies that her lover is engaged to another. To married people, it portends infidelity to the wedding-ring. 46, 8.

MASS. To dream of going to this religious celebration, is a sign that some one will either cheat you or rob your house. If a girl dreams this, let her look out that her lover does not prove to be a worthless scamp. 13.

MEADOW. (*See Field and Green.*) If you dream of walking in a green and pleasant meadow, where the grass grows regular and looks smooth, it is an excellent omen, for it denotes thrift and good luck generally. Such a dream to a farmer, is a sign of good crops and plenty of money. To lovers, it foretells a happy and speedy marriage. 72, 6.

MEANNESS. To dream you are treated in a mean and shabby manner by anybody, is a sign you will have unexpected honors thrust upon you. If a girl dreams that her lover has behaved meanly, she may be sure he will do something to command her admiration. 9, 50, 51.

MEASLES. To dream you have this troublesome disorder shows that you will be fortunate, provided you engage in some disreputable or dishonest speculation, or in a robbery of money: but to conscientious people the omen does not hold good. If a girl dreams of having the measles, it predicts that a rogue will make love to her. 33, 4.

MEAT. To dream of sweet and wholesome fresh meat is a sign you will be coquetted by a lady, and perhaps fall in love with her; but if the meat is putrid or maggoty, it foreshadows sickness and death. 8, 16.

MEDICINE. (*See Physic.*) To take medicine foretells poverty, to give any one medicine, gain. 22, 37, 8.

MELONS. To dream of ripe, fine looking melons, is an excellent omen, as it foretells good health, good luck, and much happiness. A watermelon full of black seeds denotes so much money to be paid to you. If a married woman dreams this, it promises her many children. 46.

METALS. To dream of metals has different significations and interpretations according to the metal you dream of. To enable our readers to more readily discover the meaning of their dreams, we subjoin a list of the metals with their explanations.

BRASS. To dream that you see a brass ornament, is a sign your sweetheart will be false to you. To see any one working in brass, or cleaning that metal, is a sign you will hear of the death of a distant relative who will leave you a legacy. 43, 11.

COPPER. To dream of copper, signifies that your sweetheart is deceitful and loves another, it also shows secret enemies 54, 8, 40.

GOLD. To dream of receiving gold is a good sign, and shows you will be successful in all your undertakings. To dream you pay gold betokens increase of friends. 49, 7.

IRON. For one to dream that he is hurt with iron, signifies that he shall receive some damage. 44, 5.

LEAD. To dream of lead denotes sickness, but to dream of leaden bullets good news. If you dream you are wounded by a leaden bullet it is a sign you will be successful in love. 49, 50.

QUICKSILVER. To dream of this metal is a sign your friends will all be false to you, it is also a sign of losses in property. 48, 19.

SILVER. To dream that you are presented with spoons, or any silver plate for household use, foretells that you or some near relative, will shortly marry: if you dream of buying these articles, it is a sign of poverty: to dream of silver dollars, or bars of silver, used in commerce, is a sign that you will gain money either by a legacy or speculation. 49, 6.

STEEL. To break a piece in a dream, shows that you will overcome your enemies; if you only touch it, your position in life is secure; if you try to bend it, and cannot, you will meet with many serious accidents. 41, 50.

TIN. To dream of tin is a good omen and signifies you will marry a rich wife, and make money at business. 41, 8.

ZINK. To dream of this metal denotes happiness and prosperity to the dreamer. To lovers it is a sign of success in love affairs. 48.

MIDWIFE. To see a midwife denotes revealing of secrets; to the sick, it is death. 18, 4.

MILK. (*See Pitcher and Breast.*) Dreaming of milk predicts, to a man, the love of a lady. If a newly married lady dream that she has a full breast of milk, it is a sign that she will be happily delivered of a fine child; to an old woman, it portends much money. 45, 60.

MILL. If you dream of going to a flouring-mill, where you see plenty of grain and flour, it is a good omen, as it shadows forth thrift and abundance; but to imagine in your dream that you are in any manufactory of cloth fabrics called a mill, is a sign of poverty and want. Girls who work in such places should be careful never to dream of them. 55.

MISER. To dream of a miser is a sign of waste, loss, or destruction: if you see him counting and hoarding money, it foretells you will either lose or be robbed of some: to see him patching his clothes or barn : se or barn denotes a calamity, such as a robbery or a fire. 14, 62

MISFORTUNE. To dream you have a misfortune denotes luck and success: thus, dreaming of the loss of money is a sign you will get some: if you imagine your house is burned, you will be successful in a speculation: if you dream of being robbed, it foretells a legacy or the finding of something valuable, &c. 41.

MISTAKE. If any one dreams of being vexed, annoyed, or injured by reason of making a mistake, it shadows forth disgrace. Mistaking one person for another in your dream, denotes scandal: thus if a young girl should dream that she hailed a young man as her lover, and found it was a stranger, it shows that some malicious person will talk lightly of her character. 78, 16.

MONEY. (*See Purse and Pocket Book.*) To dream of finding money is an excellent omen, as it foretells that you will soon get some: if, in your dream, you see bank bills of a large denomination, or large gold pieces, the sign is similar: to see small pieces of money is not so good, though it is a pretty fair dream. To dream of receiving money is a good omen; in love, it foretells marriage and children. To dream you lose money, is a proof you will be unsuccessful in some favorite pursuit. 18, 4.

MONKEY. To dream that you see a monkey, and are pleased with his antics, shows that you will make the acquaintance of a fool. For a girl to dream of playing with a monkey is a sign she will do something she is ashamed of, and perhaps lose her virtue. Monkeys are also a sign of law suits and secret enemies. 17, 6.

MOON. To dream of a sharp new moon with horns pointing upward is a sign you will be rich: if the horns point sideways or downward, it foretells poverty: seeing a full moon in your dream denotes a thrifty and happy marriage: a half moon shadows forth the loss of a wife or husband by death or desertion. Dreaming of seeing a half moon is fatal to the prospects of lovers. 19, 18.

MOUNTAIN. To dream of approaching beautiful smooth-looking mountains, dressed in verdure, denotes thrift and happiness, and that you will rise in the world: if the mountains look steep, rugged and rocky, it foreshadows difficulties and danger, which you may overcome by energy: to dream of successfully climbing a mountain, is a sure sign that some honor awaits you, or that you will make a good deal of money: difficulties in climbing show troubles and vexations in getting your honors or your money. 64.

MOTH. To dream of moth is a sign some one is robbing you, it also predicts slander by a supposed friend. To dream you see a moth burn its wings in a flame signifies that an enemy will die. 22.

MOTHER. If you dream of quarreling with your mother, it is a sign she will do some generous act, or confer a benefit that will delight you: to dream of fondling your mother shadows forth her loss by death, or that you will be parted from her: if you dream she makes you a present, the dream will come true so far that she will probably present you with a new brother or sister. 46, 34.

MOURNING. To dream that you are dressed in mourning for the death of a relative, is a sign that a wedding will soon take place in your family, or that of some blood relation. To see people dressed in black, and be among them, foretells an invitation to a wedding or to be present at a marriage ceremony. 32, 12.

MOUSE. (*See Trap.*) To dream of killing a mouse is a sign you will detect a thief in stealing from you: if, in your dream, you see a mouse, or a number of mice, it foretells that you will soon have thieves in the house. For a girl to dream that she pets a mouse, shows that she will have a light-fingered or dishonest lover. 75, 70.

MOUTH. Dreaming of a large mouth and big lips is a sure sign you will be kissed by some one of the opposite sex: to dream of a mouth out of shape, or with a hare lip, denotes to a woman that she will have a deformed child, and to a man that he will get into a difficulty by means of his intimacy with a woman: to dream of a small mouth and thin lips is a sign of loud and angry words, and that some one will give you a scolding. 27, 6, 3.

MOVING. To dream of moving your residence or place of business, under any circumstances, is a sign of poverty: if, in your dream, you see other people moving, it foretells that some one of your relatives will come to poverty, and you will have to assist him. 55.

MUD. To dream of getting covered with mud by having it splashed over you, is a sign that you will be belied and talked about. 29.

MULBERRIES. To dream of mulberries denotes to the maiden, a happy marriage; to the married, affection and constancy. 64, 70, 3.

MULATTO. (*See Negro.*) To see a mulatto in sleep, brings good luck; a female mulatto, dangerous sickness. 4, 11, 44.

MULE. To dream of riding a mule, or driving one, is a sign of celibacy: gentlemen or ladies who dream this may safely calculate that they will live single for the rest of their lives, unless some more vivid dream with a favorable omen should counterbalance the influence of this one. If married people dream of mules, it foretells that they will be childless. 4, 51, 66.

MUSHROOM. To dream you eat mushrooms is a sign you will live to a good old age, but to dream you see them grow, or gather them, is a sign you will get rich by a splendid speculation, and then get poor as suddenly as you got wealthy. 49, 59.

MUSIC. (*See Singing.*) To dream of hearing strains of sweet music, denotes joy and happiness. If a girl who has a lover dreams this, he will surprise her either with a splendid present, or with an invitation to go somewhere where she will be delighted and enjoy herself much. 74, 18.

MUSTARD. To dream of mustard or mustard seed, is a bad omen, and foretells sickness and perhaps death. To dream you eat mustard, is a sign your sweetheart or lover is false to you. To married persons this dream indicates domestic quarrels. 4.

MYRTLE. To dream of myrtle, is a sign you will receive a declaration of love. To the married it signifies domestic happiness. 3, 11, 33.

NAILS. To dream that one's nails are longer than usual, signifies profit, and the contrary, loss: to dream your nails are cut off, signifies loss and disgrace, and contention with friends and relations. If one dreams his nails are pulled off, it threatens with misery and affliction, and danger of death: for a man to dream he bites his nails, shows quarrels and dissensions: to dream of paring your nails, foretells a lingering sickness. 57, 8.

NAKEDNESS. To dream you see a man naked, signifies fear and terror: to dream you see a woman naked, signifies honor and joy, provided she be fair-skinned and handsome; but if she is crooked, old, wrinkled, or otherwise ill made, and black withal, it signifies shame, repentance, and ill luck. For a woman to dream she sees her husband naked, signifies success in her enterprises and a good number of children. 14.

NAPKIN. A white napkin denotes orderly conduct, which will bring happiness; a dirty napkin, disorderly behavior. 70, 6.

NAVEL. If you dream that your navel is out of shape, or looks queer, it is a sign of misfortune in connection with the opposite sex, unless you are married, in which case it denotes the birth of a child: for unmarried people to dream such dreams foretells trouble and disgrace. 35, 17.

NECK. If a woman or girl dreams that her neck is large and thick, it is a sure sign she will bear many children: if it seems smaller than usual, it denotes to a married woman a miscarriage, and to a girl the loss of her beau: if a woman dreams that her neck is fair and beautiful, it foretells that some gentleman will make love to her. 22.

NECKLACE. For a girl to dream that a gentleman presents her with a necklace, is a sign that some one meditates an attempt to seduce her: if a married woman dreams that her husband gives her a necklace, it shows that she will soon be in the family way. 69, 12, 21.

NEEDLES. To dream of needles, signifies that you will be grievously injured by the deceit of supposed friends. For a girl to dream that she pricks herself with a needle, is a sign that her beau will attempt improper liberties. 8, 49.

NEGRO. To dream of being frightened or assaulted by a negro, is a good sign, as it denotes safety: if the negro comes towards you in a pleasant and agreeable way, it shows that you will meet with a loss or be robbed: to see a grinning, pleasant-looking negro in your dream, forebodes trouble through the conduct of a dependent. 32.

NEW YEAR'S PRESENT. To dream you give a New Year's present, signifies you will hear good news. To receive one, is a sign you will soon get into trouble. 64, 19.

NIAGARA. As every one has heard of this great cataract, and multitudes have seen it, it is not strange that a good many people dream of going there: such a dream is a sign that you will be embarrassed in company by a sensation of some kind. 13, 49, 6.

NIGHT. (*See Stars.*) To dream of a clear beautiful night when the stars are shining, indicates that you will have a long and happy life and be very successful in all your undertakings. To dream you are

4

courting your sweetheart on such a night shows that she is true to you. To dream of a cloudy night portends disasters in business, and to dream of a stormy night indicates sickness. 5, 19.

NIGHTCAP. For a girl to dream that she forgot to take off her nightcap, but received company in it, is a sign she will be kissed by a strange gentleman, or that some stranger will be smitten by her charms: if a married woman dreams this, it foretells that her husband will be jealous of her, and perhaps not without cause. 70.

NIGHTINGALE. To dream of this bird signifies light amours; to hear it sing, happiness. 48.

NOBILITY. Should anybody be so foolish as to dream that they are created a Duke, an Earl, or that they have conferred upon them any patent of nobility, it is a sign of shiftlessness and poverty. If a girl dreams that a lord is in love with her, she will be apt to marry a shiftless and needy fellow. 21, 19.

NOISE. If you dream of hearing strange or mysterious noises, it is a sign that the spirit of some dead relative hovers near you, and has an influence upon your actions. 20.

NOSE. To dream of big-nosed people is generally a good omen, as such persons are usually smart and energetic. To dream of snub noses is a sign of a quarrel, or that you will be abused by somebody. 48.

NUGGET. This is an English word for a lump of gold: to dream of digging a big nugget of pure gold, is a sign of wealth and honors. Dreams relative to gold or silver promise good fortune always. 4, 11, 44.

NUN. For a young girl to dream of seeing a sober-looking nun, is a sign of celibacy; if she imagines she speaks to the nun she may safely calculate on being an old maid; if a young man dreams this, it foretells that he will suspect his sweetheart of being untrue to him, and probably discard her altogether. 29, 65.

NURSE. Dreaming of a nurse for lying-in women foreshadows luck and plenty of cash; to a farmer, such a dream prognosticates abundant crops, and to newly married people good crops of children. 28.

NUTS. To dream of nuts denotes riches and happiness; to the lover, success; if you are gathering them, it is a good omen; but if you crack them, unfavorable. 48, 6.

OAK. To dream of seeing a very large oak tree, and of gathering acorns under it, is a sign that some wealthy relative will leave you a fortune by will: if anybody dreams this who does not happen to have wealthy relations, it may turn out that somebody else will take the liberty of making a will in his or her favor; if not, a streak of good luck will come in some other way to make the matter right. 65.

OAR. If you dream of sailing in a boat, and losing one or more of the oars, it is a sign of the death of your father, mother, or guardian, or of some one to whom you look for protection: if an engaged young girl or a married woman dreams this, it foretells the death of a lover or husband. 2.

OATH. To dream of taking a solemn oath before a magistrate, or in a court of justice, foretells quarreling and litigation: even if you are a timid and quiet person, such a dream promises that some one will quarrel with you. 20.

OATS. To dream of this grain foretells a journey by land: if an engaged young girl dreams of oats, it denotes that her wedding tour is not far off. 69.

. OCEAN. (*See Sea.*)

ODD FELLOW. To dream of joining a society of this order fore-tells sickness and distress: if you are already an Odd Fellow, and dream of strife in the Lodge, and that you are in danger of being turned out, it is a sign that you will attain a higher station in life by riches or honors. 2.

OFFICER. (*See Police.*) To dream that a military officer is in your company shadows forth beggary and disgrace. If a girl dreams that she has such a person for a lover, she may calculate that her first suitor will be a poor shoat, of no account whatever. 70, 28.

OIL. To dream it is spilled on the floor, signifies damage ; to spill it on yourself, profit. 1, 41.

OLD MAN. To dream of seeing a man bowed down with age is a sign of good luck in business, and to a politician it denotes advance-ment. This is not a good dream for females, for to them it denotes want. 63.

OLD WOMAN. To dream of an aged woman is generally a good omen, as it shadows forth domestic happiness: to a married woman such a dream foretells the birth of a child: to a young girl, that she will have an offer of marriage. 3.

ONIONS. To dream of this vegetable, denotes both good and bad luck: if you are eating them, you will soon receive some money; your sweetheart will be faithful, but cross, and you will be engaged in some dispute; if you are throwing onions away, it is the forerun-ner of mischief; in love, quarrels; in trade, opposition. 5, 8, 48.

OPERA. To dream of going to the opera is a sign you will travel: if you hear a new singer that delights you, it foretells that you will make a new acquaintance on some journey: if an engaged young lady dreams of the opera, her wedding journey is thus shadowed forth. 27, 55.

OPIUM. To dream of this drug foretells sickness and poverty: if you imagine that you see some one under the influence of opium, and in danger of dying, it foretells a misfortune either to yourself or some near relative. 64.

ORANGE. To dream of having an abundance of oranges, shadows forth that you will get just so much yellow gold: if you dream of eating them, it promises you health: if you give them to friends, it foretells that you will be honored and esteemed: if a girl dreams that her lover presents her with fine-looking oranges, he will un-doubtedly bring her a fortune when she marries. 3, 12, 36.

ORCHARD. If, in your dream, you imagine you are in a fine or-chard, and the fruit looks fair and tempting, and you eat of it, it foretells that you will shortly be engaged in some pleasant adventure either of love or intrigue: if you see rotten, wormy, or scraggy-looking apples, it shows that you will be thrown into mean and low company, much to your disgrace. Such dreams are bad ones for young girls. 18, 12.

ORGAN. To dream of hearing the solemn and enchanting music of a church organ is a sad omen to young girls, as it foretells their early death: if a gentleman dreams this, it points to the death of some young girl in whom he takes an interest, and perhaps to his sweetheart, if he has one. To imagine you hear some lively tune on a street organ is also a bad omen, as it foretells that you will soon attend a funeral. 55, 3.

OVEN. (*See Baking.*)

OVERFLOW. (*See Flood.*) To dream that a river, or any stream, overflows its banks and surrounds your house with water, is a sign of wealth; that is, you will acquire riches in proportion to the quantity of water around, and the ground it covers: if you fancy that any one is drowned in the water, it foretells a misfortune in connection with your riches. 9, 66, 18.

OWL. To dream of seeing one of these birds of night in a roosting position, is a sign that you will discover an important secret that relates to yourself: to see an owl flying foretells that some secret of your own will get out. 3.

OXEN. (*See Cattle.*)

OYSTERS. If, in your dream, you imagine you are eating oysters, it denotes that you will have difficulties relative to money matters: but to rake them out of the water is a sign of money-getting: to dream of opening nice fat oysters for other people to eat is also a favorable omen, as it shows that you will have plenty of cash. 7, 53.

PAINTING. To dream of painting your house is a sign of sickness in the family, but at the same time thrift and good luck in business: if, in your dream, you see a white house newly painted outside, you will probably soon be summoned to attend a funeral: to see any other colored house newly painted, foretells that you will hear of the sickness of a friend or relative: dreaming of beautiful paintings of landscapes, portraits, &c., is an omen of bad luck and poverty. 22, 11, 5.

PALL-BEARER. For a man to dream that he is a pall-bearer at a funeral, denotes that he will be married within a year: to dream of seeing pall-bearers, is a sign you will be invited to a wedding. 49, 6.

PANCAKE. (*See Thick.*) For a girl to dream of baking pancakes is a sign that some gentleman is in love with her; and if a married woman has such a dream, she may be sure that some man, other than her husband, admires her; to dream of eating pancakes, foretells falling in love, to either sex; and if you relish them, you will be successful in your love. 36.

PANTALOONS. If you dream you have a new pair of pantaloons, it is a sign you will be prosperous; if they do not fit, and are too tight, it is a sign you will be pinched in money matters; if they are dark, it is a sign of long life, but if light, it denotes sickness. Young girls should try and not dream about pantaloons, for such an omen is very dangerous to them. 46, 8.

PANTHER. To dream that you see one of these animals, and are terrified by it, shows that you will be disgusted at the ingratitude of a friend you have served: if, in your dream, you see a tame panther, and caress it, it foretells that you have some ungrateful person in your household, (perhaps a servant,) or else a false-hearted friend. 41.

PAPER. To dream of smooth paper, is a good omen; but if it appears rumpled, it will give you much pain. To dream of paper that is wet, signifies success in love matters. 21, 18.

PARADE. To dream of a parade of soldiers, and that you are delighted with the military display, foretells that some one will deceive you: to a business man it is an omen of losses by bad debts or dull trade: to a young girl it foreshadows a gay but false lover: to a married woman it is a sign that her husband, though kind, will be false to his vows. 58, 1.

PARASOL. If a young woman dreams she has got a new parasol, it predicts for her a new lover: if she imagines she has broken her parasol, her lover (if she has one) will leave her; if not, then some male friend, in whom she placed confidence or derived advantage, will fail her: to a married woman, dreaming of a broken parasol is a very bad omen, as it predicts ruin to her husband. 34.

PARDON. To dream of asking pardon for an offence, is a bad omen under any circumstances, as it foretells humiliation and disgrace: for a criminal to imagine, in his dream, that the Governor has pardoned him, is a sign that he will not only not be pardoned, but that he will suffer much remorse and unhappiness in his imprisonment. 19, 3, 40.

PARROT. To dream that you are pleased with the chattering of one of these birds, is a sign that some deceitful person will flatter you: if an engaged young girl has such a dream, she should look sharp to the antecedents of her lover before marriage, as it is ten to one that he is not worthy of her confidence: the dream may, however, point to some other flatterer. 15, 2, 33.

PARTING. To dream of parting from friends with regret, is a sign of disappointment: if a girl dreams that her lover is going away anywhere, and she feels bad when he takes his leave, it predicts that he will not "go raving distracted with delight" the next time he comes to see her, and she will consequently be disappointed at his supposed coolness; but all this may not amount to anything more than to make her feel bad for the time being. 4.

PARTNER. (*See Ball.*) To dream that your partner in a dance slights or snubs you, is a sign that some one is enamored of you: this applies to either sex: if you dream of a particularly agreeable and attractive partner, it shows that you will quarrel with somebody of the opposite sex: for a man in business to dream of taking a partner, foretells that he will be robbed. 17, 38.

PARTY. To dream of giving a large and sumptuous party to your friends, is a sign of losses and poverty : if you imagine you go to such a party, it foretells that you will be asked to assist some one in distress.   77, 18, 42.

PASTURE. (*See Cattle.*) To dream of seeing cattle feeding in a green and rich pasture, foretells thrift and wealth: if the grass is sun-burnt and only green in patches, and the cattle look lean, the sign is the reverse; and such a dream denotes short crops to farmers. 6, 11, 66.

PATCHES. For a woman to dream of patching the clothes of her husband or children, is an excellent omen, as it denotes that each patch will be a good lump of money brought into the family.   5.

PATENT RIGHT. To dream of procuring a patent for an invention of your own, shows that you will never realize anything from it: if money is to be made by it, some one else will get the benefit: if you dream of getting a patent for some other person, it is a sign of good luck in a speculation.   33, 17.

PATHS. To dream you are walking in a broad, good pathway, denotes health and success; in love it shows you will meet with a sweetheart, who will make you happy, but if the path is crooked it foretells trouble to the dreamer.   44.

PAUPER. To dream that you visit the poor-house and see the inmates, is a sign to a woman that she will bear many children, and to a man that he will raise a large family. such a dream to a young girl foretells that she will be apt to become a mother before she is a wife. 21.

PAWNBROKER. If you dream of pawning any of your goods at a pawnbroker's, provided you have never patronized such a place, it foretells that fortune is about to smile on you, and if you take advantage of the circumstance, you will surely get rich.   To lazy and shiftless people, such a dream would not be of much account.   4, 11, 22.

PEACHES. To dream of fine, ripe, yellow peaches, denotes that you will get just so much yellow gold, which makes this dream a splendid one for gold-diggers: if the peaches you dream about are very red, or look small and wilted, it shows that your gold will turn out to be about half copper, or that your luck will not amount to much.   17, 1, 9.

PEACOCK. To dream of this proud bird, is a sign of poverty; if you imagine that he spreads his tail, and exhibits all his finery, so much the worse.   For a girl to dream of a peacock, shows that she will have an empty-headed fop for a lover, who will turn out to be as poor as a rat.   65, 54.

PEANUTS. To dream of an abundance of ground-nuts, or peanuts, shows that you will be poor, but contented, healthy and happy. If a married woman in the family-way dreams of them, it is a sign she will have a boy.   11.

PEAS. To dream of eating green peas, is a sign of health; and if you imagine that you eat crooked dry peas, it foretells both health and thrift.   If you dream of feeding any animal with dry peas, it foreshadows good luck.   6.

PEARLS. To dream of these gems, denotes poverty and misery: if a girl dreams that a lover gives her a piece of jewelry set in pearls, it shows that he will never be well off; and if she imagines that he presents her with a string or necklace of pearls, she may safely calculate that he will turn out to be a wretchedly poor man. 56.

PEARS. To dream of ripe, mellow pears, portends elevation in life, riches, honors, and constancy in love. If a woman with child dream of them, she will have a daughter. To dream of unripe, choke-pears, is a sign of misfortunes, and inconstancy in love. 33.

PEDDLER. If you dream of buying things of a peddler, it is a sign that some one will cheat you, or that one of your debtors will mysteriously disappear, which amounts to about the same thing: if a lady housekeeper dreams this, let her look sharp that her servants do not rob or swindle her in some way. 42, 13.

PEN-KNIFE. To dream of a pen-knife, is a bad omen, and foretells loss in trade, attacks by thieves, and unfaithfulness in love. 29, 47.

PENS. To dream of writing with a steel pen, is a sign you will get yourself into a bad scrape, by tattling about your friends and neighbors. If the pen be gold, it foreshadows good news, and success in business and love affairs. To dream you are making a quill pen, is a sign you have many enemies, but that you will triumph over them, and be successful in all you undertake. But this dream does not amount to much, as it is only a "set-off" to dreaming of a penknife, which is a bad omen. 28, 6.

PEPPERS. To dream of picking pepper-pods, foretells to married people smart children, if they have any. A girl who dreams this, will have a smart man for a lover, but he will not pet her much either as a sweetheart or wife. 9.

PERFUMERY. To dream of pleasant and delicate perfumes, foreshadows sluttish habits in a woman: if a lover dreams of perfumes in connection with the beloved object, it shows that when he marries, he will find her to be a slut. A girl who dreams this, will be apt to have a shiftless lover. 71, 1.

PERJURY. To dream that any one injures you by false swearing, or by perjury in court, is a sign that you will discover some friend or acquaintance to be dishonest, or guilty of a crime, or of mean conduct; if a girl dream this, it is a similar omen relative to her lover. 52.

PET. If a girl dreams she has a pet animal of any kind, (a child, of course, excepted,) it is a sign she will never marry: if she dreams of a pet child, or one whom she adores, it foretells for her a prolific marriage. 49.

PHYSIC. (See *Medicine*.) In a dream-book published 1751, is this prediction: "If any man doth dreme he taketh much physicke, it foretelleth a bad lyver, and a quarell with ye doctor; but a virgin who dremeth this dreme, will marry ye doctor first, and quarell thereafter." 37, 8.

PIANO. To dream of hearing pleasant and lively tunes on the piano, is a sign of thrift and domestic happiness; but if you dream of buying, or that any one presents you with a piano, it foreshadows poverty; it is a bad omen for a girl to dream she has got a new piano. 72.

PICKLES. If a girl dreams of eating pickles, it is a sign some old bachelor will kiss her: if a young man dreams of pickles, he will be beloved by a maid older than himself, and probably of a sour and crabbed temper. 39, 2.

PICNIC. For a young man to dream of going with a picnic party into the woods, is a sign that some silly girl will fall in love with him: if a young girl dreams this, some vain fellow will probably pay her attentions and compliments merely to gratify his own vanity. 37, 12.

PICTURES. To dream of seeing pictures is a sign of joy without profit. 48, 7.

PIES. To dream of eating pie is a sign that you will soon be in want. To dream you are making pies is a sign of pleasure and happiness. 38.

PIGEONS. To dream of pigeons is a sign of content and delight, and success in business. 39.

PIGS. To dream of seeing pigs is good; if you are in trade you will have great increase in your business from foreign parts; if you are in love, your sweetheart is thereby denoted to be of a good temper, faithful and sincere to you, and that if you marry you will become happy. 4, 12, 48.

PINEAPPLE. To dream of this fruit is a sign of gold; if you see an abundance of it, you will receive plenty of gold soon after: a young girl who dreams of pineapples will probably get a rich husband. 22, 9, 78.

PINKS. If a lady dreams of pinks, it foretells she will soon have a new bonnet that she will be delighted with: if a gentleman dreams of them, his wife or sweetheart will get a new bonnet that will please him. That's all. 34.

PINS. To dream of pins signifies that you will have small troubles all through life, but no great disasters; to dream you find a pin is a sign of success in business; if a girl dream she is pricked with a pin, she must keep a sharp look out for her lover or she may get in trouble. 3, 71.

PIPE. To dream you smoke a pipe is an omen of success in business; if the pipe goes out three times it is a sign you will meet with losses. To dream you break a pipe foretells a quarrel that will injure your prospects. 49, 7, 9.

PIRATE. To dream you are captured by pirates is a sign you will travel in foreign countries and eventually make your fortune: if a girl dreams this, it foretells that she will marry a foreigner who, dying, will leave her a fortune. 6.

PISS-ABED. To dream that you wet the bed in your sleep, is a sign you will lose something by fire: your house may not burn, but some article will either fall in the fire or be damaged by it—perhaps your servant may spoil some clothing while ironing. 5, 11, 55.

PISTOL. To dream of arming yourself with a pistol foretells that you will lose *caste*, and perhaps become poor: if a girl dreams that her lover carries a pistol, she may be sure that he is below her in social life, and therefore an unpropitious or unsuitable match. 16, 21, 57.

PITCH. To dream that you get pitch on your person is a sign that some one has been scandalizing you by telling lies: a girl who dreams this, may be sure that her fair fame has been questioned somewhere. 54, 14.

PITCHER. (*See Jug.*) To dream you drink water or milk from a pitcher is a good omen, and signifies you will be prosperous in love and business. To dream you spill anything out of a pitcher foretells losses from the treachery of supposed friends, and to dream you break a pitcher portends sickness, and accident while on a journey. To dream of breaking a pitcher is also a sign of bankruptcy through carelessness. 49, 20.

PLAINS. To dream of being on a beautiful plain signifies health, happiness and riches, but portends some crosses in love. 4, 12, 48.

> Dreams of wandering over plains,
> Walking in cross ways and lanes,
> And being in thick woods quite lost,
> Declare that lovers shall be crost.

PLANTS. (*See Blossom.*) To dream of healthy, thriving plants is a good omen, as it foretells success in life, and smart children: such a dream is an excellent one for lovers, as it denotes an early and happy marriage. 43, 14, 7.

PLASTER. For a girl to dream of having a plaster on her person is a sign that some one will offer her an insult, or perhaps make an attempt upon her chastity: if a man dreams this, the same will probably happen to his wife or sweetheart. 72, 8.

PLENTY. (*See Abundance.*)

PLOW. (*See Husbandry.*)

PLOWING. For a farmer to dream that he is plowing on smooth and even ground, denotes heavy crops, and good luck generally: if he plows up stones it is all the better, but if his plow gets hitched into a rock or stump, it denotes vexation and trouble with his good luck. 41.

PLUMS. To dream of an abundance of this fruit is a sign of health but yet you are liable to lose your life by an accident: if a girl dreams she is presented with plums, it foretells her early death. 36, 14, 77.

POCKET-BOOK. To dream of finding a pocket-book full of money is a sign of riches, but if it contains no money, it foretells a disappointment: if you dream you lose your pocket-book, it foreshadows success in business. 19, 78.

POET. If any young person should be so silly as to dream of writing poetry, it foretells poverty; and for one to dream of having a poetical lover or sweetheart, is a sign that they will fall in love with a fool. 64, 50.

POISON. To dream that you are poisoned is a sign you will get into bad or unworthy company: if you imagine that any friend or acquaintance is poisoned, it is a similar omen as regards them: if, in your dream, you think any one has given you poison to murder you, it foretells that some base proposal will be made to you. 3, 9.

POLE-CAT. If a man dream he sees one, he will marry a beautiful woman; if a woman, she will marry a handsome man. If this delightful animal make an attack on you it is a sign you will suffer from the slander of enemies. 68, 2.

POLICE. If any respectable person dreams of being arrested by police officers, it is a sign that some distinguished honor will be conferred on him: if a young girl should dream that policemen took her lover into custody, she will hear of his advancement in the world. 46, 30.

POLITE. To dream of polite people is a sign that a stranger will visit, or be introduced to you: if a girl dreams that her beau is stiff and formal in addressing her, it foretells that she will soon have a new admirer. 61.

POOR. To dream of poverty is a sign of good luck, but if you imagine you are so poor as to be induced to beg, it foretells that some one will either insult you or hurt your feelings, but yet your luck will not be impaired. 8, 2.

PORK. (*See Bacon and Ham.*)

PORTRAIT. To dream of having your portrait taken, is a sign some one will compliment your good looks; but if you are dissatisfied and think it a bad likeness, the compliment will run in a contrary direction, and you will be called frightfully ugly-looking behind your back. 12.

POUND. For a farmer to dream that any of his cattle are taken to pound, is a sign that they will increase: if he dreams of seeing strange cattle in a pound, it foretells that he will soon buy some. 19, 55.

PRAISE. To dream that any one praises or flatters you, is a sign of scandal: if a girl dreams that her lover praises her good looks or amiability, she had better discard him as a false-hearted person who cares nothing about her, but is merely flattering his own vanity. 35, 17.

PRAYER. To dream of prayer, or of joining in a prayer with others, is a sign you will ask a favor of some one who will refuse you: if you dream of hearing prayers at church, or in any public place, it shows that you will be requested to do something which you will refuse to do, and thereby make an enemy. 34, 77.

PREGNANCY. For a woman to dream that she is pregnant when she is not, is a sign of some special good fortune: she will either have a handsome present, or else her husband will be lucky in some business transaction and give her a part of the money: if a girl dreams this, it foretells that she will get married about as sudden as if the dream were a reality. 4, 11, 44.

PRESENT. (*See Gift.*) To dream of receiving a present, is usually a sign of disappointment; but if a married woman dreams that she is presented with fruit, it shows that she will soon become pregnant: if a girl imagines she is presented by her lover with gold jewelry, it predicts that he covets the possession of her person rather than her heart. 64, 21.

PRESERVES. To dream that you make or eat them, foretells the acquisition of much money and property, also health and happiness. 3, 33, 9.

PRETTY GIRL. For a young man to dream of admiring a pretty girl, is a sign he will marry a simpleton: if a girl dreams she has a nice and pretty-looking lover, she will be apt to take up with a putty-head. Here is an ancient rhyming prediction: 4, 13

> To dream you love a girl who's pretty,
> Foretells that you'll in sorrow part;
> But if you dream she's wise and witty,
> She'll be the darling of your heart!

PRICK. If a lady dreams of pricking her finger while sewing, she must put it in her mouth on awaking, and make a wish, and she will realize it within one month, provided it relates to love matters: a wish of any other kind will doubtless come true some time or other, as the omen is an excellent one: if a lady dreams she pricks herself with a pin, the omen is not so good. (*See Pin and Briar.*) 498.

PRIEST. To dream that a priest offers you service, or visits you for any purpose, is a sign that you will be robbed; if you dream you go to one for advice, it foretells that some misfortune will overtake you: any dream about a priest is a bad one. 39.

PRISON. (*See Jail.*) To dream you are put in prison, foretells that honor awaits you: but this omen does not apply to rogues or dishonest people, though such a dream by them favors their desires: if a girl dreams that her lover has gone to prison, she will soon hear of his advancement. 46.

PRIZE. To dream of drawing a prize in the lottery, is a sign of poverty and misery: if you dream that you bought a lottery ticket with a majority of odd numbers on it, you may perchance be successful with those numbers, but even numbers are worthless in dreams. To dream of getting prizes in any way is a bad omen. 4, 11, 44.

PROCESSION. To dream of seeing a long military or civic procession, is a sign that some of your friends will come to poverty and ask your assistance; if you imagine that you are in such a procession yourself, it foretells that you will either make a loss, or be very short of money. 2.

PROFIT. If a man dreams that he made a large and liberal profit by any transaction or speculation, it foretells losses and disaster. 48, 16.

PROMISE. To dream of broken promises on the part of a friend, is a sign that he will confer a benefit on you: if a girl dreams that her lover has broken his promise to marry, it foreshadows a speedy performance of the ceremony. 3.

PROPERTY. To dream of the loss of property, is a sign of good luck, and you may calculate to acquire as much as you dreamed was lost, for such dreams always work contrariwise. 45, 1, 14.

PROSTITUTE. For a young man to dream of associating with prostitutes, is a sign of poverty and disgrace: if he dreams of seeing these girls anywhere, it foretells misfortune or bad luck: for a girl to dream of them, is a sign that her chastity is in danger. 35, 9.

PROUD. To dream of proud people who disgust you, foretells that you will rise in the world: a girl who dreams this of her lover, will probably marry a rich or distinguished man. 3, 32, 13.

PUDDING. To dream of a hard-boiled plum pudding, or a hard roll of pudding of any kind, is a sign you will be invited to a dinner party; but if you imagine the pudding looks soft and mussy, it foretells that you will go to some entertainment where there will be a row. 19, 70.

PULPIT. If any one dreams of going into a pulpit, it is a sign he or she will visit a place of disrepute, as such dreams work contrariwise: for a girl to dream that she assists in ornamenting or dressing a pulpit, foretells that she will do some act that she afterwards regrets, because of an unworthy person being connected therewith. 62.

PUMP. Dreaming of a pump is an excellent omen: if you dream of pumping clear water from one, it shows that you will have good luck in business, or in a speculation: pumping dirty water is a sign of sickness. 29, 4, 20.

PUNCH. To dream of making this beverage, or of drinking it, is a sign of poverty or disgrace; if a girl dreams that her lover treats her to punch, she had better discard him at once, as he will undoubtedly turn out to be a poor and shiftless fellow. 19, 32.

PUNISHMENT. (See Stick.) To dream of punishing a child, foretells good fortune to the victim, and honors to yourself. For any one to dream of being punished by whipping, is a sign they will rise in the world, or be honored for some act. 7.

PURSE. To dream of finding an empty purse, shadows forth disappointment; if the purse has plenty of money in it, your luck will be excellent—the more money, the better fortune: if it has in it large gold pieces, or large bills, you will become rich either by marriage or inheritance. 78.

PUTTY. To dream of putty, is a sign of poverty: puttying up holes foretells losses—the larger the hole, the more extensive the loss. If you are putting glass into a window with putty, it foretells that you will soon remove into a meaner place than you now occupy. 6, 4.

PUZZLE. To dream of bothering your brains with a puzzle, foretells frivolity; if you succeed, you will do something that works to your disadvantage: if you imagine that the puzzle puzzles you, it is a sign that some silly person will do you an unintentional injury. 21, 17.

QUAIL. To dream of these birds is a good omen: if you imagine you see young quail feeding, it is a sign of thrift, particularly to farmers: to be successful in shooting them in the proper season, also foretells good luck and success in any undertaking. 76, 14.

QUAKER. To dream of business intercourse with genuine broad-brims, is a sign you will make a bad bargain. If, in your dream, you see a concourse of quakers, it foretells that you will not be fortunate in business matters. This omen is supposed to be predicated on the fact that the Quakers monopolize all the good chances when they are around. 24, 30.

QUARREL. To dream of quarreling with a stranger, is a sign you will make a new friend or acquaintance; if you imagine that you quarrel with a friend, it shows that you will soon have a pleasant and agreeable time with him: lovers who dream of quarrels, will be apt to bill and coo harder than ever. 2, 12, 24.

QUEEN. For a man to dream of seeing a queen, foretells the loss of money, either by robbery or bad debts: if he is presented to a queen, the dream is still worse in respect to losses. 39, 60.

QUICKSILVER. (See Metals.)

QUILTING. If a lady dreams of going to a quilting party, it foretells for her and her family thrift and good luck: gentlemen, who dream of being much entertained at such a party, will have the very best success in love matters. 71, 54.

QUINCES. To dream of quinces, is an excellent omen: if you imagine you are gathering quinces from trees full of fine-looking, yellow ones, it predicts that you will get just so much yellow gold, which will be a fortune. 49, 6.

QUOITS. If a man dreams he is playing quoits, it is a sign he will soon have a quarrel. If a woman dreams she is playing quoits, it foretells she will have much trouble through life. To dream of quoits, is not a good omen to lovers. 57, 3.

RABBITS. To dream of these animals, foretells many small children: if a newly married woman dreams of them it is a sign that she will have twins or triplets within a year: such a dream will not be very pleasant to a young girl unless she means to marry right sudden, for rabbits do not predict anything else but breeding children. 44, 13.

RACCOON. To dream of simply treeing a raccoon, is a good omen, for you will probably either gain a sum of money, or have it left to you as a legacy: if you imagine that you shoot the animal, and he falls to the ground, this will spoil the luck; you should stop dreaming as soon as the 'coon is up the tree. 61, 12.

RACES. (See Run.) To dream of running a race on foot and winning it, is a sign of success in any undertaking—losing it, foretells disappointment. If you dream of going to a horse-race, it predicts poverty and shiftlessness. 46, 7.

RADISHES. To dream of this vegetable, signifies that a secret will be discovered, which will occasion a muss in the family. To a girl, it is a sign she will lose her beau, and to a lover, it foreshadows he will be "cut out" by some other nice young man. 38, 13.

RAFFLE. Raffling in your dream is the same as gambling; it foretells poverty and disgrace: to dream of raffling for poultry is a sign that your family (if you have one) will want bread; if you are single, it shows that you will be apt to get seedy and loaferish. 8, 44.

RAFT. To dream of seeing a raft foretells a journey—the longer the raft, the more extensive the line of travel: if you dream of sailing on a raft, it is a sign you will travel, with good success, in distant countries. 10.

RAGE. (See *Anger*.) If you dream that you are in a great rage in consequence of a mishap, or disagreeable event, it is a sign that some pleasant episode in connection therewith will occur to put you in an excellent humor, as such dreams work contrariwise. 44, 16.

RAGGED. To dream that your clothes are ragged, indicates that a young girl will banter you: if, in your dream, you see ragged people, it is a sign that you will suffer ridicule at your next meeting with a party of ladies and gentlemen. Rags and ridicule go together in dreams. 19.

RAILROAD. To dream of traveling by railroad, foretells to people who keep house that they will break up their establishment: to young persons it indicates the loss of their home: to lovers it is a sign that if they marry they will not keep house long, if at all. 3, 11, 33.

RAIN. To dream of a gentle rain is a good omen, as it foretells success in any undertaking: if you dream of a violent rain-storm accompanied by wind and thunder and lightning, it predicts much trouble and misfortune, though ultimate success in your undertakings. 21, 72.

RAINBOW. It is an excellent dream to imagine you see a brilliant rainbow—the brighter the better: it denotes health and general prosperity: to lovers it foretells a happy marriage, and riches. A young girl who dreams of a rainbow will either get an agreeable lover or a present. 45.

RAKING. For a girl to dream of raking newly mown hay, is a sign she will be married before the hay is eaten: young fellows who dream of raking hay with their sweethearts had better get ready their necks for the matrimonial noose, as they are past praying for. 4., 11.

RAM. To dream that a ram runs at you for butting purposes, shadows forth to a young man that his society will be coveted by the girls, and that he will be fortunate in love matters generally: if a girl dreams this, she will probably have her choice of lovers, as all the young fellows around there will fall in love with her: if the ram succeeds in butting her, she will surely be taken captive and brought as Cupid's prisoner into the matrimonial ranks. 19.

RAPE. If a female (married or single) dreams of an outrage on her person, (whether attempted, or successful,) it is a sign that some one of the opposite sex is in love with her: if she is married, the dream alludes to some man other than her husband. Such dreams bode no good. 31.

RASPBERRIES. To dream of an abundance of this fruit is a sign of health and riches: if you dream you are eating raspberries, it shows that you will be engaged in some enterprise that will bring you in a good deal of cash, most of which will be spent lavishly. 3, 66.

RATS. (*See Trap and Mouse.*) To dream of rats is a sign that thieves are around: if you see any of these animals, it shows that some friend will be robbed, but if you hear them gnawing, you will suffer a loss from robbery yourself. If a girl, who has a lover, dreams of rats, she had better be careful and not let him be too free with her person, or he may rob her of that which cannot be restored. 54, 21.

RAVEN. (*See Crow.*)

READING. To dream you are reading, indicates you will be successful in your love; in trade, it is particularly propitious; but if it appear to be painful or irksome to read, it signifies that you shall not succeed without exertion. 65, 2.

REAPING. (*See Harvest.*) To dream of reaping grain is an excellent omen, as it foretells thrift and abundance, as well as plenty of money in gold; this applies to a prolific field of ripe yellow grain; if the grain is meagre and looks rusty, the sign is entirely different, as it betokens scarcity and penury. 4, 11, 44.

RELATIONS. If you dream of being annoyed at home by your relations, it is a sign that you will be the subject of much scandal: if, on the contrary, you imagine that your relatives visit you and give you great pleasure by their society, it foretells that you are talked about a good deal, but always with respect and veneration. 70.

RELIGIOUS. For any one to dream of becoming religious, foretells that they will be cheated or swindled in some way, as such a dream works contrariwise: if you dream that a minister, or any religious person, exhorts you to become pious, you had better look out sharp, for some rogue is around, contriving how to victimize you. 54.

RENT. To dream of paying your rent foretells that you will get some money unexpectedly; but if you dream that you owe it, without having the money to pay, and are worried in consequence, it foreshadows a loss of property. 3.

REPRIEVE. If a criminal under sentence of death dream of a reprieve or pardon, he may make up his mind that it is all over with him; and if any friend, who is interested in his fate, dreams this, it amounts to about the same thing. 76, 5.

REPTILE. To dream of any animal that is called a reptile, such as snakes, toads, alligators, and the like, is a sign of a quarrel: if you imagine you are bitten, it shows that you will come out second best, or badly injured either in person or reputation. If a girl dreams of a reptile, let her look sharp that her lover don't play her false. 34, 3.

RESCUE. If you dream of rescuing any one from peril, it is a sign you will rise in the world, either by means of increased wealth, or new honors: to dream that you are rescued from drowning or from any other mode of death, shows that you will go into some successful business speculation with a partner. To lovers, such a dream foretells a speedy and happy union. 64, 9.

RESIGN. If a person who holds an office, or a trust of any kind, dreams of resigning, it is a sign of advancement: to any one who cannot be advanced, it shows that he will rise above his present position in society. 41, 17.

RESUSCITATE. To dream of resuscitating a drowned person, foretells that you will engage in some enterprise that attracts public attention: if the person thus brought to life is a female, it shadows forth marriage with a lady of public fame. 16, 9, 78.

REVENGE. To dream of revenging an injury, is a sign of disgrace: if, in your dream, you imagine that you have caused any one to be locked up in prison from motives of revenge, it predicts that you yourself will be imprisoned for some degrading act. 74, 50.

REVIVAL. To dream of a religious revival, or of being where a great many people are holding a revival meeting, is a sign that you will go into a disreputable public place and lose *caste:* if you take part in the meeting, it foretells that you will come to disgrace, as all such dreams work contrariwise. 13, 57.

REWARD. To dream of receiving a reward for any act which is a public benefit, such as detecting a criminal, is a sign that you will have honors conferred upon you: if you dream of getting a reward for finding money or other property, it foreshadows good fortune and riches. 41.

RHEUMATISM. To dream of this painful disease, is an omen of health: if you imagine a friend is thus afflicted, it shows that he will soon offer to do you a favor, or benefit you in some way. 52, 16.

RHINOCEROS. To dream of this East India animal, denotes success to the man of business, but disappointment in love matters; but to dream they injure you, is unfavorable to the dreamer. If you dream you see one dead, you'll soon leave a relative. 47.

RIBBONS. For a girl to dream that she has got new, and beautiful ribbons on her bonnet or dress, is a sign some one will flatter her to her disadvantage: if she does not like the ribbon, it shows that she will hear of some scandal relative to herself; and if the ribbon is red, the scandal will impeach her chastity. 39, 6.

RICE. To dream of eating rice, denotes health: if you imagine that you see large quantities of rice, it foretells to one who does not live in a rice country, a successful and pleasant journey; and to those who live there, it predicts gain and riches. 12, 2, 24.

RICH. To dream you are rich, or that you have inherited a fortune, is a sign of poverty and bad luck; but if you imagine that some one pays you large sums of money enough to make you rich, your dream will be realized so far that you will acquire property. If a person dreams that a legacy is paid to him in money, it has an entirely different meaning from a dream that you are enriched from a legacy, but do not see the money. 15, 3.

RIDING. (*See Carriage, Stage-coach, and Gig.*) To dream you are riding, if it be with a woman, is unfortunate: in trade, decay of business; in love, disappointments; but if it be with men, then, by care, the reverse of these things will happen. Riding in a railcar, or a stage, foretells success in business matters. 6, 12, 72.

RING. For a lady to dream that a gentleman presents her with a ring, or that she has a ring belonging to a gentleman, is a sign of a wedding. If a young man dreams that he has got a lady's ring, the omen is similar. To dream of finding a ring, foretells that the person finding it will marry within a year. 4, 20.

RIOT. To dream of a public tumult or riot, is a sign of scarcity and bad crops to farmers, and dull business to tradesmen and me chanics: if any friend or relative is injured in the riot, you or they will probably suffer from misfortune, but if they are successful and pacify the crowd, it foretells that you will overcome your difficulties. 2.

RIVAL. For a lover to dream that he has a rival who annoys him, is a sign that he is in high favor with his sweetheart; such a dream to a young lady has a similar omen, and she has only to name the happy day to settle the matter to her mind. 1, 70.

RIVER. To dream of crossing a large and clear river, foretells a splendid fortune: if the water is muddy or riled, it predicts difficulties, but they will be overcome provided you get safe over the river without accident. If a girl dreams this, it is a sign she will travel somewhere and get a rich husband. 34, 20.

ROBBERY. (See Thief and Stealing.)

ROBIN. To dream of seeing robins around your house, is a good omen, as it foretells abundance to farmers and success to any one; if you do not see them, but hear them trilling, it foreshadows sickness, and perhaps death. 6.

ROCKET. To dream of seeing rockets flying in the air, foretells joy and gladness at some event about to happen: to married people it denotes the birth of a child, or the marriage of a daughter if they have one old enough. If a young girl dreams of seeing a rocket, she needn't trouble herself further, as her speedy marriage is certain. 15.

ROCKING-CHAIR. (See Chair.)

ROCKS. (See Mountain.)

ROOSTER. (See Cock.) If a girl dreams of hearing a cock crow, it foretells that she will soon have a new lover; if a lover dreams this, it is a sign that he has a formidable rival: if a married man or woman dreams of roosters, it shows that some outsider is enamored of the wife. 10, 19.

ROSE. To dream of roses is a sign of troubles: the old saying that every rose has its thorn, is exemplified in such a dream, because every rose you see brings along a trouble: dreaming of white roses signifies a marriage which will bring much vexation. 47, 9.

ROSEMARY. To the married, denotes loss of their mates and children; to the lover, trouble through his or her sweetheart. 49, 7.

ROTTEN. To dream of rotten things of any kind (except eggs), foretells sickness and death: to imagine that you handle rotten eggs, foreshadows disgrace. 35.

ROWING. To dream of rowing a boat in clear water, is a sign of good luck generally: if the water is muddy, it shows trouble and

5

difficulties which may be overcome; if a lover dreams of rowing a boat with his lady-love in it, he will doubtless make a happy match. 20.

RUDDER. To dream of a broken rudder in a boat or vessel in which you are sailing, foretells that one of the persons who you imagine are in the boat, will be drowned, or come to a sudden death. 27, 75.

ǰ RUIN. If you dream that you are looking at old ruins, or castles, or buildings, it is a sign you will travel in distant countries: to dream of the ruins of a house that has been burnt down, foretells that you will experience a loss of property: if, in your dream, you see the ruins of a house that has fallen down, it denotes the death of a friend or acquaintance. 5, 12, 60.

RUN. (See Race.) To dream of running swift, is a sign of good success in your undertakings; but if you stumble or fall, it denotes accidents or misfortune: if you imagine that you see people run, while you are still, it foretells disappointment. 7.

RUST. To dream of rust is a bad omen: rusty knives, or tools of any kind, denote the destruction of property : rusty pails or utensils are so many signs of poverty. 54.

RYE. To dream of this grain is a sign you will be fortunate in money matters; it also foretells success in love affairs: to the married it foreshadows domestic happiness. 69.

SAFFRON. To dream of gathering saffron, or of drinking a decoction of the herb, is a sign of health and wealth: if the flowers that you gather look clear and healthy, it foretells that you will get just so much gold. 19, 24.

SAILING. To dream of fair sailing on clear water, is an excellent omen, as it foretells abundance and success: heavy winds that endanger your boat, or muddy waters, point out difficulties which will probably be overcome. (See Boat, Yacht and Ship.) 20.

SAUSAGES. To dream of eating fried sausages, foretells that you will come in contact with some person who is very poor, and will be disagreeable to you: a girl who dreams this, will be very sure to get a shiftless and needy lover, and perhaps marry him if she is in much of a hurry to get married. 38, 16.

SAWING. To dream of sawing wood, or boards, foretells that you will do something that you will afterwards regret: if a young fellow dreams this, he will probably offer some indignity to his sweetheart, which he will find it hard work to get overlooked. 3, 17, 55.

SCAFFOLD. To dream of going upon a high scaffold, shows that you will rise in the world: if, in your dream, you imagine that you fall from a scaffold, or from any high place, it shadows forth a misfortune that will make you poorer: a girl who dreams of climbing upon a scaffold, will positively marry a rich man, or one of distinction, who is far above her in position. 33, 7.

SCALDED. To dream of being scalded with hot water, is usually a sign of injuries by the elements; it may foretell losses by floods, by fire, or by winds, or by thunder-storms: if you dream of scalding your tongue with hot tea, it is a sign that you will scandalize a neigh-bor with some ill-natured remark. 3, 12, 36.

SCALES. To dream you are weighing any article, is a good omen, and signifies that you will be happy and long-lived; but to dream you see another using the scales, is a sign you will be ruined by law-suits. 68, 40.

SCARCITY. To dream of a scarcity of anything is a sign that some of the article dreamed about is on its way to you; as if a farmer were to dream of a scarcity of hay, it shows that his next hay crop will be very abundant; or, if a girl should dream of a scarcity of compliments, she will probably be overwhelmed by them from gentlemen, when she next goes into company. 27, 9.

SCHOOL. To dream of attending school, is a sign of advancement and good fortune: if you dream of studying, and succeed well, it shadows forth that you will rise to a position in society above your present one: if you find it difficult to learn, you will have trouble in getting along, but will rise at last. 42, 72.

SCISSORS. To dream of a pair of scissors, is a sign of a marriage; if a girl dreams of them she will positively be married within a year: to a married woman such a dream is a bad omen, as it denotes some gay seducer will flatter her, and probably succeed in enticing her from the path of virtue. Here is an old prediction in rhyme: 47.

> To dream of scissors—a full pair,
> Tells a fair maid that soon she'll marry;
> But to a wife it doth declare
> Her chastity will e'en miscarry!

SCOLD. For a man to dream he has a scolding, shrewish wife, is a sign that he will be lucky in everything he undertakes: if a lover dreams that his sweetheart scolds at him, it is a sign that her love is strong and unalterable. 65, 16.

SCRATCH. To dream of having your face scratched, is a sign that somebody has been disparaging your good looks: if a girl imagines in her dream that she has scratched herself with a pin, it foretells that scandal is afloat relative to her conduct with her lover, or some other gentleman. 3.

SCREW. To dream of a small screw, is a good sign, and indicates success in all you undertake; but to dream of a large bed-screw portends trouble brought about by love affairs. 4, 11, 44.

SCYTHE. (*See Husbandry.*)

SEA. To dream of going to sea in a ship or steamer, is a sign that you will be fortunate in money matters: storms and perils at sea fore-tell difficulties which may be overcome: if you dream you are sea-sick, it denotes continued health. If a girl dreams of going to sea, and having a pleasant voyage, she will marry rich, and love her hus-band; but storms and perils point to quarrels with him. 6.

SECRET. If a young girl dreams that a friend has intrusted her with an important secret, it is a sign that the friend will become her enemy: if her lover tells her a secret, they will surely quarrel within a work; if she dreams of disclosing a secret to a friend, she will be much vexed at some scandal that is afloat respecting her. 4, 2, 8.

SEDUCER. If a young woman dreams that her lover's conduct is that of a gay seducer, she will find him to be very sincere in his attachment: a married woman who dreams that she is over-persuaded by a seducer to yield to his desires, will come to much honor, as such dreams work contrariwise. If a man dreams of seducing a virtuous girl, it foreshadows that he will be disgraced. 35, 8.

SEGAR. (*See Tobacco.*) To dream you are smoking a segar, is a sign you will have misfortunes and troubles with your business matters: if you imagine the fire of your segar goes out, it is a sign you will meet with losses: in love matters this dream is a bad omen. 49, 7, 9.

SEPARATION. If a woman dreams that she is about to live separate from her husband, it promises that she will shortly find herself in the family way: such a dream to a man is a sign that some woman or girl, other than his wife, is in love with him. 26, 17.

SERVANTS. (*See Domestics.*) To dream that you are robbed by your servants, is a sign that some one among them that you think the most of is deceiving you: if, in your dream, you imagine you have had your silver stolen by a servant, it shows that you will have a difficulty, and discharge one who will be replaced by a dishonest person. 71, 40, 11.

SHARK. To dream of seeing a shark in the water, is an excellent omen, as it foretells that you will escape a great danger that menaces you: if you dream of capturing the shark, you will soon thereafter get a big lump of money. Catching fish of any kind foretells money-getting. 31.

SHAVE. For a man to dream that he is shaving, is a sign he will get in debt: to dream that any one shaved you in a bargain, foretells that some debt will be paid to you which you had given up as lost. 5, 7, 54.

SHAWL. If a girl dreams of getting a new shawl, it foretells that she will soon have a new beau who will be very attentive and affable. 3, 19.

SHEEP. To dream of large flocks of sheep, is a sign of thrift and abundance, particularly to farmers, to whom the omen promises large crops: if many of the sheep have young lambs, it foretells domestic happiness and an excellent crop of children. 12, 5, 60.

SHELL. (*See Oysters and Clams.*) To dream you find an empty shell is a sign you will meet with losses in business, but if, in your dream, you imagine the shell to be full, it foretells you will be successful in all your undertakings. If you dream you are opening any kind of shell fish for others to eat it foreshadows that you will have plenty of funds. 19, 53.

SHERIFF. If you dream the sheriff is after you with a writ, or a warrant, and that you dodge and escape him, it is a sign of bad luck and losses; but if he arrests and locks you up in prison, it foretells that some good fortune is coming. Soon after such a dream you will be lucky in anything you undertake. 62, 21.

SHIFT. (*See Linen and Smock.*)

SHIP. To dream of seeing a ship under full sail, while you stand on the shore, is a sign you will soon fall in love with a pretty girl, who will favor your addresses; but if you see this ship while you are on the water in some other vessel, it shows that your sweetheart will be jealous of you. To dream of being shipwrecked and losing your property, foretells good luck in business matters, but quarrels in love affairs. 29, 8.

SHIRT. To dream that your shirt is ragged and without buttons, is a sign of poverty: if you imagine that you have a new shirt, with a stylish bosom, it foretells some disagreeable adventure in which your self-esteem will be keenly wounded, such as being placed in a ridiculous position before ladies, or before company in public. 44, 18.

SHOES. (*See Boots.*) If you dream that one of your shoes has a hole in it, it foretells that your sweetheart will offend you by favoring a supposed rival: if a girl dreams this, her lover will be jealous of her: for a young man to dream that he has lost a shoe-string, is a sign that he will be kissed by a lady with whom he had no previous acquaintance. 33.

SHROUD. (*See Corpse.*) To dream of a shroud is a sign of a wedding: to see, in your dream, a woman laid out in her shroud, foretells to a young person that he or she will either be present at a marriage, or will become a victim of Cupid's archery. 39, 11.

SICKNESS. (*See Disease.*) If you dream you have had a long sickness, and are recovering, it foretells bad luck and difficulties: should you imagine that you are sick and are going to die, the omen is the reverse, for some good fortune awaits you: if a girl dreams that she is sick abed, and her lover visits her, it foretells a smooth courtship and happy marriage. 2.

SILKS. For a lady to dream of silks and satins, and that she is having fine dresses made of those fabrics, foretells poverty and want: if she imagines that she is presented with a plain cheap dress, and is pleased with the present, it is a sign she will have some excellent luck; but if she dislikes it, it shows that she will refuse an offer that will cause her after regrets. 8, 7, 56.

SILVER. (*See Metals.*)

SINGING. To dream of singing solemn music in a choir, is a sign of the death of a young girl who is your esteemed friend or relative: to lovers, such a dream foretells the loss of sweethearts: if you imagine you are singing some lively tune by yourself, it is a sign of sorrow, though it may not be connected with any death. 34, 18.

SINGLE. If a married woman dreams that she is single, and that attentions are being paid to her by a beau, it foretells that her husband has become captivated by a new love, and will probably be false to his vows: the omen is similar to a married man who dreams that he is either a bachelor or widower. 69, 72.

SISTER. (*See Brothers.*) To dream you see your sister denotes a speedy death in your family, and that the dreamer will be long-lived; if you are in love, it is a favorable omen. 24, 8.

SKATING. To dream of skating over smooth ice, and gliding along without much effort, is a sign of success and good luck: if you are skating with ladies, it foretells that your love matters will go smoothly; if the ice be broken or lumpy, it denotes difficulties; and if you imagine you fall down, you will probably experience a misfortune or have great trouble. 4, 7, 28.

SKY. A clear sky denotes a marriage, speedy, and happy; a red sky, increase of wealth; if you ascend into the sky, you may look for much honor; a cloudy sky shows misfortune. 2, 11, 24.

SLAUGHTER-HOUSE. To dream of being in an empty slaughterhouse, shows that you are in danger, but can avoid it by precaution. To see animals slaughtered is a good sign, if the blood flow freely; if the blood does not flow, you will meet with some accident. 26, 12.

SLAVE. To dream that a favorite slave has become ungrateful, and run away, is a sign that some one has been tampering with him or her, but without effect; if, in your dream, you imagine that one of your favorite negroes has been impertinent or neglectful, and is to be flogged, and that you feel bad about it, it shows that some one will try to injure you through the medium of your slaves, and you should therefore look sharp to the characters of white people around. 62, 4.

SLEIGH-RIDE. To dream of a sleigh-ride, where the sleighing is good, and the sleigh glides free and noiseless, is an excellent omen, as it foretells success and good fortune generally, particularly to farmers: but if you imagine the sleighing is poor, and that the runners screech on the ground, it foretells trouble and unhappiness. Young men who dream of sleigh-riding with girls, stopping at taverns, drinking, getting the girls boozy, and then performing unnamable pranks, are thus forewarned that they will be poor and shiftless, as such dreams are certain omens of misery and disgrace. 67, 46.

SLIDING. (See Ice.) To dream of sliding on smooth ice, foretells good luck: if a girl dreams that a young man assists her in sliding, and that she enjoys it, she will soon get an agreeable lover: ragged or wet ice, or holes in the ice, foreshadow difficulties. If a girl dreams of falling down on the ice, and that her lover falls with her, and overtops her, they may as well go to the parson at once, and have the knot tied, as it is a sure thing to happen. 4, 28.

SMALL-POX. (See Sores.) To dream that you have this disease, foretells health and good fortune: if a lover should be so ungallant as to imagine that his sweetheart is thus afflicted, it is a sign that he will marry a great beauty; if she happens to be a beauty, it will be all right, of course; if not, he will look out for number two. 41, 32.

SMOCK. (See Linin.) If a girl dreams that she has a ragged undergarment, it foretells that some rich greenhorn will try to seduce her, and failing, will offer her marriage: if she dreams that she has a good supply of beautiful worked undergarments, it is a sign that she will sigh in vain for a lover; if she imagines that a gentleman gives her a new smock, she will be in danger of losing her chastity. 12.

SMOKE. To dream of being in a room full of smoke, foretells that you will engage in an angry controversy, and perhaps quarrel: lovers who dream of smoke, will nose out the fire when they next meet, and it will prove to be either one of anger or of lust. 76, 5.

SNAKE. To dream of snakes is a sign of an enemy, or that some one is slandering you; it also denotes quarrels and angry disputes: if an engaged young lady dreams of them, she had better ascertain positively whether her lover is all right before she marries him. 47, 50.

SNEEZE. To dream you sneeze, is a sign of long life. 55.

SNOW. (*See Sleigh-Ride and Thaw*) To dream that the ground is covered with clean, white snow, is a sign of joy and pleasure: if you walk in it, it foretells that you will go on a pleasant journey; to eat it, denotes health: if the snow is dirty, or melted in patches, you will have troubles, but they will not amount to much. To dream of a regular storm, is a sign you will be very successful in all your love and business affairs. 21, 67, 46.

SNUFF. (*See Tobacco.*)

SNUFFERS. (*See Candles.*) To dream of snuffing out a candle, is a sign of a death in the family: if you imagine that you snuff it too short, without putting it out, it foretells that you will do something that will make a female friend shed tears. 40.

SOAP. Signifies trouble in business, but it will soon depart. 66, 3, 11.

SOLDIER'S DRUM. (*See Zouave, Parade and Procession.*)

SORES. To dream of your body being covered with blotches, shows that a great fortune will fall to you. To have the arms full of sores, shows ill success in business. · 19, 74.

SOW. To dream of a sow with a large litter of pigs, denotes abundance to a farmer, but is a sign of ill-health to a tradesman or mechanic: if a girl dreams this, it foretells that she will soon marry a man in bad health. 4, 12, 48.

SPIDER. To dream that you see a spider coming toward you, is a sign that some one will soon pay you money: if you imagine that the spider spins down before your face, the omen is similar, for you will make a good lot of money in some way. If a married woman dreams of seeing a large spider, it foretells that she will have a miscarriage, which she will not be sorry for. 72, 16.

SPY-GLASS. To dream of looking through one of these instruments and observing objects at a distance, is a sign that you will enlarge your possessions; if you are a farmer, you will add to your farm; if a man of business, enlarge your business, &c.; but to a poor devil who hasn't got much of anything, it predicts that he will increase his family for the want of something else to enlarge. 14.

SQUINTING. (*See Eye.*) If a girl dreams of seeing a good-looking young man who squints, it is a sign that some one has fallen in love with her, and only waits an opportunity to demonstrate his passion: if a gentleman dreams that his sweetheart squints, it foretells that she is thinking about some one else rather than him, and would not break her heart if he refused to "come to tea." 49.

SQUIRREL. To dream of these animals is a s.gn of good fortune; they denote abundant crops to a farmer, and a.ccess to any one: if a man dreams of being bi te ¨a squirrel, it foretells that h⌐ will lose something by robbery; e catches the ai.imal when it bites him, and puts it in a cage, the omen is different, for he will h⌐ve a piece of good luck—though a robbery may be mixed up in it. 21.

STABLE. To dream of a stable denotes hospitality and good entertainment. 2, 11.

STAGE-COACH. To dream of riding in one signifies good luck in business: if you run after one you will be out of employment for a long season: to see one pass, will rid you of troublesome friends. If you are in a stage-coach and it turns over without injuring you, you will be lucky in your speculations; if you dream you are killed by the fall, you must expect misfortune. (*See Riding and Coach.*) 6, 12, 72.

STAIN. For a girl to dream of stains on her dress, is a sign of scandal : if she imagines that the stains are in front, she will be accused of an improper intimacy with a gentleman ; if on the the right sleeve, it will be insinuated that she took what did not belong to her; if on the left sleeve, some one will be disparaging her veracity. If a lover dreams that his sweetheart's dress is stained behind, it shows that she is untrue to him. 65, 13.

STARS. (*See Night.*) To dream of seeing multitudes of bright stars in a clear sky, is a sign (to a lady) that she wil' lave a great many children, and troops of good friends : to a man of business, such a dream denotes as many customers as he sees stars in a clear sky. If a girl dreams of seeing stars, and notices one or more to be brighter than the rest, those bright ones are lovers, and the small ones are her children or friends. 4, 19.

STATUE. To dream of marble statues is a sign of advancement; those who imagine that they see beautiful statuary will be sure to rise above their present position in society. 3, 13.

STEALING. (*See Thief.*) If you dream of being robbed, it is a sign that you will make a good speculation of some kind : to dream of stealing any particular article yourself, foretells that you will soon want just that thing; thus, if you imagine that you steal money, you will be badly in want of some. 49, 16.

STEEL. (*See Metals.*)

STEEPLE. (*See Tower.*) To dream of going up to the top of a steeple, and looking off at a distance, is a sign that you will increase your property or effects: if a girl dreams this, it foretells that she will marry above her present position. 6.

STICK. To hold a stick foretells mourning; to use it as a prop, instability of fortune; to see, any one with it shows that you are charitable; to receive beating with one, presicts you will better your position in life. 7, 7.

STILLBORN. If a woman dreams that she gives birth to a stillborn child, it foretells that her next child will be an uncommon bright ono: a child'ess woman who dreams this, will realize her fondest hopes. 43, 77

STING To dream of being stung by a bee or wasp, foretells an injury by unjust and scandalous reports: a young lady who dreams that a bee stings her, will probably have her chastity questioned. 64, 18.

STOCKINGS. To dream of cotton-stockings, foretells moderate happiness; of silk, poverty. To take them off, denotes the reception of money. Stockings with holes in them, signify the loss of property. 47, 71.

STORM. (See Rain, Hail and Snow.) To dream of a devastating storm, foretells losses and trouble: a violent rain-storm denotes that you will have good luck, but that misfortunes will nevertheless injure your prospects: gentle showers promise the luck without the adverse omen. 21, 72.

STOVE. To dream of a stove is a sign of wealth, if there be a fire in it; but if cold, a sign of poverty. 8, 60.

STRANGER. For a girl to dream that she is kissed by a stranger, promises her a new lover: a married woman who dreams this will probably soon present her husband with a stranger in the shape of a new baby, and he will unhappily doubt its paternity. 62, 8.

STRAW. To dream of a bundle of straw denotes abundance; if scattered about, poverty. 4, 51, 78.

STRAWBERRIES. To dream of this fruit, denotes success in love affairs, and a happy marriage. 39, 78.

SUCKLE. (See Wet-Nurse.) If a married woman dreams of suckling a child, it foretells that she will soon give birth to another: should a bachelor dream of seeing a child suckled, he had better make up his mind that he will soon have a young lady's board to pay, whether he marries or not; but as the latter would be the better course let him be looking round for a wife at once. A married man who dreams this, will soon become a happy father. 7, 9, 63.

SUGAR. To dream of sugar denotes purity: if a lover dreams that his sweetheart presents him with white loaf-sugar, it shows that her affection for him is pure and disinterested; it is therefore a good sign for him to dream of taking tea with her, as she would naturally put such sugar in his tea: to dream of sugar of any kind, or sugar candy, is an excellent omen. 19, 48.

An old prediction runs as follows:

> Dreams of sugar and sweetmeat,
> Or drinking wine with pleasure great,
> And all dreams pleasant in condition.
> Show sports of love, and love's fruition.

SUN To dream that the sun blinds you, foretells that you will be overwhelmed with good fortune: to see a beautiful bright sun, is a sign of success in anything you may undertake: a red sun denotes mishaps and accidents: if the sun looks dim and smoky, it foreshadows trouble and difficulties. To dream of seeing the sun rise brings good news and luck; the setting sun, misfortune. 2, 10, 20.

SWALLOWS. To dream of these birds, is a good omen, as it foretells health and abundant crops to farmers: if you dream of killing a swallow, it is a sign of a misfortune; if you catch the bird, you will have splendid luck and get plenty of money; but if, after capturing, you dream you let him go, a fortune will slip through your fingers. 25.

SWAN. To dream of a white swan, signifies riches; a black one, domestic sorrow. Its song denotes death. 9, 18.

SWEARING. (*See Blasphemy.*) To dream that you hear violent altercations and profane swearing, is a sign that you will lose *caste*, and go down in the world: if a man dreams that in his anger he curses and swears, it foretells that he will come to poverty. 72, 4.

SWEEPING. For a girl to dream of sweeping the house, foretells that a lover will soon make his appearance: if a married woman dreams this, it shows that some outsider is charmed with her, and may venture to make dishonorable proposals. 39, 12.

SWIMMING. To dream of swimming is an excellent omen, as it foretells success and good fortune generally: if you dream you are swimming, or bathing in clear water with ladies, it predicts that you will soon marry the one of your choice, particularly if she be present; and to dream you are naked and swimming in clear water, is a sign of excellent luck in business matters. 54, 18.

SWORD. To dream of having a sword, is a sign of poverty: if you dream of seeing a man flourish one of these weapons, it foretells you will make a loss. A young girl who imagines her lover wears a sword, had better give up all ideas of silks and satins, and learn how to cook and wash, for she will be a poor man's wife. 17.

TABLE-CLOTH. To dream of a dirty table-cloth foretells that you will have plenty to eat. 51.

TAILOR. If a girl dreams that she has a tailor for her beau, and is pleased with him, it is a sign that she will marry a softly sort of a fellow, who will allow her to be both master and mistress after marriage. Here is a popular rhyme in illustration: 19, 70.

> The maid who dreams a tailor she would wed,
> Will marry one who'll be a log in bed;
> And she'll be master, too, of all his riches,
> And, in the vulgar parlance, " wear the breeches!"

TALL. If a young lady dreams that her beau is a very tall man, it is a sign that her future husband will be a " wee bit of a fellow," and not of much account. 4.

TAMARINDS. To dream of tamarinds shows much vexation and uneasiness through a woman, bad success in trade, a rainy season, and news from beyond sea that is disagreeable: in love they denote disappointment. 77, 16.

TANNERY. To dream of being in a tannery is a sign of health and riches: if a girl dreams that her beau is a tanner, she will probably get a good husband, and one who is well off, and will live to a good old age, for your tanners are usually tough customers. 52, 7.

TAR. To dream of tar is a sign you will travel by water: if you dream you get it on your hands or clothes, it shows that you will have difficulties; and to imagine you accidentally seat yourself on tar, and get stuck to the seat, foretells that you will be detained against your will in some foreign country. 12, 6, 72.

TAVERN. (*See Inn.*)

TEA. To dream of drinking tea, or being present at a tea-party, is a sign of thrift and domestic happiness: a girl who dreams of meeting her lover at such a party, or of drinking tea with him, may be sure that he's all right, and she can close her matrimonial bargain with him at once without any risk. 61, 19.

TEARS. To dream of shedding tears of sympathy, is a sign that some one is in love with you; this applies to both sexes, but more particularly to girls who cry easy: if you imagine you cry from grief, some good fortune awaits you, and you will have riches in proportion to the tears shed: if you dream that you shed tears from vexation, it shows that you will experience a loss just in proportion to the tears, or that some one will injure your prospects by circulating a scandal. 14.

TEETH. To dream you lose your teeth, denotes the loss of friends, troubles, and misfortunes; to the lover it shows the loss of your sweetheart's affections: to dream you cut a new tooth, denotes the birth of a child who will make a figure in the world. 33, 11, 2.

TELEGRAPH. To dream of one denotes tidings from abroad, in a short space of time, and still more speedily if you think the telegraph is at work. 47, 10, 78.

TELESCOPE. (*See Spy-Glass.*) To dream of looking through a telescope at a distance over farm lands, is a sign you will either purchase a farm or inherit one: if you dream of looking at the stars, it shows that you will rise in the world—if at the moon, and you are delighted with the view, it predicts for you great riches. 7, 14.

TEMPEST. (*See Storm.*) To dream of long-continuing and great tempests, signifies affliction, troubles, dangers, losses and perils; to the poor, repose. 57, 8.

TEN-PINS. To dream of playing ten-pins, foretells disgrace; if the centre pin falls, one of the players will die; if many pins fall, all of the players will suffer loss. 10, 2, 20.

THAW. To dream of a thaw, and walking in splashy snow, foretells trouble and losses: if a young fellow dreams that he walks through splashy snow to go a courting, it is a sign that he will quarrel with his sweetheart. 34, 18.

THEATRE. For a young man to dream of taking his sweetheart to the theatre, is a sign that she will favor a new beau: if he dreams of going to the theatre alone, and seeing his lady-love among the audience, it shows that she has already seen and spoken to a gentleman that she likes better than him: if a lady dreams this of her beau, the omen is similar. 2, 4, 8.

THIEF. (*See Stealing.*) To dream that thieves break into your house and rob you, is a sign of honor or profit—the greater the robbery. the more extensive will be your good fortune: if you dream that you catch a thief and deliver him over to the officers of justice, it denotes that you will have trouble in connection with your good fortune. 49, 16, 3.

THIRST. If any one dream of thirst or of drinking water, if the water appear clear and acceptable, he will live joyfully and become wealthy; if the water be troubled, warm, or offensive, it forewarns him that without prudence, he will end his days in affliction. 20, 49.

THORN. For a girl to dream of accidentally sticking a thorn into her finger is a sign she will have a ring presented to her, probably a wedding ring: if a married woman dreams this, some outsider will make love to her by first offering a ring. If any one dreams of stick-ing a thorn in either foot or leg, it foretells improper intimacy with the opposite sex which will not end in disgrace, but in marriage: married people who dream this will do the same thing and not be found out. 39.

THROAT. For a married woman to dream that her throat is sore, or swelled, or out of order, is a sign she is in the family way; and a girl who dreams this had better be careful and keep pretty clear of the young fellows, for fear of accidents. 60, 18.

THUMB. If a girl dreams that her beau hurts her by pinching her thumb, it is a sign that if she marries him she will have to get her own living, and help to support him besides: for a man to dream of losing his thumb, or of an injury to it, foretells poverty—on the con-trary, to dream of a big thumb denotes much wealth. 36, 5.

THUNDER. To dream of heavy thunder denotes large crops to farmers: to tradesmen, mechanics, or speculators, it foretells a big business, or a successful speculation: if you are terrified by thunder, so much the better. 51.

TIGER. To dream of seeing one of these animals in a rage, is a sign that you have a treacherous friend who will endanger your rep-utation: to see, in your dream, a sleeping or quiet tiger, foretells that you will soon make the acquaintance of a treacherous or unworthy person. If a girl dreams this, she had better be suspicious of the next young man who offers her his attentions. 59, 62.

TOAD. To dream of seeing a toad is a sign of a rain storm: if, in your dream, you see multitudes of small toads, it foretells good crops to farmers, and excellent luck to anybody: if a newly married woman dreams this, it shadows forth that she will have as many smart chil-dren as she sees toads—three or four at a time, perhaps—and if she don't, her husband will beget them elsewhere. 3.

TOBACCO. For a boy to dream of chewing tobacco, is a sign of poverty, as rum and tobacco-chewing go together: to dream of smok-ing foretells waste, but is not exactly an omen of poverty, though waste always precedes that state. The best way is not to dream of using tobacco at all. If you dream of seeing large piles of tobacco, it is a sign of bad luck and loss in some speculation. To dream you take snuff is a bad omen in love affairs, but if you dream you sneeze when you take it, it is a sign of long life. 49, 7, 55.

TOMATOES. To dream of this valuable vegetable, denotes pros-perity in life; if you have children, they will thrive; if you are in love, your suit will be successful. If a maiden dreams of them, it denotes that she will marry her present sweetheart, have many children, and be very happy; to a farmer it denotes abundant crops. 78, 6.

TOMB To dream of visiting a large and magnificent tomb-stone foreshadows that you will fall in love with some one above you in social position: visiting a cemetery or grave-yard in your dream, is a sign that your turn will soon come to join the matrimonial ranks. 48.

TONGUE. If a lady dreams of having a sore on her tongue, it is a sign that she has uttered a slander. 54.

TOOTH-ACHE. To dream that you have the tooth-ache is a sign of trouble: if you imagine that you are about to have the tooth pulled, it foretells that your trouble will end by a piece of good luck; and if you dream that the tooth is out, and you have it in your hand, you will soon gain a good lump of money. 8, 5, 34.

TORCH. To see a bright torch-light at a distance in a dark night, and go toward it, foretells a successful journey; but if you stumble by the way you will experience an accident: to dream of carrying a lighted torch at night, is a sign that some distant friend will pay you a visit. 20.

TOWER. (*See Steeple.*) To dream of going upon a high tower, and looking off on a beautiful landscape, foretells that you will acquire land either by purchase or inheritance: if you look off upon the water, it is a sign of a journey by sea, during which you will acquire riches: if birds are flying around the tower, they foretell so many troubles. 58.

TRAP. To dream of setting a trap to catch rats or mice, is a sign, to a girl, that she will receive the attentions of a dishonest lover: if she dreams of catching any, she will probably marry a great scamp, or be seduced by one. 6.

TRAVELING. To dream of traveling by railroad or steamboat is a very good omen, as it denotes thrift and success in your business; but if you dream you are journeying in your own private coach, it foreshadows poverty in the end, though you may have temporary good luck: if you dream you have crossed the ocean, and find yourself in a foreign country, you may be sure that good fortune will attend all your business transactions. 6, 11, 66.

TREES. (*See Blossom.*) To dream of green and flourishing trees is an excellent omen, as it foretells riches—the larger the trees, the better the fortune: if you dream of climbing into a high tree, you will not only be rich, but will come to great distinction. If a girl should dream of seeing her lover up a tree, she will marry a wealthy and distinguished man. 4.

TRIPE. If a woman dreams of cleaning tripe, it foretells that she will either be untrue to her husband or an outrage will be perpetrated upon her: to dream of eating tripe is about as bad, for it shows to a man that he will be engaged in some affair with a female (not his wife) which will bring him to disgrace. 28, 9.

TRIPLETS. If a woman dreams that she gives birth to three children at one parturition, it foretells riches and honors: if a husband dreams that his wife is so delivered, the omen is the same: if any one dreams of seeing triplets who are healthy and well-formed, it foretells good luck and success, particularly in love matters. 49, 5.

TROUT. To dream of catching trout is an excellent omen, as it foretells that you will get money—the larger the trout, the more cash you will receive. It is stated in some of the books that to newly married people such a dream foretells the birth of a child, but I have been unable to verify this, because most young married people will have children whether they dream of trout or not. 29, 5.

TRUMPET. To dream you hear the sound of a trumpet, is a bad omen, and denotes trouble and misfortune; to the tradesman it presages the loss of business; to the farmer, bad crops; to the lover, insincerity in the object of your affections. 46, 9.

TRUNK. To dream of a full trunk, shows the necessity of economy; an empty one, signifies that you may expect to receive money. 39, 62, 1.

TUB. To dream of a tub is a bad omen: if it be filled with water, you have evil to fear; an empty tub signifies trouble; and to run against one, sorrow. 46, 9.

TULIPS. To dream of these beautiful flowers is a sign of abundance: if you imagine you see a garden full of them belonging to yourself, it foretells that you will become rich and distinguished: if a girl dreams that her lover presents her with tulips, she will undoubtedly marry well, and probably her husband will be wealthy. 48.

TURKEY. To dream of seeing a flock of turkeys denotes to a tradesman, or a farmer, that he will have a transaction which will bring him in a considerable sum in ready money: if a lover who is about to be married dreams of turkeys, he will find that his sweetheart has got a marriage portion in ready money. 72, 15.

TURNIP. To dream of turnips signifies the discovery of secrets and domestic quarrels. 29, 52.

TURTLE. To dream of turtles is a sign of long life: an engaged young lady who dreams of these animals will probably marry according to her wishes, and live with her husband until they become an old couple; but her husband will be one of the slow and easy kind. 67, 49, 5.

TWINS. To dream of having twins, brings good news, and is a sign of honor or riches; it is also a good omen in love matters if a man dreams it, but if a girl has this dream she must look out for the boys. 44, 4.

UMBRELLA. If a young girl dreams that she has got a new umbrella, it foretells a new lover: if a married woman dreams this, it is a sign that some other gentleman besides her husband is enamored of her. A man who dreams of buying an umbrella will have a narrow escape from threatened danger. 70, 30, 1.

UNDER GROUND. To dream that you go down under ground, whether into a well, a deep cellar or vault, or a cave, denotes your early death; but if you dream that you are digging in the ground, and are in a hole which you have dug, the omen is different, for it denotes riches and long life. 5, 9, 45.

UNDRESS. To see your wife undress, signifies wantonness; to undress in the presence of others, slander; to undress in your room alone, the discovery of secrets. 48, 3.

VACCINATED. To dream of being vaccinated foretells good health; and if you imagine that you have a large sore on your arm from vaccination, it is a sign that you will present to some one a liberal gift, and receive much honor. 49.

VARNISHING. To dream that your house or furniture is being, or has been, newly varnished, is a sign of a funeral; but if you imagine that you are varnishing anything, it merely foretells a loss without a death. 59, 76.

VAULT. An unexpected estate will fall to you, if you dream of a vault. 21, 18.

VEAL. To dream of veal being roasted is good; but boiled, shows sickness; and raw, a great disappointment; particularly to those who have recently formed an attachment or any new connection. 48, 2.

VELVET. If a lady dreams of new velvet dresses, it foretells poverty: velvet cushions, slippers or bonnets, are signs of waste and want. 36, 18.

VENISON. To dream of eating venison is a sign that you will travel: if you imagine you see large saddles of venison in market, it foretells a journey for business purposes which will be profitable. 42, 70.

VERMIN. To dream of any kind of vermin, is ominous of ill-luck and enemies, especially if they are in the house, or near the fireplace; but if out of the house, they are unimportant. 27, 62.

VEXATION. To dream of being much vexed, foretells the reverse, and that you will shortly be much pleased. 33, 61.

VINEGAR. To dream you drink vinegar, signifies sickness and sharp words: to use it in pickling, is a sign of gain. 29, 6, 76.

VINES. To dream of seeing or pruning grape-vines, or gathering grapes, is prosperity to persons in trade, journeys to the rich, employment to the poor, and comfort to those in affliction. 38, 17.

VIOLIN. (See *Fiddle*.)

VIRGIN. If a man dreams that he defloured a virgin, it is a sign that he will be disgraced by some act of his own: to dream of seeing the Virgin Mary, foretells that great honors await you: such a dream, to an honest business man, promises him riches and honor; but to a dishonest one, it foretells disaster. 54, 3.

VOMITING. To dream of vomiting is usually a sign of health: if you imagine that you vomit up worms, it foretells that you will have good luck in preventing a loss, or a robbery. 14, 65.

VOTE. To dream your are voting, is bad, particularly to a sick person: for a newly married woman to dream of voting, is a sure sign that her first child will be a boy, who will come to great honors. 9.

VOW. To dream that you have made a vow and broken it, is bad to all. 21, 78.

VULTURE. To dream of the vulture is unfortunate to all, except sick persons, to whom it foretells a speedy recovery. 41, 62.

WADING. If a girl dreams of wading in clear water, it is a sign that she will soon marry, and be delighted with her husband's embraces: if she imagines that the water is rily or muddy, it foretells that she will enjoy the pleasures of illicit love. If a man dreams of wading, it denotes that he will be engaged in some intrigue with a female—the deeper the water, the more difficult the realization of his wishes: muddy water denotes loose women. 20, 16.

WAKE. To dream of going to a wake where drinking and howling is going on, is a sign of poverty and misery: if a girl dreams this, it foretells her speedy marriage with a man who will turn out to be a miserable drunkard. If a young man dreams of seeing his sweetheart at a wake, he had better back out from the bargain, as she will never be of much account, and may become a drunkard. 8.

WALKING. To dream you are walking in a dirty and muddy place, foretells sickness and vexation: in love, it denotes bad temper and disappointment. 47.

WALLS. To dream you are walking on, or climbing over walls, denotes some dangerous enterprise, trouble, and vexation: if you get down without the wall falling, or hurting yourself, you will succeed; if not, be disappointed. 71, 4.

WALNUTS. To dream of them denotes riches and happiness; to the lover, success and a good tempered sweetheart. 37. 16.

WAR. To dream that war exists, and that you see bodies of troops marching, foretells quarrels and troubles in your family, if you have one, and if not, among your relatives: if you imagine you see a battle, the omen is still worse, as the quarrel will probably become public and notorious. 4, 6, 24.

WARMING-PAN. If any single person dreams that his or her bed is warmed with one of these utensils, it is a positive forerunner of their marriage: if a married woman dreams this, it is a sign that she will go to bed with a strange bedfellow (whether male or female, is not known). 16.

WARTS. To dream of warts on your left hand is a sign you will receive some money; if they are on the right hand, it foretells that you will pay away money: to dream of a wart on the nose, signifies that you will be distinguished; on the neck or bosom of a female, denotes riches. 65.

WASHING. To dream of washing, foretells change of abode, and if you wash in clear, cold water, the dream is an omen of good; but if the water is dirty or turbid, it is the reverse. If a woman dream she is washing clothes, it is a sign she will hear good news within twenty-four hours. 20, 16.

WASP. (*See Sting.*) To dream of wasps denotes thrift and abundance, particularly to farmers and those who have fruit-trees. If a girl dreams that she is stung by a mud-wasp, it foretells that she will marry a gentleman who will love her dearly. 62, 18.

WAST To dream of waste is a sign of beggary, provided you

are the cause of the waste; but if you feel bad and try to prevent it, the omen is one of losses, which may not end in beggary. 29, 17.

WATCH. (*See Clock.*) If you dream of buying a gold watch, it is a sign of poverty; but if you imagine that you are presented with one, it foretells good luck and money-getting: to dream of losing your gold watch is also a good omen, as it denotes success in business. 42, 11.

WATCHMAN. To dream of calling in one, gives confidence: to see a person taken to prison by a watchman, shows that you must be careful in conducting your business. If the watchman take hold of you, it is a very good sign. To see many watchmen together, signifies the loss of money. 67, 52.

WATER. To dream of being on the water, is good, if the water be clear; but if muddy or troubled, the reverse. To see a wide expanse of water, over or on which you wish to get, but cannot, shows that you are about to embark in some undertaking without first securing the means of success. (*See Bathing, Fountain, Pump, Pitcher, River, Rowing, Sailing, Swimming, Thirst, Washing and Well.*) 42, 18.

WATERMELONS. (*See Melons.*)

WEDDING. (*See Marriage.*) To dream of being at a jolly wedding, is a sign of a funeral: if you imagine that you kiss the bride, it foretells the death of a dear friend or relative. In an old dream-book, published 1808, it is stated that to dream of kissing the bride, is a sign of your own death, but on referring to the best authorities, I find it is necessary to dream that the bride should herself be the kissing party, and that an impressive kiss from her on the occasion denotes the death of the person kissed. 42, 78, 2.

WELL. To dream of looking into a deep well, is a sign you will find a treasure: if you dream of falling into a deep well, it foretells your death: if you imagine you draw clear water from a well, and drink it, you will surely have good fortune of some kind. 7, 14, 77.

WET-NURSE. To dream of seeing a wet-nurse suckling a child, is a sign of venery: to a married man it foretells that he will break his marriage vows; and to unmarried girls it denotes shame. 7, 9, 63.

WHALE. To dream of seeing one of these monsters alive in the ocean, is a sign that you will be in great peril of losing either your life or property: if you dream that you spear or harpoon a whale successfully, it foretells great and abundant fortune. 37, 22, 61.

WHEAT. (*See Grain.*)

WHISKERS. If a man dreams that he has very long whiskers or beard, it foretells that he will commit some folly in connection with a female; to a married man it shows that he will appear ridiculous from neglect of his wife and attentions to other women who flatter him; to a single man, that he will lose caste by foolish, though perhaps not criminal conduct toward silly girls. 78.

WHIST. (*See Cards.*)

WHITEWASH. To dream of having your house or place of busi-

6

ress whitewashed, is an excellent omen, as it promises you good health, and a good name and repute among your friends: if a woman dreams of whitewashing her house, or any part of it, it foretells that she will have a son who will be distinguished, or that some act of hers will attract public attention. 42, 77.

WHORE. If a man dreams of associating with one of this class or women, it foretells losses and disgrace: should a girl dream of playing the whore, when in fact she is chaste, it foretells her speedy mar. riage, and that she will love her husband. 19.

WHORTLEBERRIES. For a girl to dream of picking these berries in abundance, is a sign she will marry very young and get a good husband, though not a rich one: to dream of eating whortleberries, denotes health. 69, 30.

WIDOW. If a girl dreams that she is a widow, it foretells that she will have many lovers: such a dream to a married woman, denotes that some man beside her husband is in love with her. 38, 60.

WIG. To dream of wearing a wig is a good omen to a bald bachelor, as it foretells that some lady has a design to catch the poor fellow, and will not scruple as to the means she uses to accomplish it: if a young man dreams of wearing a wig, it is a sign that he will sleep with his sweetheart before he marries her. 3, 6, 69.

WILL. To dream of making your will is a sign of long life, and good fortune generally: if you imagine that you make your will to give a legacy to a lady, it foretells to a man (whether married or single) that he will marry. 22.

WILLOW. To dream of weeping willows is a sign of sickness and death: if they hang over a stream, it foretells sickness only. 12, 70.

WINE. To dream of drinking wine is a sign of poverty: if a lover dreams that his sweetheart treats him to a glass of wine, it foretells that she will be an unthrifty wife. 39.

WITCH. To dream of a witch foretells that you will leave your home and sojourn among strangers: if the witch attempts to injure you, it denotes that you will be dependent upon strangers for your support. No intelligent person believes in witches, yet a great many dream of them, and the above is the horoscope of such a dream. 17.

WOLF. To dream of being chased by one of these animals, foretells that you will be cheated in a trade or bargain: if a girl dreams of being frightened by a wolf, it shows that her lover (if she has one) is a bad man, and she had better discard him; if she has no lover, some black-hearted fellow will try to make her acquaintance. 45.

WOODCHUCK. To dream of catching one of these animals, is a sign that you will be robbed, and that the thief will be detected: if you imagine you kill the woodchuck, you will probably recover your stolen property. 36, 19.

WOODS. (See Grove and Picnic.)

WORK. (See Harvest.) To dream that you were working hard, and are very tired, is a sign of sickness: if you imagine that you see men at work, it foretells a successful business. 77.

WORMS. (*See Grub.*) To dream of fish-worms, such as are dug in the garden, is a sign of health and good fortune; dreaming of any destructive worms foretells sickness and losses: if you dream that worms spin down from a tree and light upon you, it denotes difficulties and bad luck. 65, 4, 70.

, WOUND. To dream that you are wounded by being stabbed or shot by an enemy, foretells losses and poverty; if the wounds are accidental, it still denotes losses, though your general fortune may not be affected. 13, 42.

WREN. To dream that one of these musical little birds makes her nest anywhere on your premises, is a sign of joy and riches; a girl who dreams this will make a happy match, though perhaps not a rich one, as the riches only come to the family that lives in the house. 1, 73.

WRINKLES. If a lady dreams that her face has become wrinkled, it is a sign that some one is, or has been, praising her good looks; an old bachelor who dreams this, "had better believe" that some young lady is in love with him, for there is no accounting for taste. 66, 4.

WRIST. If a girl dreams that her wrist is large or mis-shapen, it foretells that she will come to poverty after marriage; if she imagines that there is a tumor or swelling, or even a wart on it, it is a sign that she will be dependent on some one for her bread, and that person may or may not be her husband. 7, 57, 19.

WRITING. (*See Pen and Accounts.*) To dream of writing a letter, foretells that absent friends are about to visit you: if a girl dreams of writing a love-letter, it is a sign that her lover will soon return and clasp her in his arms, if she allows any such familiarities. To dream you make a blot while writing, is a sign of sickness. 14.

YACHT. To dream you see a yacht under full sail, while you are on shore, is a sign you will soon fall in love with a pretty maid, or widow. To dream you are sailing in a yacht with a pleasant breeze, is a good omen, and denotes success in business, and to lovers, happiness. Dreams of sailing on smooth water are good to all persons, but to dream the weather is stormy, predicts quarrels and strife. (*See Ship and Boat.*) 71, 29.

YELLOW. To dream of having any yellow article presented to you, is a sign you will get gold: if a girl dreams that her lover gives her yellow flowers, it foretells that she will marry rich. 60, 41.

YOKE. To dream of seeing sleek and healthy cattle yoked together and acting in harmony, is a sign of a happy marriage: if a girl dreams this, she will be apt to put her own neck in Hymen's yoke before a great while. To imagine you see yoked cattle wrangling, and trying to get their necks out of the yoke, foretells matrimonial troubles, though it still denotes wedlock to the unmarried. 6, 11.

YOUNG. If an old or middle aged person dreams that they are young, it foretells their death: for a young person to dream that he or she is a child, the omen is similar; but to dream *of youths*, is a sign that you will live to a great age. 69, 4.

. ZEBRA. To dream of seeing a zebra, is a sign of a quarrel: if you imagine that somebody presented you with one of these animals, or that you have purchased it, it foretells, to a young man, that he will marry a rich but quarrelsome wife, and that she will be constantly annoying him by bragging of her property. 39, 70, 32.

ZOUAVE. (*See Parade.*) To dream you see Zouaves, as well as other soldiers and armed men, denotes, that you will have quarrels and trouble in your family, if you have one, and if you have not, among your relatives: to the single man, this dream foreshadows that his sweetheart loves another better than himself; and to the maiden it signifies her lover will try and seduce her. 58, 1, 77.

ZINK. (*See Metals.*)

LIST OF DREAMS, WITHOUT INTERPRETATIONS, BUT WITH THE NUMBERS THEY SIGNIFY.

Afternoon, 46.
Alabaster, 13, 78, 3.
Album, 63, 18.
Alley, 2, 55.
Alloy, 9.
Alum, 62, 12.
Anchovy, 73, 1, 62.
Andiron, 33.
Apprentice, 54.
Apron, 8.
Arch, 4, 37, 9.
Archbishop, 13, 6.
Architect, 72, 3.
Armory, 54.
Army, 44.
Arrow, 37, 20.
Arrow-root, 49, 7, 8.
Ascent, 4.
Asparagus, 16, 40, 1.
Assistance, 71, 33.
Attack, 69.
Axe, 49, 74.
Band-box, 21, 44.
Bantem Fowl, 34.
Bark of Dogs, 64, 18.
Bark of Trees, 77.
Barley, 3, 19, 10.
Bar-room, 14.
Basket, 46, 31, 2.
Basque, 17.
Bass-viol, 37, 54.
Bass-voice, 53, 72, 14.

Bathroom, 11, 76, 1.
Batter, 4, 18.
Bedfellow, 72.
Bedstead, 15.
Bee-hive, 22, 1.
Beef, 27, 71, 8.
Beef, boiled, 8, 4, 32.
Beef, corned, 64, 8.
Beef, roasted, 16, 64.
Bell-ringer, 51.
Belly-ache, 78, 2.
Belly-band, 13.
Bier, 47, 6.
Billiards, 9, 6, 54.
Billiard Table, 6, 9, 72.
Birthday, *Play your age.*
Bishop, 63.
Blackbird, 41, 3.
Black-eye, 57.
Blacksmith, 35, 61, 2.
Blanket, 7, 53.
Blarny, 18.
Blind Man or Woman, 78.
Blind Man's Buff, 31.
Blue-stocking, 28, 10.
Blushing, 71, 49, 8.
Boarding-house, 65, 5.
Boasting, 4.
Boatswain, 12.
Bomb-shell, 39, 58.

Bones, 3, 9, 70.
Book-binder, 28.
Book-store, 65, 2, 11.
Borrowing, 45, 3.
Bosom, 53.
Bottle, 10, 19.
Box, 68, 13.
Box in a Theatre, 12, 4, 48.
Box-tree, 71, 6.
Box-wood, 8.
Boxing, 61.
Boxing-gloves, 16, 59, 10.
Bracelets, 78.
Brains, 37, 18, 4.
Breeches, 18, 41.
Bride, 61.
Bridegroom, 6.
Bridesmaid, 32.
Brimstone, 35, 17.
Broom, 8, 1.
Buffalo, 59.
Builder, 66, 3, 47.
Building, 77, 41.
Burglar, 7, 70.
Burr, 36, 5, 48.
Burying-ground, 69.
Button of Bone, 35, 14.
Button of Gold, 19, 1.
Button of Silver, 58.
Calendar, 40.

Calves, 68.
Camp, 78, 20, 54.
Camp-meeting, 21, 5.
Candle-stick, 2.
Capers, 46.
Capmaker, 64, 19.
Capon, 39, 14, 72.
Captain, 63, 27.
Card de visite, 1, 20.
Cardmaker, 36, 2.
Carnival, 51, 62.
Carpenter, 48.
Cartridge, 37, 1.
Cash-box, 19, 7.
Cashier, 63.
Castor-oil, 21.
Cavalry, 76.
Celestial Signs, 57, 10.
Chairmaker, 3, 15.
Chairman, 18.
Chalice, 70.
Chalk, 19.
Chamber, 37.
Champagne, 72, 60.
Champion, (of any thing,) 62.
Chandelier, 6.
Changing Money, 53, 1.
Chapel, 18.
Charcoal, 10.
Charm, 57.
Checkers, 16.
Childbed, 72, 12.
Chin, 44.
Choir, 2, 7, 14.
Church Meeting, 55, 1.
Cider, 31.
Circle, 8.
Cistern, 61, 30.
Clergyman, 29, 6.
Clerk, 5.
Cloak, 69, 70,
Cloister, 54, 9, 11.
Cloth, 34.
Cloves, 65.
Coat, 40.
Cobbler, 16.
Cock-fight, 21, 33.
Coffee, 70.

Coffee-house, 1, 17, 6.
Coffee-mill, 71, 30.
Cold, 71.
College, 16, 3.
Colonel, 64.
Color, 43, 16, 1.
Comb, 21.
Comb-maker, 47, 3.
Combing the Hair, 50.
Commander, 34.
Commandments, 41.
Commerce, 73.
Commodore, 16, 4.
Companion, 37.
Confectioner, 64, 22.
Confessions, 67.
Confidence, 58.
Conflagration, 2, 71.
Confusion, 30.
Conjurer, 48.
Conscience, 46, 19.
Conspiracy, 4.
Consume, 31.
Consumption, 75.
Convent, 32, 60.
Convention, 1, 73
Cooking, 68.
Cooking Stove, 51
Cooper, 10, 27.
Copperas, 15.
Copperplate, 48.
Coppersmith, 78, 1.
Copying, 2.
Coral, Red, 41.
Coral, White, 49.
Coronation, 16, 5.
Cot, 17, 76.
Cotton, 70.
Cotton-gin, 63, 1.
Cough, 31.
Counter, 26.
Counterfeit Money, 18.
Courage, 74.
Court, 47, 50.
Courting, 30.
Cousin, 5.
Cover, 74.
Coverlid, 1, 11.
Creek, 47, 5.

Crinoline, 68.
Crop, 4.
Cruelty, 37.
Crystal, 45.
Cunning, 18, 71.
Cup, 34.
Cup of Coffee, 14.
Cup of Tea, 43, 8.
Cup of Water, 50.
Curtains, 58.
Custom House, 19.
Cut, 1, 8.
Cutler, 40.
Dahlgren Gun, 52.
Dairy Maid, 70.
Dancing Master, 69, 2
Dandelion, 46, 18.
Delay, 64, 1.
Desert, 16, 5, 2.
Desk, 78.
Devil, 7.
Diarrhœa, 33, 52.
Distrust, 19, 8.
Divorce, 41, 70, 4.
Dominoes, 32.
Dower, 41, 6, 77.
Dragon, 13, 50.
Dressing, 43.
Drill, 5, 78, 60.
Driver, 1, 63.
Dromedary, 3.
Drug Store, 9, 16, 29
Drummer, 11, 26.
Dryness, 31.
Ducats, 70.
Dung-fork, 25, 62.
Dunghill, 77.
Ear-rings, 39, 43.
Ebony, 44.
Elbow, 52.
Election, 2, 78.
Embalming, 15, 5, 39.
Emperor, 9.
Empire, 26, 39.
Engineer, 20, 62.
Ensign, 7, 28.
Entanglement, 77.
Entrance, 39, 2, 44.
Envy, 17.

Epaulettes, 60, 65.
Errands, 19, 38.
Exchange Office, 52,45, 69.
Exile, 26.
Expulsion, 7, 13.
Extasy, 74, 47, 56.
Falsehood, 8, 11, 29.
Farrier, 2.
Fashion, 72, 1, 23.
Fast Horse, 23, 40, 2.
Father-in-law, 55.
Fencing Master, 47.
Fencing School, 77, 38.
Fig Tree, 36.
File, 5, 56.
Finding anything, 10, 32, 60.
Firebrand, 57, 1.
Fire Buckets, 39, 26.
Fire Engine, 20, 3.
Firepan, 6, 47, 52.
Fireplace, 12.
Fire-tongs, 28, 13.
Firework, 16, 32.
Fish-bone, 29, 37, 21.
Fisherman, 16.
Fish-hook, 63, 9.
Fish-market, 53, 3, 67.
Fish-net, 47.
Fish-pond, 18.
Flame, 38.
Flannel, 25, 64.
Flattery, 46, 5, 13.
Flax, 66.
Flax-dresser, 17, 46.
Flax-spinning, 9,27,69.
Foal, 4, 12.
Foreigner, 73.
Foreman, 8.
Foot, 29, 42, 3.
Fort, 11.
Founder, 47, 58, 7.
Fox, 22.
Friend, 21.
Fruit-seller, 70, 15.
Fruit Trees, 29, 57.
Furnace, 13, 39, 6.
Furniture, 45.

Gallery, 56, 61, 7.
Gardener, 16, 47.
Garland, 62, 4.
Garment, 39, 47, 8.
Garret, 4, 10, 74.
Garrison, 1, 42, 59.
Genealogical Tree, 27.
Gilder, 23, 15, 63.
Gilliflower, 53, 6, 9.
Gingerbread, 44.
Girl, 12, 19, 27.
Glass-house, 67, 73.
Glazier, 10,
Gnat, 25, 64.
Goldbeater, 37, 52.
Gold-leaves, 19.
Gooseberries, 54.
Grandfather, 77, 53, 39.
Grandmother, 68.
Gratitude, 44, 26, 21.
Greek, 5.
Grocery, 39, 27, 6.
Guardian, 21.
Guests, 13, 55.
Gymnast, 61, 28.
Hair brush, 7.
Handkerchief, 30, 65, 10.
Harness, 15.
Hatmaker, 59, 77.
Hayloft, 43, 25, 6.
Hay-wagon, 16.
Hazelnut, 2.
Head, 47, 69, 9.
Headache, 29.
Hedgehog, 15.
Helping any one, 6, 73.
Hemp, 19.
Hempseed, 64, 39.
Henroost, 23, 77, 9.
Herbs, 27.
Herdsman, 44, 29.
Hermit, 4, 9, 16.
Herring, 1, 27.
High School, 15.
High Tide, 68.
Hill, 45, 22.
Hip, 73, 5.
History, 49, 58.

Holyday, 22, 39.
Home, 10.
Homicide, 4, 37, 69.
Hoof, 56, 18, 22.
Horseshoe, 6.
Horse-cart, 59.
Hotel-keeper, 17, 34.
Housekeeper, 49.
Humpback, 77, 9.
Hunter, 69.
Husband, 31.
Hyacinth, 36, 7, 19.
Hypocrite, 55, 66.
Imitation, 42.
Impatience, 29, 31.
Inauguration, 17, 3.
Indian Corn, 10.
Ingratitude, 33, 29.
Inheritance, 9, 15.
Inkstand, 75, 69.
Inquisition, 57, 29.
Inscription, 6, 39, 73.
Interpreter, 46, 22.
Intestines, 49, 52.
Introduction, 22.
Invalid, 9, 4.
Invitation, 30, 77, 5.
Ironing, 29, 42.
Jailer, 18.
Jasmine, 2, 38.
Jeweller, 69.
Jewess, 17, 23.
Jewsharp, 70.
Journeyman, 21, 68, 6.
Judge, 9.
Juniper, 44.
Justice, 39, 47.
Kettle, 28, 51.
Kitchen, 69, 7, 74.
Kitchen-ware, 27, 39, 1.
Knifegrinder, 6, 47.
Knitting, 18, 33.
Lace String, 2.
Ladies' Maid, 35, 20.
Lame Person, 15.
Lance, 13, 19.
Lap, 26, 29.
Lapidary, 77.
Leak, 22, 49.

Leather, 15, 52.
Legislature, 42.
Lemonade, 6, 10.
Loadstone, 55.
Locks, 73, 4.
Locksmith, 2.
Locusts, 19, 61.
Lodging, 29, 21, 9.
Lodging-house, 41, 7, 56.
Lottery Ticket, 2, 12.
Maccaroni, 26.
Machine, 1, 9.
Magazine, 16, 18.
Magistrate, 49.
Mahogany, 29, 26.
Major, 5, 9.
Major General, 14, 45.
Mariner, 3.
Mark, 16.
Mason, 9, 19, 45.
Mast, 6, 39.
Master, 24, 64.
Matting, 10.
Mattress, 3, 7, 26.
Mattress-maker, 29.
Meal, 11, 19.
Measure, 52, 63.
Melancholy, 19.
Memorial, 6, 14.
Merchants, 73.
Mermaid, 41, 65.
Messenger, 13.
Miller, 25, 47.
Mine, 56.
Minerals, 39, 1.
Mineral Water, 67, 9, 77.
Mixture, 71, 6.
Model, 10.
Mole, 26, 39.
Morning, 6.
Morocco, 30, 71.
Mortar, 45.
Moss, 19, 49.
Mother-in-law, 45.
Mouse-trap, 4, 16, 64.
Murder, 53, 32, 29.
Murderer, 17.

Musician, 44, 56.
Musk, 21.
Musket, 5, 45.
Muskrat, 59.
Myrrh, 73, 9.
Necromancer, 14.
Neighbor, 78.
Nest, 29, 45.
New Moon, 38.
New Year, 18, 46.
Noon, 56, 8.
Notary, 49.
Nutmeg, 29
Oil Can, 46.
Oil Dealer, 19, 43.
Olives, 33.
One-eyed, 7.
Orator, 29, 44.
Organist, 37, 6, 3.
Ornament, 52.
Ostrich, 44, 11.
Overcoat, 15.
Package, 13, 29.
Pail, 22.
Pain, 7.
Painter, 21, 49.
Paper Mill, 41.
Parchment, 19, 28, 14.
Pardon, 6.
Parents, 29, 49.
Parson, 67.
Partridge, 46, 77.
Passion, 26.
Pastry, 4, 9.
Pasteboard, 18.
Patient, 49, 1.
Patriot, 5, 76.
Patrol, 26, 13, 44.
Pawn Ticket, 2, 9.
Pencil, 3.
Pen-holder, 71, 19.
Persecution, 56.
Perspiration, 78.
Pestle, 48, 6.
Petticoat, 22, 47, 1.
Pheasant, 1.
Philosopher, 34, 71.
Physician, 19, 33, 2.
Piazza, 6, 73.

Pickpockets, 66.
Pillory, 10, 55.
Pine Tree, 17.
Pine Wood, 29, 59.
Plane, 18.
Planet, 39, 4, 70.
Planting, 27, 74.
Plate, 9.
Pleasure, 25, 57.
Pocket, 20, 41.
Pocket Knife, 6.
Pomatum, 19.
Pool, 27, 56.
Poorhouse, 39.
Poor People, 57, 78.
Poplar Tree, 5.
Porcelain, 27, 34.
Porcupine, 49.
Postage, 5, 28.
Pot, 16, 63.
Potatoes, 72, 10, 1.
Potter, 57.
Poultry, 52.
Poultry-seller, 49, 32.
Powder, 29.
Preacher, 19, 41.
Prelate, 28, 59, 3.
Presumption, 71, 4.
Prince, 69.
Princess, 19, 44.
Print, 13.
Printer, 29, 50.
Printing Office, 69.
Printing Press, 47, 7.
Printseller, 21.
Privacy, 52, 77.
Prize-fighter, 9, 17, 49.
Professor, 15.
Prophet, 3, 38.
Prudence, 10.
Purchaser, 49, 75, 6.
Quack Doctor, 44, 2.
Quack Medicine, 19, 33.
Quadrupeds, 27.
Raisins, 21, 45.
Rake, 39.
Raw Meat, 46, 77.
Receipts, 44.
Reconciliation, 7.

Reed, 29, 64, 2.
Register, 37, 19,
Republic, 59, 1.
Resurrection, 4.
Review, 37, 57.
Riding School, 10, 44.
Rifle, 21.
Ringing Bells, 59.
Riot, 30.
Rogue, 29, 48.
Romance, 51, 13, 8.
Rope, 19, 62.
Rope-maker, 73.
Rosebud, 1.
Rose Bush, 43, 47.
Rosin, 9.
Rupture, 20.
Saddle, 2, 7.
Saddler, 37.
Sailmaker, 71, 3, 20.
Salt, 68.
Saltpetre, 15, 61.
Salve, 7.
Sampler, 13, 46.
Sawdust, 66.
Saw, 1, 63, 9.
Sawyer, 30.
Scabbard, 32, 49.
Scandal, 57.
School Teacher, 10, 78.
Scorpion, 29.
Scoundrel, 40, 42.
Scrap Book, 39, 44.
Scratch the head, 55,
    73, 22.
Scull, 29.
Sculptor, 3, 39.
Scum, 17.
Seal, 24.
Seaman, 42, 55, 31.
Seamstress, 49, 60.
Seashore, 30, 67.
Secretary, 52, 17.
Security, 12, 38.
Seed, 47.
Seed-seller, 66.
Seat, 6, 33. ·
Sentinel, 29, 64.
Separation, 32.

Sew, 43, 56.
Shame, 38, 19.
Shears, 59.
Sheep's-wool, 1, 29, 4 .
Sheet Iron, 15.
Shell-fish, 20, 45.
Shoemaker, 64, 9.
Shot-gun, 12.
Shovel, 19, 28.
Siege, 36, 48, 30.
Sieve, 77, 6.
Sign, 13.
Silk Merchant, 49.
Silk Stockings, 26, 41.
Silkworm, 67.
Silversmith, 13, 28.
Skates, 20.
Slander, 55, 6.
Sleigh, 40, 29.
Smith, 37.
Smoking, 10.
Snail, 27, 9, 47.
Snipe, 36, 46.
Snuff-box, 30, 49.
Soapboiler, 26.
Sole-leather, 64, 10.
Son, 19, 73.
Song, 40.
Soot, 74, 7.
Sorcerer, 56, 62.
Soup, 39, 41, 44.
Sparrow, 8.
Spectacles, 24, 13.
Spice, 6, 67.
Spider's-web, 39.
Spinach, 56, 49.
Spindle, 43, 10.
Spinning, 20, 69.
Spinster, 63.
Spirit, 17, 29.
Spitting, 44, 14.
Splendor, 37, 19.
Spoon, 59, 17.
Spot, 30, 47.
Sprinkling, 66.
Squandering, 78, 2.
Staff, 29, 41, 22.
Stage-driver, 11.
Stairs, 19, 39.

Stall, 42.
Stallion, 7.
Stamping, 25, 1.
Steps, 49, 16.
Step-sister, 52.
Steward, 33, 11.
Stomach, 9.
Stone, 18.
Stones, precious, 77, 2.
Street, 14, 22, 63.
Strings, 57.
Storekeeper, 10, 64.
Swelling, 42, 16.
Sweet Oil, 27.
Sweet Taste, 62, 19, 6
Swindler, 49, 28.
Swindling, 8.
Switch, 25, 42.
Synagogue, 38, 60.
Table, 11.
Tailoress, 9.
Tanner, 47, 14.
Tape, 33, 68, 20.
Tapestry, 58.
Tart, 73, 10.
Tassels, 5, 29.
Teacher, 16.
Temptation, 44.
Tenant, 78, 66.
Titles, 29, 49.
Timepiece, 25, 62.
Timber, 56.
Tongs, 30.
Tooth-pick, 3, 17, 33.
Torture, 41.
Tow, 10, 58.
Traitor, 66,
Traveller, 1, 52.
Treasure, 7.
Trembling, 41, 59, 11
Trial, 28, 42.
Triumph, 69, 3.
Trophy, 38, 17.
Tumbler, 50, 68, 44.
Turner, 59.
Turpentine, 19.
Type, 49, 69.
Under-clothes, 26.
Union, 10, 35.

Uproar, 4, 11.
Vengeance, 38.
Vermacilla, 46.
Vexation, 55, 2, 13.
Vice, 70, 19.
Victory, 68.
Village, 25, 38.
Viper, 40.
Wages, 7, 78.
Wagon, 67.
Waiter, 32.
Walls, 56, 48, 3.
Wanderer, 9, 36.
Want, 18.
Wash-house, 1.
Wash-kettle, 75, 7.
Washer-woman, 44.
Washing-tub, 30, 54.

Watchmaker, 6, 46.
Water-bucket, 29, 33, 22.
Weasel, 57.
Weaver, 10, 76.
Weaving, 66, 11.
Wedding-clothes, 23.
Wedding-cake, 3, 68.
Wedding-ring, 19.
Wheel, 47, 24.
Wheelwright, 20, 11.
Whisper, 59, 76, 4.
White, 39, 8.
White Lead, 56.
Whitewasher, 67.
Widower, 6, 45.
Wife, 70, 29.
Wig-maker, 4, 77.

Wild Animals, 25, 13.
Wild Geese, 49.
Wind, 56, 20, 2.
Windmill, 33, 10.
Wine-cellar, 18, 67.
Wine-glass, 7.
Winter, 39, 70.
Witness, 29.
Woman, 50.
Woodcock, 6.
Woodcutter, 28, 49.
Wooden Spoon, 71, 5, 6.
Woodpile, 33.
Wool, 44, 62.
Worship, 18, 44.
Wound, 3.
Wreath, 68.
Wrestling, 2.

NUMBERS FOR DREAMS OF NAMES.

Aaron, 41.
Abel, 8.
Abraham, 4.
Adam, 3.
Adolphus, 2.
Albert, 55, 8.
Alexander, 70.
Alfred, 41, 74.
Ambrose, 30, 8, 21.
Amos, 14.
Andrew, 6, 49.
Anthony, 54.
Archibald, 61.
Arnold, 9.
Arthur, 34, 19.
Augustin, 10, 75.
Augustus, 27.
Bartholomew, 9.
Benjamin, 18.
Bernard, 20.
Bertram, 49.
Boniface, 65.
Cæsar, 70.
Caleb, 29.
Cecil, 3.
Charles, 1, 10.

Christopher, 35.
Clement, 49, 7.
Conrad, 30.
Constantine, 75.
Cuthbert, 19, 47.
Daniel, 63.
David, 78.
Denis, 21, 6.
Edgar, 2, 60, 5.
Edmund, 74, 4.
Edward, 21, 8.
Edwin, 4.
Egbert, 28.
Elijah, 16.
Elisha, 14.
Ephraim, 25, 2.
Erasmus, 44.
Ernest, 72.
Eugene, 4, 13.
Eustace, 19.
Everard, 47, 3.
Ezekiel, 32, 60.
Felix, 54.
Ferdinand, 69.
Francis, 20.
Frederic, 15.

Gabriel, 17.
Geoffrey, 33.
George, 27, 13, 1.
Gideon, 75, 2.
Gilbert, 16, 30.
Giles, 27.
Godfrey, 55.
Guy, 59, 5.
Hannibal, 72.
Harold, 4, 11.
Hector, 13, 2.
Henry, 18.
Herbert, 20, 1.
Hezekiah, 17.
Horatio, 6.
Hubert, 79.
Hugh, 14.
Humphrey, 37, 6.
Jacob, 78.
James, 44, 6.
Job, 4, 10.
Joel, 30.
John, 4.
Jonah, 7.
Jonathan, 1.
Joseph, 41.

Joshua, 2.
Josias, 16.
Isaac, 58.
Laurence, 5.
Lazarus, 28.
Leonard, 4.
Leopold, 5.
Lewis, 25.
Lionel, 13.
Lucius, 77, 4.
Luke, 28.
Mark, 47, 3.
Martin, 34.
Matthew, 65.
Maurice, 3.
Michael, 7.
Moses, 34, 8.
Nathaniel, 75.
Nicolas, 6.
Norman, 10.
Obadiah, 40.
Oliver, 2, 18.
Orlando, 7.
Owen, 53.
Patrick, 5.
Paul, 14.
Percival, 11.
Peregrine, 15, 60.
Peter, 42.
Philip, 19.
Phineas, 28.
Ralph, 24, 6.
Reuben, 2, 11.
Richard, 35.
Robert, 60.
Roger, 3, 78.
Rowland, 75.
Rufus, 29.
Samson, 49.
Samuel, 76, 4, 13.
Saul, 5.
Sebastian, 34.
Simeon, 18.
Simon, 75.
Solomon, 12, 17.
Stephen, 64.
Theodore, 19.
Theophilus, 34, 5.
Thomas, 11.

Timothy, 29.
Toby or Tobias, 44.
Valentine, 50, 1, 6.
Vincent, 31.
Vivian, 5.
Walter, 11, 6.
William, 22.
Zaccheus, 1.
Zachary, 10.
Zebedee, 16.
Zedekiah, 30.

———

Adeline, 7, 17, 70.
Agatha, 9.
Agnes, 41, 2.
Alethea, 12.
Alice, 42.
Althea, 1, 70.
Amy, Amelia, 51.
Anna, Anne, or Hannah, 62.
Arabella, 78.
Aureola, 41, 6.
Barbara, 21.
Beatrice, 18.
Benedicta, 6.
Bernice, 54.
Bertha, 3.
Blanche, 1.
Bridget, 61.
Caroline, 40.
Cassandra, 5.
Catharine, 58.
Cecilia, 18, 1.
Charity, 70.
Charlotte, 8.
Chloe, 20, 4.
Christiana, 10.
Cicely, 15.
Clara, 70.
Constance, 68.
Deborah, 34.
Diana, 65.
Dorcas, 2, 18.
Dorothy, 2, 74.
Edith, 29.
Eleanor, 50.

Eliza, Elizabeth, 2.
Emily, 28.
Emma, 66, 4, 8.
Esther, 2, 17.
Eunice, 16, 52.
Eve, 41.
Frances, 17, 20, 1.
Gertrude, 75.
Grace, 69.
Hagar, 44.
Helena, 51, 6.
Isabella, 20, 71.
Jane, 22.
Janet, 2.
Joan, 4.
Joyce, 36.
Judith, 30,
Julia, Juliana, 47.
Letitia, 38, 5.
Lucretia, 7.
Lucy, 62.
Lydia, 41.
Mabel, 17, 1.
Magdalene, 4.
Margaret, 3, 41.
Martha, 20.
Mary, 3, 11, 33.
Maud, Matilda, 1, 18.
Mercy, 53, 9.
Mildred, 24.
Miriam, 3.
Nicola, 42.
Olympia, 2, 78.
Patience, 5, 2.
Paulina, 21.
Penelope, 45.
Philippa, 3.
Phœbe, 19.
Phyllis, 65.
Priscilla, 10, 11.
Prudence, 17.
Rachel, 6.
Rebecca, 45.
Rhode, 49.
Rosa, 19.
Rosabella, 11.
Rosamund, 2.
Rosecleer, 5, 14.
Ruth, 76.

Sapphira, 7, 19. |Susan, Susanna, 21. |Theodosia, 76.
Sarah, 10. |Tabitha, 4. |Theresa, 14.
Sophia, 73. |Temperance, 16. |Ursula, 1.

NUMBERS FOR DREAMS OF CARDS.

SPADES.		HEARTS.	
King,	65.	King,	54, 7.
Queen,	77, 8.	Queen,	65.
Knave,	4, 17.	Knave,	24.
Ten,	3,	Ten,	40, 11.
Nine,	19, 62.	Nine	3, 48.
Eight,	41, 6, 30.	Eight,	70, 2.
Seven,	24.	Seven,	8, 60, 3.
Six,	2.	Six,	27.
Five,	78, 12.	Five,	2.
Four,	55.	Four,	6, 21.
Trey,	30.	Trey,	45.
Deuce,	27.	Deuce,	34, 18, 4.
Ace,	77, 52.	Ace,	29.

CLUBS.		DIAMONDS.	
King,	11.	King,	65.
Queen,	22, 5.	Queen,	30, 9.
Knave,	8, 4.	Knave,	47.
Ten,	30, 1.	Ten,	3, 11
Nine,	18,	Nine,	64, 30, 4
Eight,	77,	Eight,	58.
Seven,	6, 70.	Seven,	55, 5, 1.
Six,	20.	Six,	47, 2.
Five,	74, 12.	Five,	51, 78.
Four.	58.	Four,	16.
Trey,	33.	Trey,	49.
Deuce,	24.	Deuce,	7, 12.
Ace,	51, 7.	Ace,	6.

NUMBERS FOR THE DREAMS OF DOMINOES.

Double-Six,	48.	Double-Five,	33, 8.
Six-Five,	71, 6.	Five-Four,	16.
Six-Four,	30.	Five-Three,	41, 5, 7.
Six-Three,	5.	Five-Two,	30.
Six-Two.	8.	Five-One,	21.
Six-One,	54, 2.	Five-Blank,	2.
Six-Blank,	35.		

Double-Four,	78.	Three-Blank,	30, 16, 4
Four-Three,	4.		
Four-Two,	21, 2	Double-Two,	41, 3.
Four-One,	50.	Two-One,	5, 17.
Four-Blank,	48.	Two-Blank,	2.
Double-Three,	65.	Double-One,	21.
Three-Two,	24.	One-Blank,	10.
Three-One,	16.	Double Blank,	(Don't play)

NUMBERS FOR DREAMS OF THE MONTHS.

January,	26.	July,	22.
February,	18.	August,	37.
March,	44.	September,	18.
April,	17.	October,	3.
May,	3.	November,	2.
June,	75.	December,	55.

FOR THE DAYS OF THE WEEK.

Monday,	45.	Friday,	2.
Tuesday,	18.	Saturday,	7.
Wednesday,	2.	Sunday,	1.
Thursday,	16.		

HOW TO FIND LUCKY NUMBERS WITH DICE.

This plan of ascertaining lucky numbers has always been exceedingly popular with those persons who try their fortune at the lottery. The manner of calculating a lucky number is as follows: Take two dice, and after shaking them well in a box, throw them out, being careful to note the whole number of spots on the uppermost sides of the dice, then repeat this operation and again mark down the number of spots as before. Having done this, you then consult the annexed table and find the number of your first throw, then follow the line down until you arrive at the number corresponding with your second throw on the opposite side of the table. For example, we will suppose you throw the first time, and the number of spots is equal to 4. You must then look at the top of the line and find the Roman numeral IV. You throw the second time and get 7 spots; this you will find on the outside column, at the left hand, marked VII. Then all you have to do is to place your finger on the IV. at the top of the table and follow the line down until you arrive at VII on the opposite side of the table, thus you will find the number 43, which is the lucky number. Should you come to a cypher (0) you must throw again. By following these simple directions you can get as many good numbers as you wish to play.

TABLE TO FIND LUCKY NUMBERS.

I	II	III	IV	V	VI	VII	VIII	IX	X	XI	XII
II	75	0	18	0	16	0	78	0	44	0	39
III	64	28	0	2	0	55	0	21	0	51	0
IV	1	0	70	0	32	0	29	48	35	0	12
V	53	69	0	5	40	61	0	9	42	73	0
VI	46	54	7	76	38	49	11	33	27	0	66
VII	0	58	43	8	77	0	25	67	19	3	0
VIII	50	0	22	0	65	0	72	0	36	0	47
IX	0	13	0	31	10	0	60	15	0	4	0
X	23	0	59	0	71	0	6	68	34	0	20
XI	0	74	14	52	62	24	0	30	0	17	0
XII	57	0	41	26	0	37	63	0	45	0	56

THE SHIFT CHARM.

On going to bed, take off your under garment and turn it wrong side outwards; hang it on the back of a chair, having first placed the chair facing and in front of the bed. While doing this, repeat the following lines:

Husband approach! and without fear
Sit on this chair, and thus be near
The girl your heart doth hold most dear
And if thy love is all sincere,
To her, this night appear! appear!

You must then get into bed backwards, and sleep in your night-gown without any shift. You will probably dream of seeing an agreeable young man, in which case your marriage within that year is certain. If you do not dream of a man, you will never marry. You should be alone in trying this charm, for if you speak to any one, or any one in the room speaks, it breaks it at once.

FORTUNE-TELLING WITH A PACK OF EUCHRE CARDS.

Take a pack of thirty two cards, such as is used for the game o 'uchre. Each one of these cards has its own *particular* signification ut when taken in connection with other cards its signification is termed *conditional.*

PARTICULAR SIGNIFICATION OF THE CARDS.

(SPADES.)

ACE: Disagreeable tidings—perhaps news of a death.
SEVEN: Dangerous illness, or something very unpleasant.
EIGHT: Sorrow, vexation.
NINE: Quarrels, law-suits, high words, blows.
TEN: Non-fulfilment of a wish—disappointment of a cherished hope, unforeseen accidents.

(CLUBS.)

ACE: A present, a testimonial of honor and distinction.
SEVEN: An inheritance, gain, profit.
EIGHT: Prosperity, wealth, success in business.
NINE: Proposals of marriage.
TEN: Good fortune in games of chance, in lottery speculations, finding a treasure.

(DIAMONDS.)

ACE: A letter, news—whether good or bad is determined by the nearest cards.
SEVEN: Travels, a campaign.
EIGHT: A ball, company.
NINE: Illness—if a knave lies on the right side, you will soon stand godfather.
TEN: A joyful meeting—a long lost friend returned. Of the pic true cards we will speak hereafter.

(HEARTS.)

ACE: Quiet domestic life—tranquillity.

SEVEN: Falling in Love—Love.
EIGHT: A Surprise.
NINE: Betrothal.
TEN: A Wedding.

In explaining the cards, my dear readers, to any one, shuffle the pack three times, and let the person who wishes to know his fortune cut it three times in succession. Then take up the cards, and let the person in question draw one. This drawn card you place first upon the table. Then spread out the pack in four rows, each containing eight cards. (*See Engraving.*)

The first card is of the highest significance. In the first place it indicates the character of the person inquiring, and according to the following rule:

Choleric, passionate, violent.

Sanguine, cheerful, mirthful, witty.

Phlegmatic, practical, unexcitable·

Melancholic, sentimental, poetical, talented.

As, however, the human character is never without more than one of the above named characteristics, the first card signifies the most prominent one, and the cards which lie on the right side and below it are reckoned with it, by which the meaning of the first card is either modified or corroborated.

If the person in question is a lady, and she has, for example, drawn a club, the queen of clubs is herself, the knave of clubs is her intended, the king her father, or uncle, as the case may be. The picture cards of the other black suit are her friends and relations. It is the same if she has drawn hearts or diamonds, only that in this case the picture cards of the other red suit signify her friends and relations. If the person inquiring is a gentleman, it is the same, except that he is the knave of the suit which he has drawn, and his intended the queen.

From this first card, also, you form a judgment of one's whole future course in life. If its signification is joyful, the person's life will be a happy one. If, for example, it is the ace of hearts, it indicates that the person will never be without a home, a dear and pleasant home to him; if it is the ace of clubs, he will pass through life enjoying honor and fame; if it is the ten of hearts with a female figure on

EXAMPLE OF FORTUNE-TELLING WITH AN EUCHRE PACK OF CARDS.

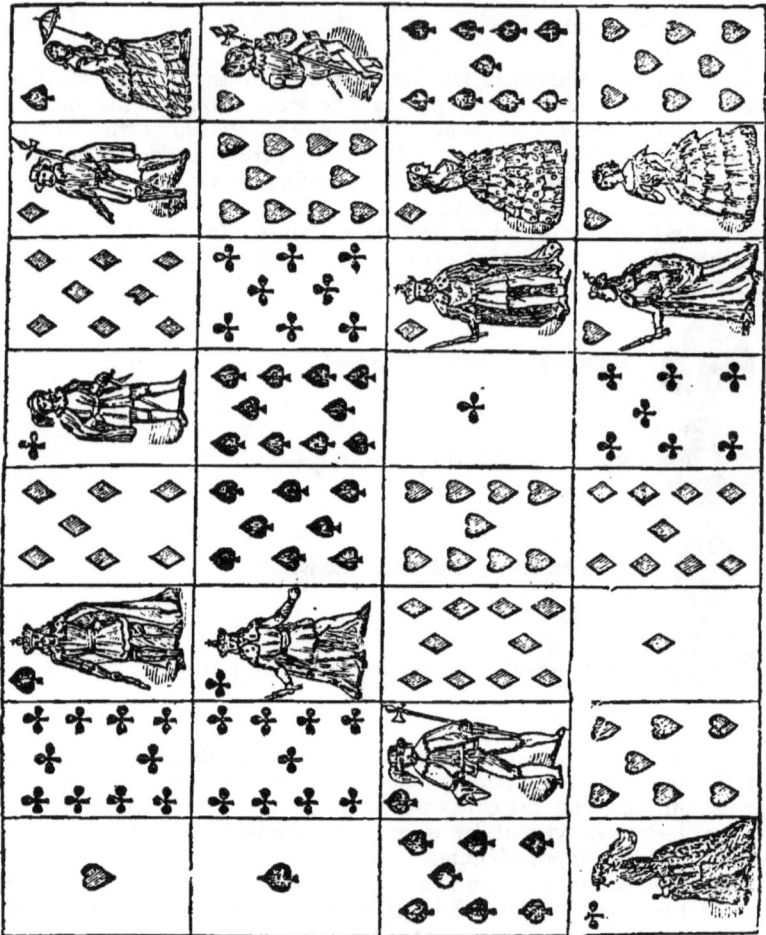

either side, it signifies two wives; if with a male figure on either side, and the person inquiring is a female, two husbands.

Thus much as to general rules. We will now instruct the reader how to explain the cards in detail. We will suppose that it is a lady who inquires of the cards, and endeavor, by means of an example, to give an accurate explanation of the method to be pursued. Spread out the cards before you, and observe carefully the different cards while you read the fortune I shall predict from them. (*See Engraving, page 96.*)

ACE OF HEARTS.—The young lady's character, it seems, is sentimental, melancholic, poetical, which three qualities are found more or *less* together. If the next card were a heart, it would indicate a temperament inclined to love. As, however, the adjacent cards are clubs and spades, of which two indeed are clubs, we conclude that the lady often displays a cheerful, sanguine disposition. yet can, at times, be very passionate. The main feature of her character, however, is the melancholic.

We will now look around for the lady herself—she is found to be the seventh card on the last row. Her lover, on the other hand, is the eighth card in the second row. As he precedes her, this signifies that she is already acquainted with him, and they seem already to love one another, as a love card lies at his side, and also one at hers; no card, however, lies between them to connect them, except the queen of diamonds. This, however, is not altogether favorable, for a queen between a loving pair signifies a rival (for a gentleman, the knave signifies the same), and can as well indicate a separation as a union, notwithstanding its similarity of color. The general rule is as follows :—If the card which connects the queen and knave is of the same color with them, it indicates a future union between the persons. (Hearts and diamonds form one color, as do clubs and spades.)

One thing more : from the cards which lie next to the knave, we are enabled to judge of the character and occupation of the lady's intended. In the present case, the cards next to. the knave of hearts are two spades, two diamonds, and one heart; his character, therefore, according to the rules already given, is choleric, yet at times melancholic and sentimental. In his daily conduct he is practical and considerate.

As to his occupation, the different colors have the following signification :

A student, probably a clergyman.

A lawyer—jurist.

A mechanic, merchant, or a person who has chosen for himself some practical career.

A capitalist, a genius who devotes himself to some favorite pursuit, also a military man.

The card at the right hand is commonly the decisive one, but as, in the present case, there is no right hand card, the one at the left takes its place; according to this, the lady's intended is a capitalist, a genius, or a military man.

We now proceed to tell the lady's fortune in its particulars.

We commence from the ace of hearts, thus: a considerable windfall will happen in your family, young lady. Either you or your parents will draw a prize in the lottery, or heaven will drop some other nice morsel into your mouth (ten of clubs).

This will give occasion to a journey, which you will take with an acquaintance (king of spades and seven of diamonds). This journey will be very agreeable to you, and especially will you enjoy yourself at a ball, to which you will be invited by a friend of your travelling companion (knave of clubs and eight of diamonds.) You will then dance a cotillion with a relative of your intended, perhaps with your own brother-in-law that is to be (knave of diamonds.)

When you return home, you will find a letter, at the sight of which you will be disturbed, the hand-writing being that of a person unfriendly to you (queen of spades, ace of spades). You open it, and behold it is a proposal of marriage (nine of clubs), and from a relative of the gentleman who invited you to the ball (king of clubs), which touches the (nine of clubs).

As, however, you promise yourself nothing but vexation (eight of spades) from this marriage, you refuse him (ten of spades), and it will soon appear that a better fortune lies before you (eight of clubs). Soon after, a wedding takes place (ten of hearts), namely, that of your sister or friend (queen of diamonds), who, therefore, does not stand between you and your intended to separate you, but to unite you. The bridegroom is the gentleman who was your partner in the cotillion at that ball (knave of diamonds). At this wedding you will among others see your intended (knave of hearts), with whom you are already acquainted. You will also meet there a gentleman, who, when you last saw him, was dangerously ill (seven of spades, knave of spades, and ten of diamonds). Your intended seizes the opportunity to offer himself to you, and you become betrothed to him (nine of hearts). You will receive a present from a relative or friend, perhaps from your brother (ace of clubs, and king of diamonds).

Something now occurs to separate you from your betrothed (nine of spades). It almost seems as if you were jealous of a lady whom he formerly loved (queen of clubs, seven of hearts). A very tender letter which he writes to you, from a bed of sickness upon which his grief has prostrated him (ace of diamonds, nine of diamonds), soon reconciles you again, and as not long after something occurs which places him in a position to support a wife in comfort (seven of clubs), the happy marriage is celebrated. Dear relatives (king of hearts, king of diamonds, and queen of diamonds) prepare for you joyful surprises, which combine to render this day an infinitely happy one.

One thing more: if the ten of hearts is the last card in the last row, the person in question will never marry; otherwise, each row counts a year. You first count the rows until you come to the nine of hearts (the betrothal), you then begin again and count to the ten of hearts (the wedding), that is, in case the nine comes after the ten.

If the nine comes before the ten, you continue to count without re-commencing.

The young lady in question will therefore be betrothed in from two to three years, and will be married in about two years after, for the nine of hearts lies in the third row, and the ten in the second row. She has then almost five years to enjoy her single life before she becomes a wife.

TO FIND OUT WHOM ONE IS TO HAVE FOR A HUSBAND.

You select the four kings from a pack, and lay them side by side in a row upon the table.

The lady who wishes to know her fortune gives to each of these cards the name of some gentleman of her acquaintance who might be likely to woo her in marriage. It is usual to pronounce these names aloud before the company. The name given to the king of hearts is, however, an exception. This secret the lady keeps to herself. To these four kings, you can also add a queen, which then denotes the old maid.

Now, take the rest of the pack, shuffle it thoroughly, let the person in question cut them three times and commence. Under each of the above named picture cards you lay a card in turn, and as often as a spade is placed under a spade, a heart under a heart, &c., that is, as often as a card of the same suit is placed under one of these picture cards, the picture card is turned from its position.

The first time it takes a direction from left to right, the second time it lies upside down, the third time it is raised again to a position from right to left, and the fourth and last time it regains its former upright position.

That one of the four kings, who, after these different changes, first resumes his upright position, is to be the happy husband. If it should happen to be the old maid, you can imagine what is in store for you.

After having learned from the cards who is to be the husband, the questions next asked are, usually: How much will he love his wife, why he marries her, and what is his profession. These questions are answered in the following manner:

Gather up the cards, shuffle them thoroughly, and let the person cut them three times. Then tell off the cards upon the table, as you recite the following sentence:

> Heartily, painfully,
> Beyond all measure.
> By fits and starts,
> Not a bit in the world.

You repeat this sentence until the king of hearts makes his appearance. If it happens that, as you lay this upon the table, you pronounce the word "heartily" he will love his future wife heartily, and so on.

Now, as to why he marries her. Count off the cards upon the table, while you repeat the following sentence:

> For love, for her beauty,
> For his parents' command,
> For her bright, golden dollars,
> For counsel of friends.

The sentence by which you discover what is his profession is the following:

> Gentleman, alderman, clergyman, doctor,
> Merchant, broker, professor, major,
> Mechanic, lawyer, shipmaster, tailor.

This method of telling fortunes is very entertaining in society, when you have not the book to find more particular answers.

A METHOD BY WHICH TO DISCOVER IF YOUR WISH WILL BE FULFILLED.

Take a pack of cards, shuffle it, and let the person inquiring cut three times; then place singly five cards upon the table, and upon each of these cards another, taken from the top, and so on, until the pack is exhausted, and the cards are divided into five nearly equal heaps.

The person in question now selects a suit, spades or clubs, &c.—or a card may previously be drawn to determine the suit.

Suppose diamonds is the chosen suit: you take up the first heap, and throw away all the cards until you come to a matadore of diamonds. (The matadores are the ace, king, queen, knave and ten.) You do the same with the other heaps. If any one of the heaps does not contain a matadore, you cast it entirely aside.

The heaps which are left you now place one upon another in order, beginning at the left hand, and, without shuffling them, you lay them in five heaps, and proceed as before. This time there are, of course, fewer cards, beside matadores, than before. After having cast aside the cards which you meet with before finding a matadore, you take up the heaps, and, without shuffling them, lay them in five heaps, for the third time. This third and last time, you must, if your wish is to be fulfilled, be able to discard all the cards except the matadores. If any other cards are left in the heaps, your wish will not be granted.

TELLING FORTUNES BY DOMINOES AND DICE.

The telling of fortunes by the spots on Dominoes and Dice is a very ancient custom, and has always been practised by the most celebrated astrologers and fortune-tellers. The calculations have all to be made by drawing a horoscope from each domino and the spots on each side of a die; therefore the process is exceedingly tedious. We have given in the following pages the results of three years' experimental labor on this subject; not constant labor, for there are but a few hours in each year when the stars are in the right position to draw the horoscope of any particular domino. A good many of the signs predicted here have been proved to be correct within the personal knowledge of the writer, and he doubts not they will all be found to be accurate.

METHOD OF TELLING FORTUNES WITH DOMINOES.

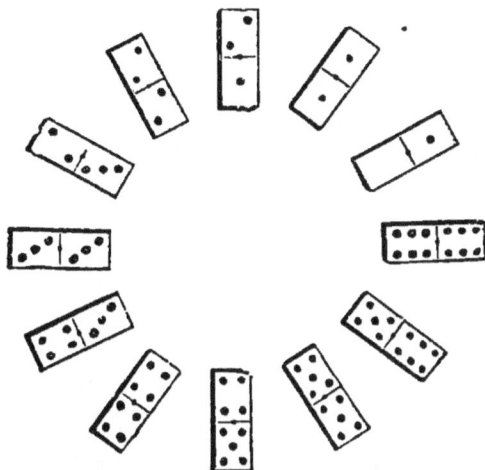

Shuffle the dominoes well on a smooth table, with their faces downward, then draw one and see what it signifies according to the description given below.

It is useless for any person to draw more than three dominoes at one time of trial, or in one and the same month, as they will only deceive themselves. Shuffle the dominoes each time of choosing; to draw the same domino twice makes the answer stronger.

Be very particular and do not attempt to tell your fortune by dominoes on *Friday* or *Monday*.

SIGNIFICATION OF THE DOMINOES.

DOUBLE-SIX. Denotes much riches by speculation, and a happy and prolific marriage. It is not good to farmers as far as relates to crops and success in their calling, but it foretells that their lands will rise in value, and that they can make money by selling out. If a girl turns this domino to learn her fate in matrimonial matters, it is a sign she will marry rich, and have a large family of children.

SIX-FIVE. If you are in search of employment, this domino shows that you will succeed by proper perseverance. If in love, do not be discouraged by any rebuffs, for success awaits you. If you have planted a crop, or about to plant one, it will yield nobly. In money matters exclusively, you may not be fortunate, as the domino is not lucky for money. If your wife is about to give birth to a child, and you try your fortune with special reference to such birth, this domino foretells its early death. If you are about to buy real estate, you will be lucky in the purchase—if to buy silverware, jewelry, or a watch, you will get cheated. If you expect a legacy, you will probably be lucky and get it.

SIX-FOUR. This domino denotes early marriage and much happiness; the sexes of the children will be about equally divided, and they will live, but will leave home early—the girls to marry, and the boys to do for themselves. It denotes neither poverty nor riches.

SIX-THREE. This domino denotes constancy and affection. It is an excellent domino for lovers, who will marry early, and enjoy much happiness. It is also a sign of riches and honors; and no troubles of any account will mar your fortune. There is some danger, however, that you will die at middle age, but if you survive that period you will live to a good old age.

SIX-TWO. Is an excellent domino for lovers, as it foretells a happy marriage. A gentleman turning this domino, will get an orderly and economical wife, and a lady will have equal good fortune in a thrifty and industrious husband. Those who turn this domino for luck in business matters, will realize all and more than they expect. To dishonest and selfish people, however, the domino is fatal. If it is turned to determine the result of any scheme that is not fair and above-board, it foretells ill-success and exposure. To a married lady who expects to present her husband with an heir, it presents a beautiful and healthy child, and one who will excel as a mathematician, and (if a boy) will probably become distinguished.

SIX-ONE. This domino foretells to young people that they will marry twice, and the second marriage will be the happiest of the two. To married people it is a sign they will be better off in middle age than when young, and that one child will be faithful and remain with them, while the others will seek their fortunes away from home.

SIX-BLANK. If you turn this domino you will hear of the death of an esteemed friend, or an acquaintance—will experience the loss of a relative or member of your family—or some one will die in whom you are interested. To a farmer, or the owner of horses or other animals, it may denote the loss of some of the animals rather than human beings; but it foretells death in some shape, and may even mean to warn you of your own decease.

DOUBLE-FIVE. Is a decidedly lucky domino in everything you undertake. It foretells success in all enterprises, but does not assure you that you will become rich.

FIVE-FOUR. This domino shows to a lady that she will probably marry a poor man, have a large family of children, and then become a widow. He may be pretty well off, to appearance, when she marries him, but if it be so, she will find that he has debts and expensive habits that will bring him to poverty and the grave. It is not a good domino for money matters, for if you have lost money, or if people owe you, the turning of this domino shows that you will not be apt to get the cash. To a farmer it is a sign of good crops; but it is also a sign that something unfortunate will occur in connection with the farm—such as cattle lost or injured, or property of some kind destroyed.

FIVE-THREE. Denotes ample means, without any other peculiarity of fortune. If you turn this domino you may calculate you will never be poor, and may become quite wealthy. But to one already wealthy, it shows that though he may not become poor, he will never be any better off than he then is, and perhaps not so well off. To young people the domino denotes comfortable circumstances after marriage, but not over-zealous love. It shows no positive bad luck in love matters, at the same time that it does not assure you of devoted attachment of your proposed partner for life, of either sex. On the whole, it is a pretty fair domino for any one to turn.

FIVE-TWO. If you are in love, you will probably be unfortunate: for though you may get the person you want, and an apparently happy marriage may follow, it will prove an unhappy one in the end. Nevertheless, your happiness may continue for some time after marriage. To a gentleman this domino foretells a thrifty and industrious wife, though one with an unhappy temper or disposition. To a single lady it denotes thrift and independence as long as she remains single. If a man is engaged in a speculation, or is about starting any new enterprise, he will not be likely to succeed. If you are a candidate for office, you will be defeated. On the whole, this is not a lucky domino for gentlemen, though for ladies it is a pretty fair one.

FIVE-ONE. Is a jolly domino for persons fond of excitement. It predicts that you will receive an invitation to a dinner, or social gathering, or to some place where you will enjoy yourself. If a married lady turns this domino it is a sign she will present her husband with a triple addition to his family—all boys. To a young lady it predicts a beau, who will not be rich or refined, but rather a rough customer, and she will discard him and marry another. If you expect to earn or to receive money, this domino is one of disappointment.

FIVE-BLANK. If a man turns it, he will be either a gambler or a rich rogue, if he has brains enough, and if his intellect is not sufficient, he will probably be a small swindler, or the favored lover of a lewd woman, or both. Although these will be his characteristics, yet circumstances may place him in a different position; but he will always be mercenary, selfish, impudent, and without pride of character. To a girl this domino foretells an unhappy marriage, and misfortune by that means; but if she remains single, and keeps clear of lovers, she will avoid the ill omen.

DOUBLE-FOUR. Is a good and smooth domino for lovers, for farmers, and for laboring people of all kinds. On the contrary, lawyers, doctors, or professional men who turn it, will probably have a spell of hard times to encounter. To little girls and boys it predicts that they will soon be invited to a party, and have much pleasure. If any one is about to give a party, and turns this domino, he or she may count on a first-rate time, for everything will go on well, and the party will be a decided success. It likewise predicts that a wedding will come off very soon.

FOUR-THREE. Those who turn this domino will marry young, live happily, and will not probably have more than one child that will live. It denotes neither poverty nor riches. To a couple who are childless, it is a sign of a second marriage. If a married person who as children turns this domino, it is a sign that the family will be reduced by death or long absence.

FOUR-TWO. Foretells a change in your circumstances, condition, family, relations, or your ideas. It is not known what the change will be, but that there will really be a change, fate has ordained. It may be nothing at all serious, or it may be something that will affect your whole life. For instance, a young person who turns this domino may get married—that will be an important change, but whether the marriage will be a happy one, is not known. A married person may lose their partner—a man may fail in business, or may become pious and join the church—a family may break up housekeeping and take board, or may lose a favorite child. Indeed, a thousand little incidents may occur in life which will cause a change in your usual routine. To farmers and persons who work hard for a living, the change will probably be a favorable or happy one. To rich and lazy people it will be an unfortunate one. To any other than these two classes it is uncertain what the nature of it will be. If you have offended your lover, or any particular friend, this domino shows that you will soon make up and become stronger friends than ever. It is a lucky domino for farmers in business matters, although it does not point out any particular good fortune that awaits them.

FOUR-ONE. Those who turn this domino will marry happily, and no uncommon event will mar their nuptials: the omen connected with it usually points to childless couples who are well off; and I find that where children are born, the parties will lose their wealth and position in proportion to the number of their offspring, which will never exceed four. In most cases there will be no children, but ample means.

FOUR-BLANK. Is an unfortunate domino for lovers, as it foretells quarrels and separations, old maids and old bachelors. A girl who has a lover, and turns this domino to find out his peculiarities, had better look somewhere else at once, for she will certainly either lose or discard him. It is the same with a gentleman—he will never marry the girl he then expects to, and may be jilted. To married people the domino gives a prolific promise. A married lady who turns it will probably have twins or triplets at her next maternity. If you think to entrust a secret to a friend, this domino denotes that it will not be kept. It also foretells that your future husband or wife will be a very credulous person—perhaps a believer in Spiritualism or some other absurd doctrine.

DOUBLE-THREE. Denotes immense riches, but has no allusion to matrimony. It is an excellent domino for any one to turn, as it points to money in abundance, and does not intimate any unhappiness: therefore, the person who turns it will get plenty of cash, and be happy or not, as fate may ordain.

THREE-TWO. Is a fortunate domino in the following cases: marriage, love-making, recovering stolen property, going on a journey, entering into a speculation, planting a crop, collecting a debt, or making a purchase. This domino shows also that you may be lucky in collecting some old claim or debt that you had given up as lost. It is bad for gamblers, for a woman about to give birth to a child, and for peddlers.

THREE-ONE. A young girl who turns this domino will be in danger of losing her chastity; therefore let her be careful. A married woman turning it will have an outside admirer who will flatter her with a view to an improper intimacy. To a man it foretells the loss of money through his illicit intercourse with the opposite sex. It is not a favorable domino to any one.

THREE-BLANK. This domino denotes that your sweetheart is artful and deceitful. If you get married, your wife will be either shrewish, or vain and unprincipled, and perhaps run away and disgrace you. To a girl it foretells a putty-head of a husband—one who is easily influenced, and whom she can wind round her finger. If you turn this domino, it is a sign you will soon be invited to a party and there make a new acquaintance, with whom you will afterwards have a quarrel. If a married man or woman turns it, it predicts a family quarrel.

DOUBLE-TWO. The turning of this domino denotes success in love matters and much happiness in the married state, together with good children who will live and be prosperous. It also denotes success in any undertaking, and thrift, though not great riches.

TWO-ONE. The turning of this domino denotes to a lady that she will marry young, and that her husband will die, leaving her a large property, and childless. For a long time she will be a gay, rich widow, but will be caught at last, and marry happily. To a young man it denotes a life of luxury; he will never marry, but will be a favorite of the ladies, and have several mistresses. It is not a good domino for business men, as it foretells losses by failures.

TWO-BLANK. The turning of this domino denotes poverty and bad luck. To a marriageable young woman it predicts a poor, dissipated and dishonest husband. On the birth of a child—if a boy, it is a sign that he will be poor and shiftless, and perhaps dishonest—if a girl, that she will not marry well. It is not a bad domino for a girl who lives unmarried, for she may do very well alone. It is a domino of good luck to thieves and bad people. If they turn it, it is a sign of success in any dishonest undertaking. Should you turn this domino in reference to a journey, it shows that you will go in safety. It predicts an easy deliverance in case you are attacked and should be obliged to defend yourself.

DOUBLE-ACE. Denotes affectionate constancy and happiness in the marriage state. It is an excellent domino to turn, both for lovers and married people, as besides the above it indicates a competency of this world's goods.

Double-Blank. To turn this domino is the worst sign in the whole set, and is only favorable to misers, usurers, gamblers, and unprincipled cheats and seducers. To any heartless, selfish person, the turning of this domino foretells good luck—to all others disappointment. We hope that no young girl turning a domino to ascertain her fortune as to marriage will turn this one, for it surely foretells disappointment and sorrow. If she has a lover, and should he marry her, he will desert her afterwards. In business matters, too, it is decidedly unfavorable, and is a sign that your business will decrease. If you are wanting a situation, you will not be likely to get it, and if anything is lost or stolen, it will not probably be recovered again. It is generally a pretty bad domino for decent people—but a good one for all the dishonest ones, who, if they have got anything by trickery and fraud, will be apt to enjoy it.

METHOD OF TELLING FORTUNES WITH DICE.

Take three dice, shake them well in the box with your left hand, and then cast them out on a board or table, on which you have previously drawn a circle with chalk; count the number of spots on the uppermost sides of the dice, and look at the signification of the numbers, as given below. Be careful and do not attempt to tell your fortune on Mondays or Wednesdays, as they are unlucky days for dice. To throw the same number twice at one trial, shows news from abroad, be the numbers what they may. If the dice roll over the circle, the number thrown goes for nothing, but the occurrence shows sharp words, and if they fall to the floor, it is blows; in throwing out the dice, if one remains on top of the other, it is a present of which I leave the ladies to take care.

SIGNIFICATION OF THE SPOTS ON DICE.

Three. If a young girl throws this number, (three aces,) it foretells that she will have numerous lovers, and if she marries will have a good crop of children, and then become a widow. To a young man it denotes that he will never marry, but will be a great favorite of the ladies, and probably a gay seducer. If a married person throws it, he or she will become a widower or widow, as the case may be.

Four. To throw this number denotes frivolity in love matters. Unmarried persons who throw it will have many lovers or sweethearts, and will not be fully satisfied with either. It foretells to a married woman that her husband admires the sex generally quite as much as he does her; but it also denotes that she will have many children, and that both herself and husband will live to raise them.

Five. To throw this number of spots of the dice, foretells good luck in a land speculation to any one who is about buying lands. It is a very good number for farmers, prognosticating a fortunate season to come. To lovers it shows that some obstacle will present itself to their marriage, or else that they will quarrel. In a family it is a sign that some person will soon visit there that is not welcome. . If you are about to go a journey, and throw this number, you will meet some one who will bother you, or that you dislike, or else some disagreeable accident will happen; but the accident will not be serious.

SIX. If a girl throws this number, (three deuces,) it denotes that she will be of gay disposition and have many lovers, but will never marry; if she escapes illicit connections, she will be fortunate, and probably get some money by will. To a young man it denotes that he will marry a gay wife, who will be of loose principles; and also that he himself will keep a mistress, and perhaps become a gambler. He will not be poor as long as he is young and attractive, but he will either die young or become poor in middle age. To gamblers, the throwing of this number is a sign of success in winning money.

SEVEN. If a man throws this number it foretells that he will never marry, but will be lucky in business speculations. A young lady who throws it will be apt to marry a wealthy husband, though he may not be an agreeable companion. To farmers and mechanics it is not a particularly bad number, though it does not promise them much success, and it foretells that they will have pretty hard work to keep even with the world.

EIGHT. This is the miser's throw; those who throw it will probably be well off, though not rich. It foretells a miserly or stingy disposition, and a character too close in money matters to be very prosperous. If a girl throw this to test the character of her lover, she may be assured that he will not be poor, though it is possible he may lead her an unhappy life from his selfish and penurious habits.

NINE. If you throw this number with the dice with reference to your future husband or wife, be assured that you will be lucky in your choice. It foretells an orderly, energetic and industrious person. I should not want a better wife than this number predicts. To a young girl it does not promise riches with a husband, but it foretells thrift and plenty, and that she may be rich, too. It is a fair business throw also—foretelling pretty good luck in everything except games of chance, and predicting bad luck in such games.

TEN. If a young girl throws this number, she will not marry very soon, and perhaps not at all; but she will have good luck in other matters, and rise above her present position in society. If a man throws it, he will get a rich wife. It is a favorable number to the male sex in love matters. A married woman who throws it will rise in the world, or have a legacy left to her.

ELEVEN. This throw foretells extravagance and fondness of show and display. Those who throw it, or for whose fortune it may be thrown, will probably have the command of means, but all will be spent in gimcracks, parties of pleasure, and in adorning the person; and though they may not come to poverty, they will leave nothing but debt to their heirs. To laboring people it denotes that they will be always in debt, and live above their means.

TWELVE. Shows that an event of some kind is soon to occur in your affairs, either for good or evil. To a farmer or a laboring man it will probably be fortunate, but it may be otherwise. To a banker, money-dealer, or a jeweler, it is generally a bad omen—to other trades, uncertain. It has no special reference to love matters.

THIRTEEN. I hope no virtuous young girl will ever be so unfortunate as to throw this number, unless she be possessed of a resolution as firm as a rock, for it foretells that she will be sorely tempted to become profligate. It is emphatically the throw of an unchaste female. If a man throws this number, it is a sign that he will never marry, but will associate with harlots, or live with a woman who is not his wife; if he throws it with a view to discover the character of his lady-love, he may guess the result.

FOURTEEN. This is the gambler's throw, and denotes dishonesty and an unprincipled disposition in men, and misfortune in women. If a man throws it, he will be either a gambler or a rich rogue, if he has brains enough, and if his intellect is not sufficient, he will probably be a small swindler, or the favored lover of a lewd woman, or both. Although these will be his characteristics, yet circumstances may place him in a different position, but he will always be mercenary, selfish, impudent, and without pride of character. To a girl this number foretells an unhappy marriage, and misfortune by that means; but if she remains single, and keeps clear of lovers, she will avoid the ill omen.

FIFTEEN. If you are a speculating character—a buyer of lottery tickets or lottery policies, or are engaged in any games of chance, such as gambling, horse-racing, shooting at a mark, betting, or in fact any scheme that you expect to win money by, this number foretells bad luck and discomfiture. If you try to test your luck in any such matters, and this number turns up, you may be sure you will lose, and had better give up at once. If you want to buy land, you will be apt to get a good bargain and be fortunate. This number foretells good luck to a farmer putting in his crops, and the same to a girl choosing a husband; for though she may not get a rich man, yet he will be industrious, thrifty, comfortable, and good-hearted. To consumptive people this throw is not a favorable one, as in many cases it predicts a short life to them.

SIXTEEN. This is an unlucky number to a merchant, a banker, or a mechanic. It foretells bad luck of some kind, though it is generally a forerunner of a brisk and profitable business. An excellent run of business may come first, and the bad luck afterwards, or vice versa, but the misfortune is sure to come in somewhere. To a farmer this throw foretells abundant crops, and to a gold-digger good luck and plenty of the precious metal. A young girl who throws it will get a thrifty husband, and have a numerous family.

SEVENTEEN. If you are a girl, and think of getting married, you will be apt to lose your lover unless he is a farmer, a gardener, a well-digger, a gold-miner, a brewer, a coal-heaver, a grave-digger, or some occupation that makes him use a shovel a good deal. If you think of marrying any such man, this throw is a good one. For a man of any other occupation, it foretells disappointment. To a young man, this number shows that by perseverance and industry he will do well in the world—that his luck will be good if he only tries his best to get along. If you have had anything stolen from you, or have lost valuable property while walking or riding, this throw is unfavorable; you will probably never recover what you have lost.

EIGHTEEN. People who throw this number may congratulate themselves, as it foretells riches, honors, and a happy and contented life. It predicts unexceptionable prosperity in all kinds of business, good luck in love matters, and advancement to those who are honorably ambitious. To rogues and dishonest people it is an omen of discomfiture, detection and punishment.

PALMISTRY,

OR TELLING FORTUNES BY THE LINES OF THE HAND.

Many people think the predictions from lines in the hand are all guess-work, but it is a mistake, for they are determined by simple rules and long observation. Let us explain the matter:
In the first place each finger has its name.

(1) Forefinger :	Jupiter	♃
(2) Middle finger :	Saturn	♄
(3) Ring finger :	The Sun	☉
(4) Little finger :	Mercury	☿
(5) Thumb :	Venus	♀

Each hand has five main lines.

(1) The Life line :	L. Vitalis.
(2) The Natural line :	L. Naturalis.
(3) The Table line :	L. Mensalis.
(4) The Liver line :	L. Hepatica.
(5) The Wrist line :	L. Rascetta.

(*See Engraving.*)

1. LINEA VITALIS.

If this line is wanting or nearly so, it is by no means a good sign. It signifies a feeble understanding, a faint heart, and a short, sickly life. This, however, is not the signification in every case; it often indicates, especially with the ladies, changeableness of feeling, a disposition easily influenced by others, and a proneness to enthusiasm.

The length of life is in proportion to the length of the line of Life. It begins be-tween ♃ and ♀, and it is here that you commence with the prophecy.

Each knot in this line denotes an obsta-cle, or, at least, something momentous in life. Each crossing by smaller lines, some unpleasant occurrence. The larger the cross, the greater the misfortune.

In most cases one or more lines run from the Natural line to the line of Life. This indicates the partner of one's life. The point where the junction takes place denotes the point of time of the marriage. If this occurs near the commencement of the line, of course the marriage will take place early in life. If two lines unite with the line of Life it indicates two husbands (or wives). If no line joins it, the person will remain unmarried.

The clearer and more distinct the line of Life, the happier the person's life. When it is fine, deep and sharply defined, it denotes an energetic, and at the same time a noble character.

2. LINEA NATURALIS.

A regular length and good appearance of this line denotes excellent digestive organs. Large crosses occurring in its course signify impru-dence, precipitation.

3. LINEA MENSALIS.

If it is well defined it indicates an amorous temperament; if accom-panied by a side line, it signifies good fortune in love and wedlock. If it is very broad, happiness in domestic life. If it is interrupted it denotes that sad calamity, infidelity.

4. LINEA HEPATICA.

If it is complete and tolerably long, it promises robust health, a clear understanding, and good humor. If it throws out branches near its commencement it signifies wit, acuteness, presence of mind, a spirit of mischief, perhaps falsehood.

5. LINEA RASCETTA.

When it is complete and unbroken, it denotes good fortune in all matters of importance.

From the ring finger (Solis ☉) there commonly runs one or more lines into the Linea Mensalis. These denote the various inclinations of the heart. If but a single line is actually visible, and if this is deep and long, the person loves or will love faithfully and warmly If a number of smaller lines are found in its place, the person is inconstancy itself, a butterfly roving from flower to flower. Add up all these little lines, and the sum will give you the number of times the person will fall in love.

PHRENOLOGY AND PHYSIOGNOMY.

The science of Phrenology teaches how to discover from the formation of the skull the qualities of the soul, and to draw conclusions as to the character of an individual. The whole head, accordingly, is divided into organs. The following are the principal ones, and are all that are necessary for the reader's instruction. To enter more deeply into the subject would exceed our limits.

1. Memory.
2. Causality.
3. Benevolence.
4. Approbativeness.
5. Painting.

6. Energy.
7. Imagination.
8. Inclination to Melancholy.
9. Mischievousness.

(*See Engraving.*)

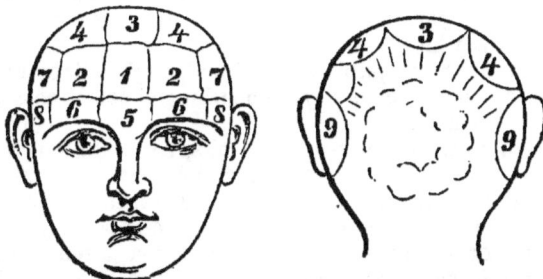

According as these organs are more or less elevated and well formed that peculiarity of character which they indicate is more or less present.

PHYSIOGNOMY, OR THE FEATURES OF THE HEAD AND FACE, teaches us to judge of the character of a person and of events connected with his destiny from the shape, color and expression of his features. If my fair readers would like to know how many husbands they are to have, they have only to knit their eyebrows closely together, and count the folds of the skin formed by this movement.

If they wish to see how many years they have to live, let them elevate their brows as much as possible, and then count the cross folds in the forehead. Subtract the number found from one hundred, and the remainder is the number of the years which it is allotted you to pass upon this earth.

OF THE NOSE A bold, projecting nose, usually called a Roman nose, denotes an enterprising temper. In general a large nose is a good sign. A long nose is a sign of good sense, a stumpy one generally indicates the contrary. A perfectly straight nose denotes a high and noble spirit, unless the expression of the eyes contradicts this judgment, and then it denotes great stupidity. A turned up nose signifies a spirit of mischief, wit, forwardness, that is, if it is not too stumpy. A very small nose indicates good nature, yet at the same time a complete want of energy. A red nose denotes a cheerful temper, or an inclination to drink, as all the world knows.

OF THE LIPS. Very thick lips indicate either great stupidity or very great genius. Very fine thin lips denote falsehood, especially if they are usually compressed. Swelling lips, if generally compressed, denote great decision of character, a philosophical turn of mind, and oftentimes somewhat of obstinacy. A mouth always open says as plain as words can speak, "I am a calf."

OF DIMPLES. Dimples in the cheeks signify roguery. But the dimple in the chin the God of Love has himself imprinted with his own divine finger.

OF THE EYE. The soul, however, dwells particularly in the eyes, and the faculty is inborn with every man to understand their language without ever having studied it. At least it should be so; the eyes should be like an open book, which all may read and understand. But as all eyes are not to be trusted, and will sometimes lead you astray, I will give you, my dear readers, a few rules to guide you in your path through life.

A clear eye, with the pupil in continual, slightly tremulous movement, denotes a good memory, yet something of selfishness with slowness of comprehension.

An eye which, while the person speaks, roves hither and thither, denotes a deceiver. Very quiet eyes which have an imposing effect upon you, and embarrass you by their great repose, signify great self-command, yet, at the same time, great self-complacency.

Eyes which ordinarily appear impressive, yet often suddenly flash forth a clear pleasant light, denote true-heartedness and honesty, coupled with a sound understanding.

Eyes which have always an inquisitive expression in them, and then suddenly, when they turn to address a person, have an exceedingly kind expression, are not to be trusted. This indicates a suspicious temper, and he who does not trust his fellow-man, can seldom himself be trusted.

An eye in which the white has a yellowish tinge, and is streaked with reddish veins, denotes vehement passions.

Very blue eyes, betray a temper inclined to coquetry.

Gray eyes, intelligence.

Greenish, falsehood, and a disposition to tittle-tattle.

Yellowish, great phlegm.

Black, a passionate and lively temperament.

Brown, a kind, good, happy disposition.

A pair of eyes which looks every one cheerfully and frankly in the race, with an air of simple joy and unaffected innocence, yet, when surprised, droops to the ground, with a certain sly bashfulness, or, when offended by another's glance, turns aside blushing and confused, such a pair of eyes, indicates an amiable character, a faithful heart, a sound understanding, and a pure soul.

A being with such a pair of eyes we cannot help loving, let the eyes be black, brown, blue, gray, green, or yellow, let the nose be stumpy, and the features ill-shaped, no one can help regarding their possessor with a feeling of hearty kindness and good will, if not with actual love.

OF THE EYE-BROWS. Upright eye-brows are amiable; the eye-brows hanging over, indicate an effeminate person; the brows very hairy, denote an industrious, affectionate man; the brows extending to the temples, usually signify a slovenly man.

OF THE EARS. Open ears usually indicate but little reason; great ears not too much wisdom; very small ears foolishness; square ears of medium size, prudence.

OF THE NOSTRILS. The nostrils thick and strong, betoken strength; it round, fair, and drawn in length, they are a sign that the person is merry and courageous; if narrow and round, they are mostly indica-tive of an envious and foolish person.

OF THE MOUTH. A very large mouth, with the upper lip hanging over, usually signifies a foolish, unsteady person, a rash man and a babbler. A mouth not too large, indicates a bold and courageous man; and a small mouth, a clever man.

OF THE FACE. A lean face is an indication of a wise man; the face plain and fat, denotes a person addicted to strife. The face without any rising and swelling, indicates a penurious person; a sad face sometimes denotes foolishness, and at other times wisdom; a fat face indicates a man to be inclined to untruth; a round face signifies folly; a great face denotes a man slow about business; a well-proportioned face indicates a person to have virtuous qualities.

OF THE NAILS OF THE FINGERS. Broad nails show the person to be bashful, fearful, but of gentle nature. When there is a certain white mark at the extremity of them, it shows that the person has more honesty than subtlety. White long nails denote much sickness, but are sometimes indicative of strength and deceit. If upon the white anything appears at the extremity that is pale, it denotes short life; but if the white is clear and smooth, it signifies long life.

OF THE HEAD. A large head shows a person stupid, and dull of apprehension; also a very small head signifies the same; but the head of a man being neither great nor small, is the prognostic of a wise man; for all extremes are irregular and a deviation from nature, and experience has made it manifest, that a great head and small members do always produce great indiscretion and folly in either man or woman; but we must also consider the several parts of the head; and first,

OF THE FOREHEAD. A large forehead shows a liberal man; but

8

the forehead narrow, denotes a foolish person; a long forehead shows one apt to learn; a high forehead, swelling and round, is a sign of a crafty man, and a coward; a forehead full of wrinkles, shows a man to be envious and crafty.

But in forming your opinions of men from these or other indications, you should always bear in mind that there is no rule without an exception.

FORTUNE-TELLING BY MOLES.

These little marks on the skin, although they appear to be the effect of chance, or accident, and might easily pass with the unthinking for things of no moment, are nevertheless of the utmost consequence, since from their color, situation, size, and figure, may be accurately gathered the temper of, and the events that will happen to the person bearing them; though moles are, in their substances, nothing else than excrescences, or ebullitions which proceed from the state of the blood whilst the fœtus is confined in the womb, yet they are not given in vain, as they are generally characteristic of the disposition and temper of those that bear them; and it is also proved by daily experience, that from the shape, situation, and other circumstances, they bear a strong analogy to the events which are to happen to a person in future life. But before I presume to give any directions to those who are to form the prognostic, who are desirous to be duly enabled to pronounce an infallible judgment, I shall, in the first place, teach you herein the common prognostications by moles found in the various parts of the body, according to the doctrine of the ancients. And, first, it is essentially necessary to know the size of the mole, its color, whether it be perfectly round, oblong, or angular; because each of these will add to or diminish the force of the indication. The larger the mole, the greater will be the prosperity or adversity of the person; the smaller the mole, the less will be his good or evil fate. If the mole is round, it indicates good; if oblong, a moderate share of fortunate events; if angular, it gives a mixture of good and evil; the deeper the color, the more it announces favor or disgrace; the lighter, the less of either. If it is very hairy, much misfortune may be expected; if but few long hairs grow upon it, it denotes that your undertakings will be prosperous.

We shall further remark only, that moles of a middling size and color are those which we are now going to speak of. The rest may be gathered from what we have just above mentioned, but as it may frequently happen that modesty will sometimes hinder persons from showing their moles, you must depend upon their own representation of them for your opinion.

— ·· -

SIGNIFICATION OF MOLES.

ARM. (*Right or Left.*) Show a courteous disposition, great fortitude, resolution, industry, and conjugal fidelity; it foretells that the person will fight many battles, and be successful in all; that you will be prosperous in your undertakings, obtain a decent competency, and live very happy—it denotes that a man will be a widower at forty, but in a woman it shows that she will be survived by her husband.

ANKLE. Shows an effeminate disposition, given to foppery in dress, and cowardice in a man; but in a woman it denotes courage, wit, and activity—they foretell success in life with an agreeable partner, accumulation of honors and riches, and much pleasure in the affairs of love.

ANUS. Around outside this place, a mole predicts that you will be indolent, shiftless and poor, though of good capacity.

ARM-PITS. You will be very good looking, will become rich, and be benevolent.

BACK. If just below either of the shoulder blades, it signifies that you will have misfortune and defeat in the enterprises you may undertake.

BELLY. Shows an indolent, slothful disposition, given to gluttony, very selfish, addicted to the pleasures of love and drink, negligent of dress, and cowardly; it denotes small success in life, many crosses, some imprisonment, and travelling, with losses by sea; but it foretells that you will marry an agreeable partner of a sweet temper, have children, who will be industrious and become very respectable in life.

BOSOM. Shows a quarrelsome and unhappy temper, given to low debauchery, and exceedingly amorous, indolent and unsteady; it denotes a life neither very prosperous nor very miserable, but passed without many friends or much esteem.

BREAST. A mole on the right breast shows an intemperate and indolent disposition, rather given to drink, strongly attached to the joys of love; it denotes much misfortune in life, with a sudden reverse from riches to poverty—many unpleasant and disagreeable accidents, with a sober and industrious partner—many children, mostly girls, who will all marry well, and be a great comfort to your old age; it warns you to beware of pretended friends, who will harm you much. A mole on the left breast shows an industrious and sober disposition, amorous, and much given to walking; it denotes great success in life and in love, that you will accumulate riches, and have many children, mostly boys, who will make their fortunes by sea.

A mole under the left breast under the heart, shows a rambling, unsettled disposition, given to drinking and little careful of your actions; very amorous, and much given to indulge indiscriminately in the pleasures of love, in a man. In a woman it indicates sincerity in love, industry, and a strict regard for character; in life it denotes a varied mixture of good and bad fortune, the former rather prevailing; it denotes imprisonment for debt, but not of long duration. To a woman it denotes easy labors, and children who will become rich, live happy and respected, and marry well.

BUTTOCKS. Signifies shiftlessness and poverty, though a good capacity; it is a sign that you will be too lazy to do anything for yourself.

CHEEK. A mole on either cheek, shows an industrious, benevolent and sober disposition, given to be grave and solemn, little inclined to amorous sports, but of a steady courage and unshaken fortitude; it denotes a moderate success in life, neither becoming rich nor falling into poverty—it also foretells an agreeable and industrious partner, with two children, who will do better than the parents.

CHIN. A mole on the chin shows an amiable and tranquil disposition, industrious and much inclined to travelling, and the joys of Venus; it denotes that the person will be highly successful in life, accumulating a large and splendid fortune, with many respectable and worthy friends, an agreeable conjugal partner, and fine children, but also indicates losses by sea and in foreign countries.

EAR. On either ear it denotes riches in man or woman. If on the lower tip of the ear, keep off the water, or you will be drowned.

ELBOW. A mole on either elbow shows a restless and unsteady disposition, with a great desire for travelling—much discontented in the married state and of an idle turn; it indicates no very great prosperity, rather a sinking than rising condition, with many unpleasant adventures, much to your discredit—marriage to a person who will make you unhappy, and children who will be disobedient, and cause you much trouble.

EYE. A mole on the outside corner of either eye shows a sober, honest, and steady disposition, much inclined to the pleasures of love; it foretells a violent death, after a life considerably varied by pleasures and misfortunes; in general it foreshadows that poverty will keep at a distance.

EYEBROW. A mole on the right eyebrow signifies a sprightly, active disposition, a great turn for gallantry, much courage, and great perseverance; it denotes wealth and success in love, war and business; that you will marry an agreeable mate, live happy, have children, and die in an advanced old age, at a distance from home. On the left eyebrow, temple, or side of the forehead, shows an indolent peevish temper, a turn for debauchery and liquor, little inclined to amorous sports and very cowardly; foretells poverty, imprisonment and disappointments in all your undertakings, with undutiful children, and a bad-tempered partner.

FINGER. On either finger of either hand, it shows that you will be a thief, or a dishonest person in some way, and never wealthy.

FOOT. A mole on either foot shows a melancholy and inactive disposition, little inclined to the pleasures of love, given to reading and a sedentary life; they foretell sickness and· unexpected misfortunes, with many sorrows and much trouble, an unhappy choice of a partner for life, with disobedient and unfortunate children.

FOREHEAD. If the mole is in the centre of the forehead it predicts an active, industrious disposition, success in business, riches, honors, a happy marriage, and a son who will be distinguished. But if the mole is on the side of the forehead, the signification is not s) favora‧ ble, particularly if on the left side. (*See Eyebrow.*) On the right side of the forehead, or right temple, shows an active and industrious disposition, much given to the sports of love; it denotes that she will be very successful in life, marry an agreeable partner, and arrive at unexpected riches and honors, and have a son, who will become a great man.

GROIN. On the right groin denotes riches and honors, but to be accompanied with disease. On the left groin, you will have the sickness without the wealth.

GULLET. On that part of the throat called the gullet, it predicts that you will be distinguished in some way and become rich.

HAND. Moles on either hand, if not on the fingers, denote wealth, industry and energy in either sex. You will also be fortunate and happy in your children.

HEART. Over the heart, denotes wickedness, poverty and a hasty, headstrong disposition. (*See Breast.*)

HEEL. Shows a spiteful and malevolent disposition, but a person of much energy, who may be successful in what he undertakes; that he will be greatly talked about behind his back.

HIP. A mole on either hip shows a contented disposition, given to industry, amorous and faithful in engagements, of an abstemious turn; it foretells moderate success in life, with many children, who will undergo many hardships with great fortitude, and arrive at ease and affluence, by dint of their industry and ingenuity.

KNEE. A mole on the left knee shows a hasty and passionate disposition, extravagant and inconsiderate turn, with no great inclination to industry and honesty, much given to the pleasures of Venus, but possessed of much benevolence; it indicates good success in under‧ takings, particularly in contracts, a rich marriage, and an only child. On the right knee, shows an amiable temper, honest disposition and a turn for amorous pleasures and industry; it foretells great success in love, and the choice of a conjugal partner, with few sorrows, many friends, and dutiful children.

LEG. Moles on either leg show a person of a thoughtless, indolent disposition, of an amorous turn, much given to extravagance and dissipation; it denotes many difficulties through life, but that you will surmount them all; it shows that imprisonment will happen to you at an early age, but that in general you will be more fortunate than otherwise; you will marry an agreeable person, who will survive you, by whom you will have four children, two of which will die young.

LIPS. A mole on either lip shows a delicate appetite, a sober disposition, and much given to the pleasures of love, of an industrious and benevolent turn; it denotes that the person will be successful in undertakings, particularly in love affairs—that you will rise above your present condition, and be greatly respected and esteemed—that you will endeavor to obtain some situation, in which you will at first prove unsuccessful, but afterward prevail.

MONS. If a woman have a mole here, she will become the mother of a great genius, or else the wife of a distinguished personage. It is also a sign of riches.

MOUTH. (*See Lips.*)

NAVEL. On a woman it denotes many children, a good husband, and an abundance of this world's goods. On a man it is a sign he will be lucky in all he undertakes, become very rich, and that he will have a son who will be distinguished.

NECK. In front of the neck is a good sign; you will rise to unexpected honors and dignities, or become rich. On the back of the neck it denotes misfortune. On either side of the neck it foretells that you will become wicked or quarrelsome; and if on the right side, behind the ear, it is a sign that you will be hung.

NIPPLE. In woman it is a sign that she will have a child that will become famous and distinguished in the world. In man it denotes that he will be fond of women, and spend much of his life in amours, to the neglect of his proper business.

NOSE. Moles on any part of the nose, show a hasty and passionate disposition, much given to amorous pleasures, faithful to engagements, candid, open, and sincere in friendship, courageous and honest, but very petulant, and rather given to drink; it denotes great success through life and in love affairs—that you will become rich, marry well, have fine children and be much esteemed by your neighbors and acquaintance—that you will travel much, particularly by water.

NOSTRIL. Inside the nostril shows that you will be energetic and persevering, and well off in the world; that you will get a good wife or husband when you marry.

PRIVATE MEMBERS. Moles on these parts show a generous, open and honest disposition, extremely disposed to gallantry, and the joys of Venus, given to sobriety, and of undaunted courage; it denotes great success in the latter part of life, but many and severe misfortunes in the former, which will be borne with fortitude; it also foretells a happy marriage and fine children, who will be happy, thrive well, and grow rich and respectable: in man it shows that he will have natural children, who will cut a great figure in life, but he will experience much plague and vexation from their mother.

SHIN. (*See Leg.*)

SHOULDER. On the left shoulder shows a person of a quarrelsome, unruly disposition, always inclined to dispute for trifles, rather indolent, but much inclined to the pleasures of love, and faithful to the conjugal vows. It denotes a life not much varied either with pleasures or misfortunes; they indicate many children, and moderate success in business, but dangers by sea. On the right shoulder shows a person of a prudent and discreet temper, one possessed of much wisdom, given to great secrecy, very industrious, but not very amorous, yet faithful to conjugal ties; it indicates great prosperity and advancement in life, a good partner, and many friends, with great profit from a journey to a distant country, about the age of thirty-five.

SIDE. On either side, near any part of the ribs, shows an indolent,

cowardly disposition, given to excessive drinking, of an inferior capacity, and little inclined to the pleasures of love; it denotes an easy
life, rather of poverty than riches, little respected, a partner of an
uneven and disagreeable temper, with undutiful children, who will
fall into many difficulties.

STOMACH. If in the pit of the stomach, it shows a person of fop-
pish disposition, with little common sense, though much industry; it
also denotes riches. If lower down on the stomach, it is a sign that
you will promise more than you will perform, but will nevertheless be
highly esteemed.

THIGH. On the right thigh, it shows the person to be of an agreeable temper, inclined to be amorous, and very courageous: it also denotes success in life, accumulation of riches by marriage, and many
fine children, chiefly girls. On the left thigh, shows a good and benevolent disposition, a great turn for industry, and little inclined to
the pleasures of love: it likewise indicates many sorrows in life, great
poverty, unfaithful friends, and imprisonment by the false swearing
of some one.

THROAT. It predicts a fortunate and wealthy marriage to either
sex. (*See Neck.*)

TONGUE. If a man shall have a mole on his tongue, it foretells
that he shall marry with a rich and beautiful woman of great celeb-
rity. On a woman's tongue it denotes reserve of manner and wisdom; also a fortunate marriage.

WRIST. Moles on the wrist, or between that and the finger ends,
show the person to be of an ingenious and industrious turn, faithful
in his engagements, amorous and constant in his affections, rather of
a saving disposition, with a great degree of sobriety and regularity in
his dealings. It foreshows a comfortable acquisition of fortune, with
a good partner, and beautiful children, but some disagreeable circumstances will happen about the age of thirty, which continue four or
five years. In a man, it denotes being twice married—in a woman
only once, but that she will survive her husband.

TO CHOOSE A HUSBAND BY THE HAIR.

BLACK. Generally healthy, but apt to be cross; fond where he
fixes his attachment, and likely to make a good husband, and be careful of his family: but if short and curly, is usually of an unsettled
temper, apt to show a want of prudence and carefulness in early life.

WHITE OR FAIR HAIR. Usually of a weak and sickly constitution,
fond of music, and will cut no great figure in the world.

YELLOW. Fond, but inclinable to jealousy; and not always industrious.

LIGHT BROWN. Sensible and good-humored, careful and attentive,
and, if saving of his income, generally makes a good husband; but
is apt to be otherwise.

DARK BROWN. Neither very good nor very bad, middling in all respects, but may be regarded as a pretty good character.

VERY DARK BROWN. Of a robust constitution, and of a grave dis-position, but sometimes not very good-tempered and sensible, and kind to a good wife.

RED. Will be cunning, artful, and fond of female companions; and generally of a lively temper, and sometimes careless of money.

SIGNIFICATION OF THE NAILS.

BROAD NAILS. The person that hath the nails thus, is of gentle nature, good, and pusillanimous, and a great fear to speak before great persons, or those by whom they are in subjection; as also being guilty of extreme bashfulness.

If about these nails there happens to be an excoriation of the flesh, which is commonly called points—in these large nails it signifies the party given to luxury, yet fearful, but usually given to excess.

When there is at the extremity a white mark, it signifies ruin through negligence. The party has more honesty than subtlety.

WHITE NAILS. He that hath the nails white and long, is sickly, and subject to much infirmity by fevers; he is neat but not very strong, because of his indispositions, much addicted to the company of women by whom he will be greatly deceived.

NARROW NAILS. The person with such nails, is desirous of attaining knowledge in the sciences; but is never long at peace with his neighbors. But if to narrowness they add some degree of length, the person will be led away by ambitious propensities, always aiming at things which he will be unable to obtain.

ROUND NAILS. These declare a hasty person, yet good-natured and very forgiving; a lover of knowledge, liberal sentiment, doing no one any harm, and acting by his own principles, but too proud of his own abilities.

LONG NAILS. When the nails are long, the person is of a good-natured turn, but placing confidence in no man, being from his youth familiar with duplicity, but not practising it, from his strict adherence to virtue.

FLESHY NAILS. This description of nail indicates an idler, loving to sleep, eat, and drink; not delighting in bustle and busy life; one who prefers a narrow income without industry, to one of opulence to be acquired by activity and diligence.

LITTLE NAILS. Little round nails discover a person to be obstinately angry, seldom pleased, inclining to hate every one, as conceiving himself superior to others, though without any reason.

PALE OR LEAD-COLORED NAILS. A melancholy person, one who through choice leads a sedentary life, and would willingly give up all things for the sake of study, and to improve in the learned and metaphysical branches of philosophy.

RED AND SPOTTED NAILS. Choleric and martial, delighting in cruelty and war; his chief pleasure being in plundering towns, where
every ferocious particle in human nature is glutted to satiety.

When you find any black spots upon the nails, they always signify
evil, as white ones are a token of good.

FORTUNE-TELLING BY TEA OR COFFEE GROUNDS.

TO POUR OUT THE GROUNDS OF A TEA OR COFFEE CUP.—Pour the
grounds of coffee or tea into a white cup, shake them well about in
it, so that their particles may cover the surface of the whole cup;
then reverse it into the saucer, that all the superfluous parts may be
drained, and the figures required for fortune-telling be formed.

The person who acts as the fortune-teller, must always bend his or
her thoughts upon him or her who is to have their fortune told, and
on their rank in life, and profession, in order to give plausibility to
the predictions. It is not to be expected that upon taking up the cup,
the figures will be accurately represented as they are in reality, but
it will be quite sufficient if they bear some resemblance to any of the
emblems; and the more fertile the fancy is of the person that inspects
the cup, the more he or she will discover in it.

In other respects, every one who takes a pleasure in this amusement, must be a judge under what circumstances he or she is to make
changes in point of time—speaking, just as it suits, in the present, the
past, or the future; in the same manner, their ingenuity ought to
direct them when to speak more or less pointedly with regard to sex.

THE ROADS, or separate lines, indicate ways; if they are covered
with clouds, and, consequently, in the thick, they are said to be infallible marks, either of many great or future reverses. But if they
appear in the clear and serene, are the surest token of some fortunate
change near at hand; encompassed with many points or dots, they
signify either a gain of money, or long life.

THE RING signifies marriage; if a letter is near it, it denotes to the
person that has their fortune told, the initial of the name of the party
to be married. If the ring is in the clear, it portends happy and
lucrative friendship; if surrounded with clouds, the contrary. But if
the ring appear at the bottom of the cup, it forebodes the probability
of a separation.

THE LEAF OF CLOVER is, as well here as in common life, a lucky
sign. Its different position in the cup alone makes the difference;
because, if it be on the top, it shows that the good fortune is not far
distant; but it is subject to delay, if it be in the middle or at the
bottom. Should clouds surround it, it shows that many disagreeables
will attend the good fortune; in the clear, it prognosticates serene
and undisturbed happiness.

THE ANCHOR. The emblem of hope and commerce, implies successful business carried on by water and by land, if on the bottom of the cup; at the top and in the clear part, it shows constant love and fidelity; but in thick and cloudy parts, it denotes inconstancy.

THE SERPENT, always the emblem of falsehood and enmity, is like-wise here a general sign of an enemy. On the top or in the middle of the cup, it promises to the consulting party that by his always act-ing properly, his enemies will not be able to triumph over him; if in the thick or cloudy part, he must watch his temper and actions very carefully, to prevent great troubles.

THE COFFIN. The emblem of death, prognosticates the same thing here, or at least a long and tedious illness, if it be in the thick or turbid. In the clear, it denotes long life; if in the thick, at the top of the cup, it signifies a considerable estate likely to be made by cau-tious industry.

THE DOG, being at all times the emblem of fidelity or envy, has also a two-fold meaning here. At the top, in the clear, it signifies true and faithful friends: if the image be surrounded with clouds and dashes, it shows that some whom you take for your friends are not to be depended on; but if the dog be at the bottom of the cup, take much care not to excite any person to envy or jealousy, or you will have to dread the effects of both.

THE LILY. If this emblem be at the top, or in the middle of the cup, it signifies that the consulting party either has, or will have, a good spouse; if it be at the bottom, it denotes anger. In the clear, the lily further betokens a long and happy life; if clouded, or in the thick, it portends trouble and vexations.

THE CROSS, in general, predicts adversities; if it be at the top, and in the clear, it indicates that the misfortunes of the party will soon be at an end, or that he will, by careful conduct, easily get over them; but if it appear in the middle, or at the bottom of the thick, the party must expect many severe trials; if it appear with dots, either in clear or thick, it promises recompense for sorrow.

THE CLOUDS. If they be more bright than dark, you may expect a good result from your hopes; but if they are black, you may give it up. Surrounded with dots, they imply success in trade, if you are saving, and not too venturesome; the brighter they are, the greater will be your happiness.

THE SUN, is an emblem of the greatest luck and happiness, if in the clear; but in the thick, it denotes a great deal of illness; surrounded by dots or dashes, it foretells that, without much circumspection, an alteration will soon take place.

THE MOON. If it appear in the clear, it denotes high honors; in the dark or thick parts, it implies disappointment and sadness, which will, however, pass without great prejudice. But if it be at the bottom of the cup, the consulting party may expect, by industry and prudent conduct, to be very fortunate.

THE STAR denotes happiness, if in the clear, and at the top of the cup; if clouded, or in the thick, it signifies long life, though exposed to various troubles. If dots are about it, it foretells fortune and respectability. Several dots denote good children; surrounded by dots, it predicts that, without good bringing up, they may cause you grief and vexation.

MOUNTAINS. If it present only one mountain, it indicates the favor of people of rank; but several of them, especially in the thick, are signs of powerful enemies; in the clear, they signify the contrary, or friends in high life.

THE LETTER. Signifies both pleasant and unpleasant news. If this emblem is in the clear part, it denotes the speedy arrival of welcome news; surrounded with dots, it announces the arrival of a remittance of money; but hemmed in by clouds, it forebodes some melancholy or bad tidings, a loss, or some other accident; if it be in the clear, and accompanied by a heart, lovers may expect a favorable letter; but in the thick it denotes the contrary.

THE TREE. One tree only is indicative of good health; a group of trees in the clear part, betokens misfortunes, but which may be avoided by carefulness and industrious habits; several trees, wide apart, promise that your wishes will be accomplished; if they be en compassed by dashes, it is a token that your fortune is in its blossom, and requires only your own care and prudence to bring it to maturity; if the trees be accompanied by dots, it is a sign of riches.

THE CHILD. In the clear part it bespeaks innocent intercourse be tween the consulter and another person; in the thick part it signifies crosses in love matters, and requires your utmost care to prevent great expenses; and a family without means of support.

THE WOMAN. Signifies much joy in general. If in the clear, this emblem shows very great happiness; but in the thick part it cautions against jealousy. If dots surround the image, it shows children and wealth.

THE PEDESTRIAN. Denotes in general a merchant, good business, pleasant news, or the recovery of lost things. It denotes to the female a kind and industrious husband; it also signifies some engagement, and a short journey.

THE RIDER OR HORSEMAN. Denotes a letter, good news from abroad, a good situation, or the like; it also foretells that a fortune is to be obtained by care and industry.

THE MOUSE. As this animal lives by stealth, it also is an emblem of theft or robbery; if it be in the clear, it shows that your loss will be easily prevented; but if in the thick, you must use your utmost watchfulness.

THE ROSE, OR ANY OTHER FLOWER. Usually indicates success in science or art by study; if married, good children may be expected, and all the happy fruits, if they have but a good education and good examples.

THE HEART. If it be in the clear, it signifies future pleasure. It promises joy at receiving some money, if surrounded with dots. If a ring or two hearts be together, it signifies that the party may expect to be married; if a letter is perceptible near it, it shews the initial of the person's name.

THE GARDEN, WOOD, OR BUSH. Signifies a large company. In the clear and with leaves, it indicates good friends; in the thick, encompassed with streaks, or if without leaves, it is a token of the caprices of fortune, and warns the consulting party to be cautious whom they take for their friends.

THE ROD. Predicts differences with people about matters relating to legacies; in the thick, it denotes some affliction, which will require your utmost care to avert.

THE BIRD IN GENERAL. In the clear, it signifies that the disagreeables and troubles with which you will have to combat, will only be surmounted by persevering in doing good; in the thick, it is a sign of good living; also a speedy journey, or voyage, which, if there be dashes, is likely to be to a distance.

FISH IN GENERAL. Imply some lucky event by water, if in the clear, which will either happen to the consulter, or be the means of improving his affairs. If they are in the thick, the consulter may expect to fish in troubled water. Surrounded with dots, his destiny warns him to use diligence, temperance and frugality.

THE LION, OR ANY FEROCIOUS BEAST. At the top, in the clear, it signifies prosperity in your intercourse with people of quality. At the bottom it warns the consulter to shun such intercourse and do nothing to excite any person to envy his fortune.

WORMS. At the top, or in the middle of the cup, they denote good luck in trade and in matrimony; below they warn you against rivals in courtship, and against enviers in your trade and profession.

THE STYLE. If combined with an hour-glass and in the thick, it denotes imminent dangers of all kinds; in love, disappointment; but in the clear, it signifies that your sweetheart is faithful and affectionate toward you, and that you are likely to live a long and happy life.

CHARMS AND MAGIC PROGNOSTICA-TIONS.

Herewith I give a few mysterious magic formulas and prognostications, for the most part hitherto known only to wise old men and women, some of which I have had confided to me by learned astrologers, and a few were revealed to me by Madame Le Normand, a celebrated fortune-teller, in whose predictions the Emperor Napoleon put great confidence.

TO PREPARE A LOVE POTION.

The following substances must be gathered in silence when the full moon is in the heavens: Three white rose leaves, three red rose leaves, three forget-me-nots, and five blossoms of Veronica.

All these things you must place in a vessel, then pour upon them five hundred and ninety-five drops of clear Easter water, and place the vessel over the fire, or what is better still, over a spirit-lamp. This mixture must be allowed to boil for exactly the sixteenth part of an hour.

When it has boiled for the requisite length of time, remove it from the fire, and pour it into a flask. Cork it tightly, and seal it, and it will keep for years without losing its virtue.

That this potion is certain in its effect I myself will guarantee, for I have gained more than thirty hearts by its help. Three drops swallowed by the person whose love you desire, will suffice.

ANOTHER MEANS TO COMPEL LOVE.

Take a healthy, well-grown frog. Place it in a box which has been pierced all over with holes with a stout darning needle or gimlet. Then carry it in the evening twilight to a large ant-heap, place it in the midst of the heap, taking care to observe perfect silence.

After the lapse of a week, repair to the ant-heap, take out the box, and open it, when in place of the frog you will find nothing but a skeleton. Take this apart very carefully, and you will soon find among the delicate bones a scale shaped like that of a fish and a hook. You will need them both. The hook you must contrive to fasten in some way or other into the clothes of the person whose affections you wish to obtain, and if he or she has worn it, if it is only for a quarter of a minute, he will be constrained to love you, and will continue to do so until you give him or her a fillip with the scale.

This method is over three thousand years old, and it has been practised by thirty-thousand of our ancestors with the most complete success.

FOR A GIRL TO ASCERTAIN IF SHE WILL EVER MARRY.

Borrow a wedding-ring from a young married woman—the more recently she has been married the better—and do not tell her, or let her suspect your purpose; wear this ring on the third finger of your left hand at least three hours after sunset before you retire to rest. When you are ready to go to bed, take half a sheet of pure white paper, with no rule marks or anything upon it, lay down the ring on the paper, and mark round it so as to make a circle exactly its size: you then write within the circle, "With this ring I hope to wed:" write your name over the top, and your age underneath; fold the paper with a three-cornered love-letter fold, and put it under your pillow. Before getting into bed, suspend the ring by a hair of your head over the pillow so that it will hang about six inches above your face. You will then dream of your future husband if you are ever to marry. If you dream of several men, the one whose appearance pleases you best will be the man. If you dream of women or girls exclusively, you will never marry. Sometimes it may happen that your dream is confused, and you have no clear recollection of it, or perhaps you may not dream at all, in which case you must continue the charm, by keeping the paper under your pillow for three nights; but the ring is not necessary after the first night.

THE STRAW SIGN.

If you find a blade of straw lying in your chamber, you may expect visitor that same day. If there is one grain upon the straw, the visitor will be a gentleman, if not, a lady.

THE SCISSOR OR KNIFE PROGNOSTIC.

If a pair of scissors, a knife, or any other pointed instrument falls accidentally from your hand, and sticks in the floor, so that it remains upright, you may make every preparation for company, for be assured they will not fail to come.

THE CAT PORTENT.

When the cat licks and trims herself, it is a sign of visitors, but this is probably known to most of my readers already.

SIGN OF VISITORS.

Finally, a fourth sign of approaching visitors is the crying of the magpie. Magpies, as is well known, are the most inquisitive creatures upon the face of the earth. They fly from place to place, and listen to everything. When they find out that any persons have concluded to pay you a visit, they fly to you at full speed, and bring you the news, for they are as chattering as they are inquisitive. They perch themselves upon your house, or upon a tree which may stand near it, or on the grass, and there sit and chatter until they think you must have understood them. Therefore, always give heed to these wise birds, for it is well to know when you are to expect visitors.

THE NEW MOON.

On first seeing the new moon, if you happen to look at it over your right shoulder, you may make a silent wish, and you will realize it. If a girl thus observes the new moon, and desires to see her future husband, she must repeat to herself (so as not to be heard by any one) the following lines:

> New moon, new—pray let me see
> Who my husband is to be:
> The color of his hair,
> The clothes he is to wear,
> And the happy day that he'll wed me!

If she is to be married that year, she will positively see the man of her choice before the wane of the full moon.

THE KEY AND BOOK CHARM.

To find out the two first letters of a future wife's or husband's name, take a small Bible and the key of your front street-door, and having opened to Solomon's Songs, chap. viii., ver. 6 and 7, place the wards of the key on those two verses, and let the bow of the key be about an inch out of the top of the Bible; then shut the book, and tie it round with your garter, so as the key will not move, and the person who wishes to know his or her future husband or wife's signature, must suspend the Bible, by putting the fore-finger of the right hand under the bow of the key, and the other person in like manner on the other side of the bow of the key, who must repeat the following verses, after the other person's saying the alphabet, one letter to each time repeating them.

It must be observed, that you mention to the person who repeats the verses, before you begin, which you intend to try first, whether surname or Christian name, and take care to hold the Bible steady; and when you arrive at the appointed letter, the book will turn round under your finger, and that you will find to be the first letter of your intended's name.

Solomon's Songs, chap. viii., ver. 6 and 7.

"Set me a seal upon thine heart, as a seal upon thine arm; for love is strong as death, jealousy is cruel as the grave; the coals thereof are coals of fire, which hath a most vehement flame.

"Many waters cannot quench love, neither can the floods drown it; if a man would give all the substance of his house for love, it would be utterly contemned."

CARD CHARM.

Draw all the face cards from the pack and put them into your stocking on a Friday night, placing the stocking under your pillow. You must find out by the Almanac the precise time the sun rises on Saturday morning, and at that moment draw a card. A king denotes a speedy marriage; a queen means delay or celibacy; a Jack is a gay seducer who will give you trouble. Diamonds are riches, hearts true love, spades thrift, and clubs poverty.

THE SPIDER OMEN.

It is considered an ill omen when one sees a spider *in the morning.* The earlier in the morning, and the larger the spider, the greater the evil which threatens you. It is *within doors,* however, and chiefly *in one's own chamber,* that the spider has this signification—out of doors they forebode no harm. The *wood spider* especially, is not much to be dreaded; what I have said above refers particularly to the *house spider*. Never, on any account, kill a wood spider. By such an act you would only draw upon yourself the hatred of the whole race of witches, and sooner or later you would suffer from it.

When found *in the evening*, a spider signifies good luck. The smaller the spider, the greater the good fortune. I will here teach you the following rhyme:

> "Matin, chagrin,
> Soir, espoir."

Little spiders have much less evil in them than the others, and those called daddy-long-legs are always messengers of good luck.

THE STRING TOKEN.

If your shoe-tie or apron string breaks, your sweetheart is thinking of you.

SIGN WHEN YOUR RIGHT EAR TINGLES.

If your *right ear* tingles, some one is speaking *well* of you, if the *left ear* tingles, some one is speaking *ill* of you. To find out who this some one is, you must call out aloud the names of your acquaintance, one after another. The name at which the tingling ceases is the name of the person.

SIGN WHEN YOUR NOSE ITCHES.

If your nose itches early in the morning, you will on that very day hear a piece of news.

STRANGE BED.

Lay under your pillow a prayer-book, opened at the matrimonial service, bound round with the garters you wore that day, and a sprig of myrtle on the page that says "*With this ring I thee wed*," and your dream will be ominous, and you will have your fortune as well told as if you had paid a dollar to an astrologer.

THE SIGN OF A SNEEZE.

If any one tells you anything, and you are shortly after obliged to sneeze, you may be sure that what was told you is true.

THE DEATH-TICK.

If you hear a wood-tick or death-watch ticking anywhere in the house, you must try to get rid of it as soon as possible, or you will speedily hear of a death which will greatly afflict you.

THE CRICKET.

If there is a cricket in the house, be careful on no account to disturb it. Think of Dickens' *Cricket on the Hearth.*

AN OMEN OF RICHES.

When an *ant-heap* gathers in your house, it signifies *coming wealth* —you may, however, destroy the nest.

THE FROG PROGNOSTIC.

If the first *frog* that you see in the spring of the year is sitting upon *dry ground*, it signifies that, during the same year, you will shed as many tears as the frog would require to swim away in.

THE CANDLE TOKEN.

When a large red token forms in the flame of a candle-wick, it signifies that the one who first sees it will soon receive a letter.

THE STAR AUGURY.

When you are out of doors on a starlit evening, and shooting stars appear, turn your face upward to the stars, and utter in a whisper the wish nearest your heart. If a star shoots while you do this, you may be sure that the wish will be fulfilled.

HOW TO BE SURE OF A PARTNER AT A DANCE.

When you wish to be sure of many partners at a dance or ball, let a little brother or sister, or any other person *hold a thumb for you*—that is, keep her hand closed like a fist for a quarter of an hour, holding her *thumb* between the *fore* and *middle finger*, while she thinks of you, and wishes you good luck. This proceeding has a wonderful effect.

THE BRIDE'S OMEN.

If you would have fair weather on your wedding day, you must always faithfully feed the cats. It is true it is a common error when persons think that it forebodes evil when it rains upon the bride *in her bridal dress*. This is no evil omen, but the contrary. But, above all things, let her be careful not to allow her *shoes to get wet*. If my young readers would take the trouble to read Frederika Bremer's work called "The House," they would find in it a confirmation of this warning.

TO KNOW IF A WOMAN WITH CHILD WILL HAVE A GIRL OR BOY.

Write the proper names of the father and the mother, and of the month she conceived with child, and likewise adding all the numbers of those letters together, divide them by seven; and then, if the remainder be even, it will be a girl, if uneven, it will be a boy.

THE CROW SIGN.

If you wish to know how matters will go with you during the year, you must take good heed of the first *crow* that you see in the spring. If, when you first see it, it is *flying*, it signifies that you will take a journey that will be longer or shorter, according to the distance which the bird flies before it alights. It may also signify a complete *change of abode*, perhaps by a wedding. If you first see the bird *sitting*, you will remain at home; if *cawing*, much that you do not think of will happen to you; if upon *one leg*, fortune will not smile upon you.

9

THE RABBIT AUGURY.

If, when in the open field, or upon the highroad, a *rabbit runs across your path*, it signifies that something *unpleasant* will happen to you.

THE SHEEP AND SWINE TOKEN.

If you are going to pay a visit, and you meet with *sheep*, you will be very *welcome*; but if you meet with *swine*, you will be *unwelcome*.

A CHARM AGAINST NIGHTMARE.

If you wish to be secure against the nightmare in your sleep, place your shoes side by side upon the floor, at the foot of the bed, so that the toes will point *not* toward the bed, but in the contrary direction, as if they were *going from it.*

WHAT A SPIDER WEB FORETELLS.

If you are walking with a young man at a time when the so-called gossamer, those snow-white spider's threads, are floating about in the air, and one of these delicate fibrous veils sweeps by, *and forms a band between you and him*, it is a sign that feelings of a tender nature will some day bind you to each other.

HOW TO GET A SWEETHEART.

If a thick, long spider's web hangs anywhere from the ceiling, you must sweep it down as soon as possible, for it signifies a *suitor*, and the one that gets the web will have him.

WHAT A PRICK IN THE FINGER SIGNIFIES.

If you are sewing upon a new dress, apron, &c., &c., and you prick your finger with the needle so as to bring blood, it is a sign that when you first wear the garment you will receive many kisses.

EASTER WATER.

In speaking of a love potion, I made mention of *Easter water*; many of my readers have, I suppose, never heard of this singular kind of water. I will explain it to you. It is water which is drawn from the river upon Easter morning, before the sun has shone upon it. To obtain it, therefore, you must rise on Easter morning while it is still quite dark, take your way to the river in silence, fill your pitcher in silence, and then make your way home in silence, without looking behind you. You may then go to bed again and have your sleep out. This Easter water has this peculiarity: *it will keep sweet throughout the whole year.* You can, therefore, fill as many bottles with it as you please, cork them tightly, and lay them away. Besides its use in the above-named love potion, it is beneficial in various maladies, especially in diseases of the eye, and, in addition to this, it is an approved cosmetic.

THE RYE CHARM.

If you would have bread and cake in plenty during the whole

year, hang a full sheaf of rye and a full sheaf of wheat upon a pole outside the door, on Christmas morning, so that the birds may come and feed from it.

NUMEROUS METHODS OF TELLING FOR TUNES ON NEW YEAR'S EVE.

The evening which of all others is the most adapted for witchery, is New Year's eve. It is a very ill practice to spend this evening at *a ball*, and it is an acknowledged fact that ill luck, more or less, follows a person throughout the year, who has *danced the old year out and the new year in.*

You should spend New Year's eve with a small circle of near and dear friends, around a punch-bowl, while you seek to inquire what the future has in store for you. In the first place this may be done with *melted lead or wax.* Some of you, perhaps, are acquainted with this method of inquiring of the future, yet there may be many among your number who are still ignorant of it. Now, as it is of the highest interest in the world that these should know the process, I will here give, for their benefit, a short explanation of it, which the others may skip over.

THE LEAD AND WAX SPELL.

Take a good-sized piece of lead or wax, (the former is better,) place it in a melting-ladle, and dissolve it over the coals, or over a spirit-lamp, into which you have poured a little alcohol. You must then take a vessel full of water, (a bowl is best, that is not too deep nor too shallow,) and pour into it the lead or wax, and from the various figures which it forms in the water you endeavor to tell your fortune.

THE SAUCER CHARM.

The following is another method: you take four saucers; in one you put a *ring*, in another a *sprig of myrtle*, in the third a *piece of money*, and in the fourth *nothing*. The individuals composing the company must now walk around the table, blindfold, one after the other, and choose one of the saucers, which, in the mean time, have been changed as to place. Those among the company who choose the ring, will be *betrothed* in the course of the year; *myrtle* signifies wedlock, the *piece of money wealth*, the *empty saucer* no change of circumstances.

HOW TO TELL THE FIRST LETTER OF YOUR FUTURE WIFE OR HUSBAND'S NAME.

If you wish to know the letter with which your future wife or husband's name commences, write all the letters of the alphabet, separately, upon small pieces of paper, put these pieces in a box, and draw one out blindfold.

All this may be done before twelve o'clock. Exactly at the stroke of midnight, however, you can summon up your future husband or wife, and behold his or her image *up the chimney.*

THE CANDLE SPELL.

The following is another method: Take *two candles,* go a little before twelve o'clock into an adjoining chamber—no one on any account must follow you—place yourself before the *mirror,* and exactly as it strikes *twelve,* call out your own name in full, *three times.* When the last sound has died away, you will see in the glass your future husband looking over your shoulder.

The company may not remain together after twelve o'clock. When the old year is out and the new year in, you must embrace, and kiss each other, and then go home. You must not yet go to bed, however, but must first devote an hour to solitude, to reflect upon all which the past year has brought with it, and to commit to writing the chief occurrences, as well as the state of your minds. It would be well to keep a book for this purpose, in which you should read and write only on a new-year's eve, and at other times keep carefully stored away. I have always done this, and I can assure you, that it is with a feeling of sad, sweet interest, that I now read, each new-year's eve, of the eighty-nine years of my life.

THE NUTSHELL WITCHERY.

Among the witcheries which you may perform on a new-year's eve, there is one to which I have not alluded. Each person of the company, to wit, takes a *nutshell,* and, after lighting a *wax taper,* places it in the shell. A basin of water is then brought. You now place the nutshells, with the burning tapers in them, in the basin. Some will incline toward each other as they float along, others will repel each other, until, at last, all are extinguished or sunk. What conclusions in reference to the future, are to be drawn from the various movements of these tiny magic skiffs, your own quick wits will tell you.

THE BRIDGE OMEN.

After you have gone home, and have devoted an hour to the solitary task which I counselled you (see CANDLE SPELL), take a *glass of water,* cut a small *chip of wood,* and lay it crosswise upon the glass, so that it stretches like a bridge, from one end to the opposite one. Then place this glass under your bed. The consequence will be that you will dream during the night that you are walking over a bridge, and that you fall into the water. A gentleman, however, appears and rescues you. This same gentleman, whom you will see very distinctly, be careful to remember, for he is your future husband. A gentleman can make the same experiment, and he will dream the same thing, with the difference only, that it is a lady who rescues him, and she is to be his future wife.

THE HAIR SPELL.

If you wish any person to think of you, pluck a hair from your head, and blow it out into the air toward that quarter of the heavens in which the person lives, while, at the same time, you call out the name of this person *three times*, at the top of your voice. During this you must be entirely alone, and must have thought intently upon the person for, at least, a quarter of an hour beforehand. At the same instant he will experience a strange unearthly shudder or thrill, and his thoughts will turn irresistibly toward you.

SIGN WHEN YOU WET YOUR APRON.

When you are washing, if you are apt *to wet your apron* a great deal, it is a sign that your future husband will be a tippler. Take good heed therefore!

THE NAIL TOKEN.

If a person has nails that are all bitten to pieces, and gnawed close to the quick, it signifies an evil, malicious character, and you have every reason in the world to be on your guard in your intercourse with such a person.

HOW TO DETERMINE THE LUCKY AND THE UNLUCKY DAYS OF ANY MONTH IN THE YEAR.

Ascertain from the Almanac the day on which a full moon occurs, and count the number of days from that to the end of the month: you then multiply the number of days in the month by the number ascertained as above, and the total will give you the lucky days (subject to a further test hereafter explained), which must be reckoned this wise: if the total happens to be, say 516, the lucky days of that month would be the 5th and 16th, and if it should be 561, the days are the same, for you must always transpose the figures, when they will work together. Suppose that instead of 516, the total should be 399: as neither of these figures can be paired, the lucky days from that total are the 3d and 9th, and the 9th would be considered doubly lucky, if no tests worked to the contrary.

The unlucky days are determined in precisely the same manner, by multiplying the number of days in the month by the number which had passed previous to a full moon.

After working out your list of lucky days, in the manner above described, you must then test them, in order to be sure that there are no opposing influences. You can do this by calculating the unlucky days. Should you find that any day of the month which was designated as lucky came also in the list of unlucky days, the latter preponderates, and you must strike it from the lucky list.

This plan of demonstrating lucky and unlucky days is very ancient, and has been tested to such an extent that it is considered accurate by most astrologers. In old times, before the mass of the people understood much about figures, the professional fortune-tellers demanded a large fee for casting the lucky days of any month, which they accomplished in the manner above described.

Lucky marriage days for girls were cast in the same manner, except that the age of the girl was used as the multiplicator, or multiplier, instead of the number of days in the month. The result was determined similarly, and also by a test of the unlucky days. Thus, if a girl is 18 years old, and thinks of marrying in October, she takes up an Almanac and ascertains the day of the full moon in that month. It occurs on the 24th, and there are 31 days in the month: this leaves 7 for the multiplier. She multiplies this by her age, 18, and the result is 106, which shows the lucky days in that month for her to marry are the 10th and 6th, unless they are destroyed by the test, which is determined as follows: There are 23 days before the 24th, and she must multiply 23 by 18, which gives 414, and shows that the 4th and 14th are the only unlucky days for her to marry; and as they do not conflict with the lucky days, the 6th and 10th may be considered as genuine lucky days for that month, reckoning the moon to have fulled on the 24th. In determining her age, she should reckon any period over half a year a full year.

THE DIVINING ROD:

OR, HOW TO TELL WHERE TO DIG FOR WATER AND ALL KINDS OF METALS.

So early as Agricola, a celebrated conjuror who lived in ancient times, the divining rod was in much request, and has obtained great credit for its discovering where to dig for metals and springs of water; for some years past its reputation has been upon the decline, but lately it has been revived, and with great success, as I have myself found from numerous experiments that its effects are more than imagination, and to enable others to do the like, I have laid down some short rules, as follows:

DIRECTIONS FOR CHOOSING RODS. The hazel and willow rods, I have by experience found, will actually answer with all persons who are in a good state of health, if they are used with moderation, and at some distance of time, after meals, when the operator is in good spirits. The hazel, willow, and elm are all attracted by springs of water. Some persons have the virtue intermittently; the rod in their hands will attract one half hour, and repel the next. The rod is attracted by water, all metals, coals, amber, and lime-stone, but with different degrees of strength.

The best rods are those from the hazel, or nut-tree, as they are pliant and rough, and are best cut in the winter months; a shoot that terminates equally forked is to be preferred, (*See Fig.* 1,) about two feet and a half long; but as such a fork is rarely to be met with, two single ones of a length and size may be tied together with thread, and they will answer as well as the others. (*See Fig. 2.*)

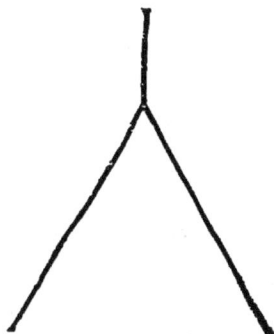 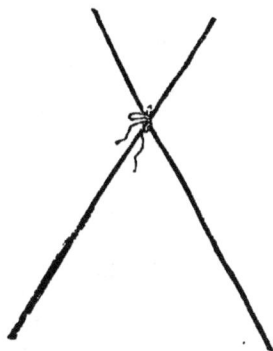

Fig. 1. Fig. 2.

The most convenient and handy method of holding the rod is with the palms of the hands turned upward, and the two ends of the rod coming outward; the palms should be held horizontally as nearly as possible; the part of the rod in the hands ought to be straight, and not bent either backward or forward; the upper part of the arm should be kept pretty close to the sides, and the elbows resting on them, the lower part of the arm making nearly a right angle with the upper, though rather a little more acute; the rod ought to be so held that, in its working, the sides may move clear of the little fingers. The position of the rod, when properly held, is much like the following figure, (*see Fig.* 3,) where the distance between the four downward lines is the part supposed to be held in the hand.

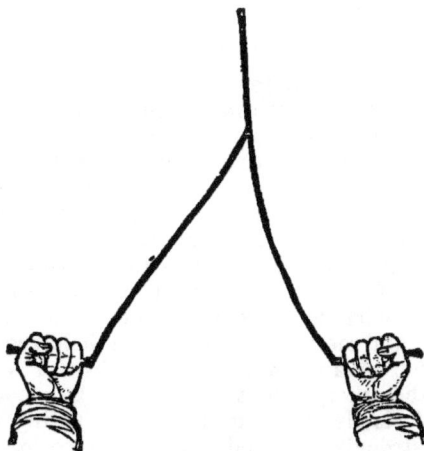

Fig. 3.

The best manner of carrying the rod is with the end prolaided in an angle of about eighty degrees from the horizon, as by this method of carrying, the repulsion is more plainly perceived than if it was held perpendicularly. But after all the directions that can be given, the adroit use of it can only be attained by practice. It is necessary that the grasp should be steady, for if, when the rod is going, there should e the least succession or counteraction in the hands, though ever so small, it will greatly impair, and generally totally prevent its activity, which is not to be done by the mere strength of the grasp, for provided this be steady, no strength can stop it.

As soon as the person's foremost foot comes near the attracting body, the end of the rod is repelled toward the face. (*See Fig. 4.*) Then open the hands a little, replace the rod, and approach nearer, and the repulsion will be continued until the foot is on or over the attracting body. When this is the case, the rod will first be repelled a little, viz., two or three inches, and then be attracted toward it.

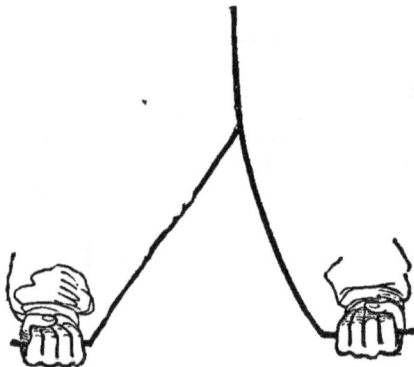

Fig. 4.

When it hath been drawn down, it must not be thrown back without opening the hands, a fresh grasp being necessary to every attraction, but the least opening of the hand is sufficient. As long as the person stands over the attracting body, the rod continues to be attracted, but as soon as the fore foot is beyond it, then the rod is drawn down backward to the face. Metals have different degrees of attraction: gold is strongest, next copper, then iron, silver, tin, lead, bones, coals, springs of water and lime-stone. To make common experiments, set the foot on a piece or coin of any of these metals, having the rod in your hands as before directed. In using the rod to discover springs and metals, let the person hold the rod as already directed, and then advancing north or south with a slow pace, just one foot before the other, at first the rod may be repelled, but as the person advances slowly, and comes over the spring, or vein of ore, the rod will be strongly attracted. The divining rod is sometimes called *Divina Virgula*, and sometimes *The Luck Rod*.

JUDGMENTS DRAWN FROM THE MOON'S AGE.

1. A child born within twenty-one hours after the new moon will be fortunate and live to a good old age; whatever is dreamt on this day will be fortunate and pleasant to the dreamer; various undertakings will succeed on this day.

2. This is a very lucky day for discovering things lost or hidden; the child born on this day will thrive, but the dreams are not to be depended upon.

3. A child born on this day will be fortunate through persons in power, and all dreams will prove true.

4. This day is bad; persons failing on this day rarely recover; the dreams will have no effect.

5. This day is favorable to begin a good work, and the dreams will be tolerably successful; the child born on this day will be vain and deceitful.

6. The dreams of this day will not immediately come to pass; and the child born will not live long.

7. Do not tell your dreams on this day; if sickness befall you on this day you will soon recover; the child born will live long, but have many troubles.

8. Dreams of this day will come to pass; business begun on this day will prosper, and anything lost will be found.

9. This day differs little from the former, the child born on this day will acquire great riches and honor.

10. This day is likely to be fatal; those who fall sick will rarely recover; the child born on this day will be devoted to religion, and of an engaging form and manner; if a female, she will possess an uncommon share of wisdom and learning; this day is good to begin a journey, to marry, or to engage in business.

11. Dreams on this day are fortunate; and the child born will live long, and be very sensible; but a person who falls sick on this day rarely recovers.

12. Dreams on this day will quickly prove true.

13. If you ask a favor on this day, it will be granted.

14. The sickness that befalls a person on this day is likely to prove mortal; what was lost yesterday may be found to-day.

15. The child born on this day will be of ill manners and unfortunate; it is a good day for dealing in merchandise.

16. The child born on this day will be foolish; it is an unlucky day to marry, or to begin any kind of business on.

17. The child born on this day will be very valiant, but will suffer hardships; if a female, she will be chaste and industrious, and live respected to a great age.

18. This day is dangerous; the child born will be dishonest.

19. Dreams on this day will be vain and untrue; the child born will grow up healthy and strong, but be of a selfish and ungentle turn of mind.

20. The child born will be fortunate, and of a cheerful countenance,

religiou3, and much beloved; any kind of business begun on this day will be unfortunate.

21. The child born on this day will be of an ungovernable temper, forsake his friends, wander in a foreign land, and be unhappy through life; it is a happy day to marry on; and all business begun on this day will be successful.

22. The child born on this day will be wicked, meet with many dangers, and come to an untimely end; it is a very unfortunate day, and threatens everything with disappointment and crosses: whoever falls sick on this day seldom recovers.

23. Dreams on this day are certain; and the child born on this day will be rich and greatly esteemed.

24. This day is favorable for dreams; and the child born will be of a sweet and amiable disposition.

25. This day is bad for dreams, and those who fall sick on it, are in great danger; the child born on this day will be its parents' delight, but will not live to any great age.

26. This day is good for dreams, but children born on it will experience many hardships, though in the end, they may turn out happily.

27. This is a very unfortunate day to look for anything that is lost, but a child born on this day will make a great stir in the world, either as a statesman, soldier, physician, or clergyman.

28. A child born upon this day will live to be a rich and truly good man if born before noon, but if born after that hour, it is to be feared that he will be dissipated or worthless.

29. Dreams on this day are not worth a moment's attention, for rest assured they will never be fulfilled. Never buy a lottery ticket on this day.

TO KNOW THE TEMPER AND DISPOSITION OF EVERY ONE.

THE SIGNS OF A CHOLERIC DISPOSITION ARE,

1. The habit of the body hot in touch, dry, lean, hard, and hairy.
2 The color of the face, yellow.
3. A natural dryness of the mouth and tongue.
4. The thirst great, and frequent.
5. Activity and inquietude of the body.
6. The pulse hard, swift, and often beating.
7. The spittle bitter.
8. The dreams are most of yellow things, of brawls, of fights and quarrels.

THE SIGNS OF A SANGUINE CONSTITUTION ARE,

1. The habit of the body hot in touch, fleshy, soft and hairy.
2. The color of the body fresh, sanguine and lively.
3. A natural and constant blush in the face.
4. The pulse soft, moist, and full.

5. The spittle sweet.

6. Dreams most commonly of red things, of beauty, feasting, dancing, music, and all jovial and pleasing recreations.

7 A continual habit of pleasantness and affability.

8. Often affected with jests, mirth, and laughter.

THE SIGNS OF A PHLEGMATIC CONSTITUTION ARE,

1. The habit of the body, cold and moist; in touch, soft, fat, gross, and not hairy.

2. A constant natural whiteness, or wanness in the face.

3. The pulse soft, slow, and rare.

4. The thirst little, and seldom desiring drink.

5. The dreams usually are of white things, floods, inundations, and accidents belonging to water.

6. Sleep, much and frequent.

7. Slowness and dulness of the body to exercise.

THE SIGNS OF A MELANCHOLY CONSTITUTION ARE,

1. The body in touch, cold, dry, lean, and smooth.

2. The body of a dark, dull, gloomy, leaden color.

3. The spittle in small quantities, and sour.

4. Pulse little, rare and hard.

5. They dream of terrible things, as ghosts, wild beasts, etc.

6. Greatly oppressed with fear.

7. Constancy in the performance of the thing intended.

THE SIGNS OF A GENEROUS PERSON ARE,

1. The forehead large, fleshy, plain and smooth.

2. The eye moist and shining.

3. The countenance expressing joy and content.

4. The voice pleasant.

5. The motion of the body, slow, etc.

THE SIGNS OF AN ILL-NATURED PERSON.

1. The form of the body meagre and lean.

2. The forehead cloudy, sullen and wrinkled.

3. The eye cast down and malicious.

4. A nimble tongue.

5. Walking a short, quick, uneven pace.

6. A secret murmuring to himself as he walks.

SIGNIFICATION OR LANGUAGE OF THE FLOWERS.

No Book on Fortune-telling and Dreams would be complete without the signification of the flowers. If we dream of, or have those smiles of nature given to us, we should at once consult the language of Flora and ascertain what our dream or present signifies.

It is no new thing to attach a sentiment or meaning to each flower

In Eastern lands flowers have a language which all understand. It is that "still small voice" which is powerful on account of its silence. It is one of the chief amusements of the Greek girls to drop these symbols of their esteem or scorn upon the various passengers who pass their latticed windows, and the traveller can read upon Egyptian rocks accounts of the conquests of that ancient people recorded by foreign plants. Accompanying, we give a complete dictionary of the meaning of the flowers.

ACACIA BLOSSOM. Come to my heart!

ACONITE—BLUE. Flatterer! are you to be trusted?

ACONITE—YELLOW. Your caprice is unendurable.

ALPINE ROSE. Love must venture; timidity can never win.

AMARANTH. The earthly only can become the spoil of the grave, love is immortal, and belongs to heaven.

ANEMONE. My thought by day, and my dream by night.

ANEMONE-WOOD. Your cruelty is destroying me.

ANISE. You must mend your manners.

APPLE BLOSSOM. Who plucks the blossoms, destroys his hopes of fruit.

APRICOT BLOSSOM. Are you always so gay, so trifling?

ASTER. Weep no longer—you will find him again above the stars.

ASPEN-LEAF. Your heart beats for every one, therefore no heart beats for you.

AURICULA. Who would not love you?

BALSAM. Splendor dazzles, grace alone enchains.

BALSAM-ROSE. Let my image dwell always in your heart.

BARLEY. Come again to-morrow.

BEAN BLOSSOM. Forgive me, I misunderstood you.

BIRCH BRANCH. How sweetly are sorrow's tears dried up on the bosom of a sympathizing friend.

BLACKBERRY BRANCH. Contentment and love.

BLUE-BOTTLE. Be simple and humble, and life will always appear to you in heavenly colors.

BOXWOOD. I hope continually.

BUCKWHEAT BLOSSOM. Not idle show, quiet domestic virtues alone ensure lasting happiness.

BURR. Like seeks like.

BUTTER-CUP. Your presence is consoling to me.

CABBAGE-LEAF. When you come again, come sober.

CAMOMILE. Could you, then, love anybody beside yourself?

CARNATION. How I burn!

CENTAURY. You seek money only—I will not waste my love upon you.

CHERRY BLOSSOM. When will love tinge your cheeks?

CHESTNUT BLOSSOM. Always as to-day.

CLOVER BLOSSOM. I will live for you.

COLUMBINE. Your words sound well, but what says your heart?

CROWN-IMPERIAL. Let me be your slave, and I am happy.

CUCKOO-FLOWER. I like not long complainings.

CURRANT-TWIG. Whoever loves me must share my sorrow, and respect my grief.

CYPRESS. When my heart is broken, and I lie in the cold grave, give me at least a tear.

DAFFODIL. Let me not pine!

DILL. Love strengthens—I will protect you.

ELDER BLOSSOM. Your fidelity is destined to a sweet reward.

FIG-LEAF. I am ashamed.

FLAX. Do you love me for myself?

FOX-GLOVE. None but a fool could be as forward as you.

GILLIFLOWER. Where you are, it is always spring.

GRAPE-VINE. Fear not! Love conquers!

GRASS. Love for love, truth for truth.

HAZEL-TWIG. Forgive me!

HEART'S-EASE. Because I feel friendship for you, you imagine that I love you—you are in error.

HEATHER BLOSSOM. I ask only for your friendship.

HELIOTROPE. Give me proofs of your love.

HONEY-SUCKLE. Eternal fidelity! When shall we meet again?

HYACINTH-SINGLE. When I am dead, you will regret your cruelty.

HYACINTH-DOUBLE. Heaven shines in your eyes; the angels listen to your words.

HYDRANGEA. And you could so soon forget me!

IMMORTELLE. True love is unchangeable.

IRIS. Why have you disturbed the peace of my heart?

IVY. I am ever true.

JASMINE. Can calm, domestic happiness content you?

LARK-SPUR. Your love is my aim.

LAUREL. You have my heart.

LEMON BLOSSOM. Give me hope!

LILY-TIGER. My heart burns.

LILY-WHITE. Angel, let me adore you.

LINDEN BLOSSOM. I am favorably inclined to you.

MAPLE-TWIG. What is more painful than to be misunderstood by one you love?

MARIGOLD. I like you not.

MARSH-MALLOW. To fondle is not to love.

MIGNONNETTE. Not beauty, but goodness of heart is my choice.

MULLEN. If you love me, I envy not a king's crown.

MUSHROOM. Away! go home, and cry about it!

MYRTLE BLOSSOM. Be constant; sweet is the reward of love.

MYRTLE BRANCH. Will you be my wife (husband)?

NETTLE. Beware! coquetry has its penalty.

OAK-LEAF. My fidelity bids defiance to every storm.

OATS. Return.

OLEANDER. True until death.

PARSLEY. You are in love with me.

PEONY. You are too vain—and of what?

PINE. In vain you strive to gain my confidence—stern fate has made me rude and silent.

PINK-CARTHUSIAN. Why so reserved?

PINK-VARIEGATED. Friendship is all that I can feel for you.

POMEGRANATE BLOSSOM. A kiss.

POPPY. I cannot endure you—you are too stupid.

POTATO BLOSSOM. Modest worth surpasses outward show.

PRIMROSE. Give me your love—I will cherish it faithfully and in secret.

RANUNCULUS. Where you are there is my home.

RIBBON GRASS. Give me a kiss.

ROCKET. Sleep visits not my eyelids; I wake and long for you.

ROSE—MONTHLY. Every month you have a new love.

ROSE—RED. You pass like a conqueror through the world.

ROSE—WHITE. Beautiful are you in childlike innocence, more beautiful will you be when warmed by the breath of love.

ROSE-BUD. Your presence fills me with heavenly longing.

ROSE-LEAF—RED. Yes!

ROSE-LEAF—WHITE. No!

ROSEMARY. You were absent—life departed; you returned—I live again.

SNOW-DROP. You have kindled the first sparks of love in my bosom.

STRAWBERRY. Not earthly rank gives happiness, but worth and amiability.

SWEET-PEA. Your name is inconstancy.

SWEET-WILLIAM. Light and hasty impressions are soon effaced.

THISTLE. Your words offend me; you have deeply wounded me.

THYME. I have not understood you.

VERONICA. What would this world be without you?

VIOLET. I love you for your gentle modesty.

WINTERGREEN. Remain constant and true—then we will meet again.

WOOD-SORREL. You brighten my existence as the stars brighten the night.

THIRTY PHYSIOLOGICAL SIGNIFICA-TIONS.

STRENGTH OF BODY is known by a stiff hair, large bones, firm and robust limbs, short muscular neck, firm and erect, the head and breast high, the forehead short, hard, and peaked, with bristly hair, large feet, rather thick than broad, a harsh unequal voice, and choleric complexion.

WEAKNESS OF BODY is distinguished by a small ill-proportioned head, narrow shoulders, soft skin, and melancholy complexion.

THE SIGNS OF LONG LIFE are strong teeth, a sanguine temperament, middle stature, large, deep, and ruddy lines in the hand, large muscles, stooping shoulders, full chest, firm flesh, clear complexion, slow growth, wide ears, and large eyelids.

SHORT LIFE may be inferred from a thick tongue; the appearance of grinders before the age of puberty, thin, straggling and uneven teeth, confused lines in the hand, of a quick but small growth.

A GOOD GENIUS may be expected from a thin skin, middle stature, blue bright eyes, fair complexion, straight, pretty strong hair, an affable aspect, the eyebrows joined, moderation in mirth, an open, cheerful countenance, and the temples a little concave.

A DUNCE may be known by a swollen neck, plump arms, sides, and loins, a round head, concave behind, a large fleshy forehead, pale eyes, a dull heavy look, small joints, snuffing nostrils, and a proneness to laughter, little hands, an ill-proportioned head, either too big or too little, blubber lips, short fingers, and thick legs.

FORTITUDE is promised from a wide mouth, a sonorous voice, grave, slow, and always equal, upright posture, large eyes, pretty open and steadfast, the hair high above the forehead, the head much compressed or flattened, the forehead square and high, the extremities large and robust, the neck firm though not fleshy, a large corpulent chest, and brown complexion.

BOLDNESS is characterized by a prominent mouth, rugged appearance, rough forehead, arched eyebrows, large nostrils and teeth, short neck, great arms, ample chest, square shoulders and a froward countenance.

PRUDENCE is generally distinguished by a head which is flat on the sides, a broad square forehead, a little concave in the middle, a soft voice, a large chest, a thin hair, light eyes, either blue, brown or black, large eyes, and an aquiline nose.

A GOOD MEMORY is commonly attached to those persons who are smaller, yet better formed in the upper than the lower parts, not fat but fleshy, of a fair, delicate skin, with the poll of the head uncovered, crooked nose, teeth thick set, large ears with plenty of cartilage.

A BAD MEMORY is observable in persons who are larger in their superior than inferior parts, fleshy, though dry and bald.—N. B. This is expressly contrary to the opinion of Aristotle, who says that the superior parts being larger than the inferior signify a good memory, and *vice versa.*

A GOOD IMAGINATION AND THOUGHTFUL DISPOSITION is distinguished by a large prominent forehead, a fixed and attentive look, slow respiration, and an inclination of the head.

A GOOD SIGHT is enjoyed by those persons who have generally black, thick, straight eye-lashes, large bushy eyebrows, concave eyes, contracted as it were inwards.

SHORT-SIGHTED PEOPLE have a stern, earnest look, small, short eyebrows, large pupils and prominent eyes.

SENSE OF HEARING: those who possess the same in perfection, have ears well furnished with gristle, well channelled and hairy.

THE SENSE OF SMELLING is most perfect in those who have large noses, descending very near the mouth, neither too moist nor too dry.

A NICE FACULTY OF TASTING is peculiar to such as have a spongy, porous, soft tongue, well moistened with saliva, yet not too moist.

DELICACY IN THE TOUCH belongs to those who have a soft skin, sensible nerves, and nervous sinews, moderately warm and dry.

IRASCIBILITY is accompanied by an erect posture, a clear skin, a solemn voice, open nostrils, moist temples, displaying superficial veins, thick neck, equal use of both hands, quick pace, blood-shot eyes, large, unequal, ill-ranged eyes, and choleric disposition.

TIMOROUSNESS resides where we find a concave neck, pale color, weak-winking eyes, soft hair, smooth plump breast, shrill tremulous voice, small mouth, thin lips, broad thin hands, and small shambling feet.

MELANCHOLY is denoted by a wrinkled countenance, dejected eyes, meeting eyebrows, slow pace, fixed look, and deliberate respiration.

AN AMOROUS DISPOSITION may be known by a fair, slender face, a redundancy of hair, rough temples, broad forehead, moist shining eyes, wide nostrils, narrow shoulders, hairy hands and arms, well-shaped legs.

GAYETY attends a serene open forehead, rosy agreeable countenance, a sweet musical tone of voice, an agile body and soft flesh.

ENVY appears with a wrinkled forehead, frowning, dejected, and squinting look, a pale, melancholy countenance, and a dry, rough skin.

INTREPIDITY often resides in a small body, with red curled hair, ruddy countenance, frowning eyebrows, arched and meeting, eyes blue and yellowish, large mouth, and red lines in the hand.

GENTLENESS AND COMPLACENCY may be distinguished by a soft and moist palm, frequency of shutting the eyes, soft movement, slow speech, soft, straight and lightish-colored hair.

BASHFULNESS may be discovered by moist eyes, never wide open, eyebrows frequently lowered, blushing cheeks, moderate pace, slow and submissive speech, bent body, and glowing ears of a purple hue.

TEMPERANCE OR SOBRIETY is accompanied with an equal respiration, a moderate-sized mouth, smooth temples, eyes of an ordinary size, either fair or azure, and a short, flat body.

STRENGTH OF MIND is signified by light, curled hair, a small body, shining eyes, but a little depressed, a grave intense voice, bushy beard, large broad back and shoulders.

PRIDE stands confessed with arched eyebrows, a large prominent mouth, a broad chest, slow pace, erected head, shrugging shoulders, and staring eyes.

LUXURY dwells with a ruddy or pale complexion, downy temples, bald pate, little eyes, thick neck, corpulent body, large nose, thin eyebrows, and hands covered with a kind of down.

LOQUACITY may be expected from a bushy beard, broad fingers, pointed tongue, eyes of a ruddy hue, a large prominent upper lip, and a sharp pointed nose.

PERVERSENESS may be dreaded, when we perceive a high forehead, firm, short, thick, immovable neck, quick speech, immoderate laughter, fiery eyes, and short fleshy hands and fingers.

DICK & FITZGERALD,

PUBLISHERS, NEW YORK.

*** The Publishers, upon receipt of the price, will send any of the following books by mail, POSTAGE FREE, to any part of the United States. In ordering books, the full name, post-office, county and State should be plainly written.

Inquire Within for Anything You Want to Know; or,

Over 3,500 Facts for the People. "Inquire Within" is one of the most valuable and extraordinary volumes ever presented to the American public, and embodies nearly 4,000 facts, in most of which any person living will find instruction, aid and entertainment. As a book to be kept in the family for reference it is unequaled, comprising, as it does, all kinds of books of information in a single volume.

It is a Doctor, a Gardener, a School-master,
A Dancing-Master, an Artist, a Naturalist,
A Modeler, a Cook, a Lawyer,
A Surgeon, a Chemist, a Perfumer,
A Dyer, a Brewer, an Architect,
A Bookkeeper, a Confectioner, a Laundress,
A "Hoyle," a "Letter-Writer,"

A " Ready Reckoner," and a House-keeper.

IT ALSO CONTAINS

Tables of Weights and Measures,
Interest Tables from $1 up to $10,000,
Innumerable Tables on Curious and Interesting Subjects,
All Kinds of Family Amusements and Recreations.

It might strike the casual observer as something incredible, if not impossible, that such an immense and varied amount of matter could be crowded into a book of the merely nominal price of a dollar and a half; but the work contains 436 large pages of small type, closely printed in double column, and a perusal of it will convince the most skeptical that the only thing to be wondered at in it, is the extremely low price at which it is offered.
Bound in extra cloth, with gilt side and back.......................$1.50

The Perfect Gentleman. A book of Etiquette and Eloquence.

Containing information and instruction for those who desire to become brilliant or conspicuous in General Society, or at Parties, Dinners or Popular Gatherings, etc. It gives directions how to use wine at table, with Rules for judging the quality thereof, Rules for Carving, and a complete Etiquette of the Dinner Table, including Dinner Speeches, Toasts and Sentiments, Wit and Conversation at Table, etc. It has also an American Code of Etiquette and Politeness for all occasions. It also contains all the necessary information relating to the Rules of Etiquette to be observed in fashionable and official society at Washington, and this alone makes it valuable to any one who visits that city, either for pleasure or business. It also contains, Model Speeches, with directions how to deliver them, Duties of the Chairman at Public Meetings, Forms of Preambles and Resolutions, etc. It is a handsomely bound volume of 335 pages...................................$1.50

McBride's New Dialogues. Especially designed for School

and Literary Amateur Entertainments; containing entirely New and Original Dialogues, introducing Irish, Yankee, and other eccentric characters. By H. ELLIOTT MCBRIDE.

CONTENTS.

A Happy Woman.	An Uncomfortable Predicament.
The Somnambulist.	The Opening Speech.
Those Thompsons.	The Cucumber Hill Debating Club.
Playing School.	Married by the New Justice.
Tom and Sally.	Bread on the Waters.
Assisting Hezekiah.	An Unsuccessful Advance.
A Visit to the Oil Regions.	When Women Have Their Rights.
Breaking up the Exhibition.	Only Another Footprint.
Turning Around.	Rosabella's Lovers.
A Little Boy's Debate.	A Smart Boy.
The Silver Lining.	A Heavy Shower.
Restraining Jotham.	Master of the Situation.
A Shoemaker's Troubles.	

The marked favor with which the four preceding volumes have been received suggested the necessity for an increased variety of new eccentric and characteristic pieces, to form an addition to the repertoire contained in "McBride's Comic Dialogues," "McBride's All Kinds of Dialogues," "McBride's Humorous Dialogues," and "McBride's Temperance Dialogues." They are all written with a view to develop dramatic talent, and abound in quaint humor, Dialect Drolleries, and telling stage "situations." 16mo, 178 pages, illuminated paper cover..................30 cts.
Bound in boards...50 cts.

Dick's Book of Toasts, Speeches and Responses. Contain-

ing Toasts and Sentiments for Public and Social Occasions, and specimen Speeches with appropriate replies suitable for the following occasions:

Public Dinners,	Friendly Meetings,
Social Dinners,	Weddings and their Anniversaries,
Convivial Gatherings,	Army and Navy Banquets,
Art and Professional Banquets,	Patriotic and Political Occasions,
Manufacturers' Meetings,	Trades' Unions and Dinners,
Agricultural and Commercial Festivals,	Benedicts' and Bachelors' Banquets,
Special Toasts for Ladies,	Masonic Celebrations,
Christmas, Thanksgiving and other Festivals,	Sporting Coteries,
	All Kinds of Occasions.

This work includes an instructive dissertation on the Art of making amusing After-dinner Speeches, giving hints and directions by the aid of which persons with only ordinary intelligence can make an entertaining and telling speech. Also, Correct Rules and Advice for Presiding at Table. The use of this work will render a poor and diffident speaker fluent and witty—and a good speaker better and wittier, besides affording an immense fund of anecdotes, wit and wisdom, and other serviceable matter to draw upon at will. Paper covers. Price......................30 cts.

How Boggins Was Cured. An intensely ludicrous sketch,

pictorially expressed; showing how Mr. Boggins, who had been reduced to a despairingly crippled state by rheumatism and a complication of other causes, was induced to submit to the wonderful effects of a course of dynamo-electro magnetic therapeutics, tracing the magical and potent effects of the treatment, and the heroic efforts he made while submitting to the doctor's system of pathology; until, crowned with complete success, he is able to throw aside his crutches and is restored to perfect health and pristine agility. An entirely new and original series of sketches. Funny! is no name for it. Small quarto. Illustrated............10 cts.

Le Marchand's Fortune-Teller and Dreamer's Dictionary.

Containing a complete Dictionary of Dreams, alphabetically arranged, with a clear interpretation of each Dream. Also showing how to tell fortunes by the Lady's Love Oracle. How to foretell the Sex of Children. How to tell any Person's Age. To know who your future Husband will be, and how soon you will be Married. How to tell Future events with Cards, Dice, Tea and Coffee Grounds, Eggs, Apple Parings and the Lines of the Hand. Illustrated with wood engravings. 144 pages. Bound in boards....40 cts.

Fontaine's Golden Wheel Dream-Book and Fortune-Teller.

Being the most complete book on Fortune Telling and Interpreting Dreams ever printed. This book informs you how to TELL FORTUNES with the *Golden Wheel, Cards, Dice and Dominoes;* how to find where to dig for water, with the celebrated DIVINING ROD; together with Twenty Ways of Telling Fortunes on New Year's Eve. It is illustrated with engravings, and contains a large Colored Lithographic Engraving of the *Golden Wheel,* which folds up. 144 pages, bound in boards.....................40 cts.

Pettengill's Perfect Fortune-Teller and Dream-Book; or, The Art of Discerning Future Events.

This is a most complete Fortune-Teller and Dream-Book. It is compiled with great care from authorities on Astrology, Geology, Chiromancy, Necromancy, Spiritual Philosophy, etc., etc. Among the subjects treated of, are—Casting Nativities by the Stars, Telling Fortunes by Lines on the Hand, by Moles on the Body, by Turning Cards, by Questions of Destiny, by Physical Appearances, by the Day of Birth, etc. A book of 144 pages. Bound in boards...40 cts.

Mother Shipton's Fortune-Teller; or, Future Fate Foretold by the Planets.

Being the 900 Answers of Pythagoras to the Questions of Life's Destiny. Derived from the Mystic Numbers and Letters of the Planets. Containing the Emblematical and Mystical Wheel of Fortune and Fate, colored. 115 pages, paper covers......................30 cts.

Mother Shipton's Oriental Dream-Book.

Being a reliable interpretation of Dreams, Visions, Apparitions, etc. Together with a History of Remarkable Dreams, proven true as interpreted. Collected and arranged from the most celebrated masters. 16mo, paper covers.....30 cts.

The Everlasting Fortune-Teller and Magnetic Dream-Book.

Containing the Science of Foretelling Events by the Signs of the Zodiac; Lists of Lucky and Unlucky Days; List of Fortunate Hours; the Science of Foretelling Events by Cards, Dice, Dominoes, etc.; the Science of Foretelling anything in the Future by Dreams; and also containing NAPOLEON'S ORACULUM; or, The Book of Fate......................30 cts.

Mother Carey's Dream-Book and Fortune-Teller.

Containing the method of Fortune-Telling with Cards; a complete Dreamer's Dictionary; the Science of Palmistry, or telling Fortunes by the Lines of the Hand; how to tell a Person's Character by a list of Lucky and Unlucky days and hours; how to tell with Cards which of Three Ladies has the best Husband. Mathematical Tables for telling any Person's Age..15 cts.

Aristotle's Book of Fate and Dictionary of Dreams.

Containing Dreams and their Interpretations; the Signification of Moles on Men and Women; one hundred and eighty-seven Weather Omens; Hymen's Lottery and Aristotle's Oraculum, or Book of Fate...........15 cts.

The Egyptian Dream-Book and Fortune-Teller.

Containing an Alphabetical list of Dreams, with their signification and their lucky numbers. Illustrated with explanatory diagrams. Boards, cloth back 40 cts.

The French Wine and Liquor Manufacturer. A Practical

Guide and Receipt Book for the Liquor Merchant. Being a clear and comprehensive Treatise on the Manufacture and Imitation of Brandy, Rum, Gin and Whisky, with Practical Observations and Rules for the Manufacture and Management of all kinds of Wine, by Mixing, Boiling and Fermentation, as practiced in Europe; including complete instructions for Manufacturing Champagne Wine, and the most approved methods for making a variety of Cordials, Liquors, Punch, Essences, Bitters and Syrups, together with a number of Recipes for Fining, Flavoring, Filtering and Coloring Wines and Liquors, and instructions for Restoring and Keeping Ale and Cider. Also containing the latest improvements for Manufacturing Vinegar by the Quick Method. To which is added a collection of Descriptive Articles on Alcohol, Distillation, Maceration and the use of the Hydrometer; with Tables, Comparative Scale, and 14 important Rules for Purchasing, Reducing and Raising the Strength of Alcohol, etc. Illustrated with descriptive diagrams and engravings. Adapted for the Use and Information of the Trade in the United States and Canada. By John Rack, Practical Wine and Liquor Manufacturer. Bound in cloth....$3.00

Bartender's Guide. Containing Recipes for Mixing American,

English, French, German, Italian, Spanish and Russian Drinks—such as Juleps, Punches, Cobblers, Slings, Cocktails, etc. By Jerry Thomas, late Bartender at the Metropolitan Hotel, New York, and Planter's House, St. Louis. To which is appended a Manual for the Manufacture of Cordials, Liquors, Fancy Syrups, etc., containing Recipes after the most approved methods now used in the Distillation of Liquors and Beverages, designed for the special use of Manufacturers and Dealers in Wines and Spirits, Grocers, Tavern-keepers and Private Families—the same being adapted to the trade of the United States and Canada. The whole work containing over 700 valuable recipes. A large book, bound in cloth.............$2.50

The Independent Liquorist; or, The Art of Manufacturing

all kinds of Syrups, Bitters, Cordials, Champagne, Wines, Lager Beer, Ale, Porter, Beer, Punches, Tinctures, Extracts, Brandy, Gin, Essences, Flavorings, Colorings, Sauces, Catsups, Pickles, Preserves, etc. By L. Monzert, Practical Liquorist and Chemist. Every Druggist, Grocer, Restaurant, Hotel-keeper, Farmer, Fruit Dealer, Wine Merchant, should have a copy of this work. It gives the most approved methods, and a true description of the manner in which our most popular beverages are prepared, in such plain terms that the most inexperienced person can manufacture as well as the practical man, without the aid of any expensive apparatus. 12mo, cloth $3.00

The Bordeaux Wine and Liquor Dealer's Guide. A Treatise

on the Manufacture of French Wines and Liquors, with full directions to the Liquor Dealer how to manage his Liquors, Wines, etc., etc. A book of great value to every person who deals in Foreign and American Spirituous Liquors, or Foreign Wines, Cordials, etc. It tells exactly how all kinds of them are made. The directions are simple and easily understood. It also
› tells how to make all kinds of Ales, Porter and other fermented liquor, how to manage Cider, etc. 12mo, cloth......$2.50

Lacour on the Manufacture of Liquors, Wines and Cordials,

Without the aid of Distillation. Also, the Manufacture of Effervescing Beverages and Syrups, Vinegar and Bitters. Prepared and arranged expressly for the Trade. By Pierre Lacour. By the use of this book every man can make all kinds of liquors, wines, cordials and vinegar and syrups at home, without the use of any apparatus of any kind. The work is by the French chemist, Lacour, of Bordeaux. We would advise all who are concerned in the liquor business to get the work. Bound in cloth.......$2.50

Dick's Games of Patience; or Solitaire with Cards. New and
Revised Edition. Containing Sixty-four Games. Illustrated with Fifty explanatory full-page Tableaux. This treatise on Solitaire, a pastime which is steadily gaining in popularity, embraces a number of new and original Games, and all the Games of Patience at present in favor with the most experienced players. This comprehensive work contains the following Games :

Auld Lang Syne.	The Beleaguered Castle.	The Fourteens.
Tam O'Shanter.	The Citadel.	Napoleon's Favorite.
The Four Seasons.	The Exiled Kings.	The Fifteen Puzzle.
Simplicity.	Penelope's Web.	The Contra-Dance.
The Gathering of the Clans.	Napoleon's Square.	The Betrothal.
	The Court Yard.	The Reinforcements.
Napoleon at St. Helena.	The Windmill.	The Reserve.
The Calculation.	Leoni's Own.	The Frog.
The Surprise Party.	La Nivernaise.	The Pyramid.
The Four Kings.	The Four Corners.	The Quadrille.
The Clock.	The Baker's Dozen.	The Chatelaine.
The Garden.	The Salic Law.	The Order of Precedence.
The Queen's Audience.	The Sultan of Turkey.	The Congress.
The Phalanx.	The Fortress.	Thirteen Down.
The Idle Year.	The Hemispheres.	The Octagon.
The Chameleon.	The Elevens.	Light and Shade.
La Belle Lucie.	The Chester Game.	St. Louis.
The Shamrocks.	The Shah of Persia.	Rouge et Noir.
The House in the Wood.	The Empress of India.	The Blondes and Brunettes.
The House on the Hill.	The Zodiac.	
The Grand Duchess.	The Blockade.	The Royal Cotillion.
The Constitution.	The Besieged City.	Nestor.

Each game is carefully and lucidly described, with the distinctive rules to be observed and hints as to the best means of success in play. The Tableaux furnish efficient aid in rendering the disposition of the cards necessary to each game plain and easily comprehensible. The difficulty usually attending descriptions of intricate games is reduced, as far as possible, by precision in method and terseness of expression in the text, and the illustrations serve to dispel any possible ambiguity that might be unavoidable without their aid. The work is attractive in style and elegant in execution, and will prove an interesting companion for many a solitary hour. Quarto. 143 pages. Board cover...75 cts.
Cloth...$1 00.

Dick's Parlor Exhibitions, and How to Make them Suc-
cessful. Containing complete and detailed directions for preparing and arranging Parlor Exhibitions and Amateur Performances. It includes :

Tableaux Vivants.	Popular Ballads illustrated by appropriate action.
Living Portraits.	
Living Statuary.	Charades of all kinds.
Dame History's Peep Show.	Parlor Pantomimes.
Shadow Pantomimes.	Punch and Judy.

AND FIFTY OTHER DIVERTING PARLOR PASTIMES AND AMUSEMENTS.

It contains also a full Catalogue of the celebrated "ART EXHIBITION," and a practical treatise on the wonderful SCIENCE OF SECOND-SIGHT, by the aid of which all the startling effects and achievements of second-sight may be performed by any one possessing a tolerable retentive memory.
This work is thoroughly practical and gives the fullest instructions for preparing and lighting the stage, the construction of the FRAMES FOR LIVING PORTRAITS, and shows how each performance can be presented with complete success. It is illustrated with numerous engravings explaining the text. 150 pages, paper cover....................................30 cts.
Bound in boards, cloth back................................50 cts

Popular Books sent Free of Postage at the Prices annexed.

Walker's Rhyming, Spelling and Pronouncing Dictionary
of the English Language. Containing

I. *The whole Language arranged according to its terminations.*

II. *Every Word explained and divided into Syllables, exactly as pronounced.*

III. *Multitudes of Words, liable to a double pronunciation, fixed in their true sound by a Rhyme.*

IV. *Many of the most difficult Words rendered easy to be pronounced, by being classed according to their endings.*

V. *Numerous classes of Words ascertained in their pronunciation, by distinguishing them into perfect, nearly perfect and allowable Rhymes.*

To which is added critical and practical Observations on Orthography, Syllabication, Pronunciation, an Index of Allowable Rhymes, with Authorities for their usage, etc. Royal 12mo, 700 pages.................$3.00

Book of Household Pets. Containing valuable instructions
about the Diseases, Breeding, Training and Management of the Canary, Mocking Bird, Brown Thrush or Thrasher, Blue Bird, Yellow Bird, Scarlet Tanager, Bobolink, Baltimore Oriole, European Black Bird, Blue Jay, Blue and Yellow Macaw, Carolina Parrakoet, Cockatoo, Green and Gray Parrot, and the rearing and management of all kinds of Pigeons and Fancy Poultry, Rabbits, Squirrels, Guinea Pigs, White Mice and Dogs; together with a Comprehensive Treatise on the Principle and Management of the Salt and Fresh Water Aquarium, with instructions how to make, lay the foundation and stock the Tank. Illustrated with 123 fine wood-cuts.
Bound in boards, cloth back.....................................50 cts.

Chesterfield's Art of Letter-Writing Simplified. A Guide to
Friendly, Affectionate, Polite and Business Correspondence. Containing a collection of valuable information relative to the Art of Letter-Writing, with clear instructions how to begin and end Correspondence, Rules for Punctuation and Spelling, etc., with numerous examples of Letters and Notes, with several important hints on Love-letters.................15 cts.

The Life, Crime and Capture of John Wilkes Booth. With
a full Sketch of the Conspiracy of which he was the Leader, and the Pursuit, Trial and Execution of his Accomplices, together with an original Poem on Abraham Lincoln. By George Alfred Townsend, a Special Correspondent. Illustrated on the cover with a fine portrait of the Assassin, and also containing Plans, Maps, etc. Octavo.....................25 cts

The Hindoo Fortune-Teller and Oracle of Destiny. Containing Ten Methods of Telling Fortunes with Cards, a complete system of Fortune Telling with Dice, together with Sixty-seven Good and Bad Omens, with their interpretation.................................15 cts.

The Combination Fortune-Teller and Dictionary of
Dreams. A Comprehensive Encyclopedia explaining all the different methods extant by which good and evil events, are foretold, containing 400 pages, and illustrated with numerous engravings and two large colored lithographs. 16mo, cloth.....................................$1.25

The Play-Ground; or, Out-Door Games for Boys. A Book
of Healthy Recreations for Youth, containing over a hundred Amusements, including Games of Activity and Speed, Games with Toys, Marbles, Tops, Hoops, Kites, Archery, Balls; with Cricket, Croquet and Base-Ball. Splendidly illustrated with 124 fine wood-cuts. Bound in boards....50 cts.

10,000 Wonderful Things. Comprising the Marvelous and
Rare, Eccentric and Extraordinary, in all Ages and Nations. Enriched with hundreds of illustrations 12mo, cloth, gilt side.................$1.50

Allyn's Ritual of Freemasonry.

Containing a complete Key to the following Degrees: Degree of Entered Apprentice; Degree of Fellow Craft; Degree of Master Mason; Degree of Mark Master; Degree of Past Master; Degree of Excellent Master; Degree of Royal Arch; Royal Arch Chapter; Degree of Royal Master; Degree of Select Master; Degree of Super-Excellent Master; Degree of Ark and Dove; Degree of Knights of Constantinople; Degree of Secret Monitor; Degree of Heroine of Jericho; Degree of Knights of Three Kings; Mediterranean Pass; Order of Knights of the Red Cross; Order of Knights Templar and Knights of Malta; Knights of the Christian Mark, and Guards of the Conclave; Knights of the Holy Sepulchre; The Holy and Thrice Illustrious Order of the Cross; Secret Master; Perfect Master; Intimate Secretary; Provost and Judge; Intendant of the Buildings, or Master in Israel; Elected Knights of Nine; Elected Grand Master; Sublime Knights Elected; Grand Master Architect; Knights of the Ninth Arch; Grand Elect, Perfect and Sublime Mason. Illustrated with 38 copper-plate engravings; to which is added, a Key to the Phi Beta Kappa, Orange and Odd Fellows Societies. By Avery Allyn, K. R. C. K. T. K. M., etc. 12mo, cloth....$5.00

Lester's "Look to the East." (Webb Work.)

A Ritual of the First Three Degrees of Masonry. Containing the complete work of the Entered Apprentice, Fellow Craft and Master Mason's Degrees, and their Ceremonies, Lectures, etc. Edited by Ralph P. Lester. This complete and beautiful Pocket Manual of the First Three Degrees of Masonry, is printed in clear, legible type, and not obscured by any attempts at cypher or other perplexing contractions. It differs entirely from all other Manuals, from the fact that it contains neither the passwords, grips, nor any other purely esoteric matter, with which Masons, and Masons only, are necessarily entirely familiar. It affords, therefore, a thorough and valuable guide to the regular "work" in the above degrees, divested of everything that any member of the Fraternity would object to see in print, or hesitate to carry in his pocket. It gives the correct routine of

Opening and Closing the Lodge in each Degree.	The Entire Ceremonies of Initiating, Passing and Raising Candidates.
Calling Off and calling On.	The Lectures all Ritually and Monitorially Complete.
Calling the Lodge Up and Down.	

Bound in cloth..$2.00
Leather tucks (pocket-book style), gilt edges...................... 2.50

Duncan's Masonic Ritual and Monitor;

or, Guide to the Three Symbolic Degrees of the Ancient York Rite, Entered Apprentice, Fellow Craft and Master Mason. And to the Degrees of Mark Master, Past Master, Most Excellent Master, and the Royal Arch. By Malcom C. Duncan. Explained and Interpreted by copious Notes and numerous Engravings. It is not so much the design of the author to gratify the curiosity of the uninitiated, as to furnish a Guide to the Younger Members of the Order, by means of which their progress from grade to grade may be facilitated. With the aid of this invaluable Masonic Companion, any mason can, in a short time, become qualified to take the Chair as Master of a Lodge. Nothing is omitted in it that may tend to impart a full understanding of the principles of Masonry. This is a valuable book for the Fraternity, containing, as it does, the Modern "Work" of the order. No Mason should be without it. Bound in cloth..................... ....$2.50
Leather tucks (pocket-book style), with gilt edges.................. 3.00

Lander's Expose of Odd-Fellowship.

Containing all the Lectures complete, with regulations for Opening, Conducting and Closing a Lodge; together with Forms of Initiation. Charges of the various Officers, etc., giving all the work in the following Degrees: 1st, or White Degree; 2d, or Covenant Degree; 3d, or Royal Blue Degree; 4th, or Remembrance Degree; 5th, or Scarlet Degree...25 cts.

Martine's Manual of Etiquette and Perfect Letter-Writer.
For the use of both Ladies and Gentlemen. A great many books have been printed on the subject of Etiquette and correct behavior in society; but none of them are sufficiently comprehensive and matter-of-fact to suit the class of people who may be called new-beginners in fashionable life. This book explains in a plain, common-sense way, precisely how to conduct yourself in every position in society. This book also contains over 300 sensible letters and notes suitable to every occasion. It has some excellent model letters of friendship and business, and its model Love-Letters are unequaled. If any lady or gentleman desires to know how to *begin* a love correspondence, this is just the book they want. This volume contains the same matter as "*Martine's Hand-Book of Etiquette*" and "*Martine's Sensible Letter-Writer*," and, in fact, combines those two books bound together in one substantial volume of 373 pages. Cloth, gilt..................$1.50

Frost's Original Letter-Writer, and Laws and By-Laws of
American Society, combined. Being a complete collection of Original Letters and Notes upon every imaginable subject of every-day life, and a condensed but thorough treatise on Etiquette and its Usages in America. By S. A. Frost. This book consists of Miss Frost's two celebrated works on Etiquette and Letter Writing, bound together in one substantial volume. Anybody who wants a book that will tell them how to appear to advantage in society, or how to write a letter on almost any subject, should send for a copy of this valuable work. 16mo, 378 pages, extra cloth...........$1.50

One Hundred and Thirty Comic Dialogues and Recitations.
Being Barton's Comic Recitations and Humorous Dialogues, and Spencer's Comic Speeches and Dialogues, combined in one volume. This capital book contains an endless variety of Comic Speeches, Humorous Scenes, Amusing Burlesques and Diverting Dialogues. It embraces French, Dutch, Irish, Ethiopian and Yankee Stories, and from its fruitful pages may be selected enough fun to make any entertainment a success. Bound in cloth...$1.50

Frost's School and Exhibition Dialogues. Comprising Frost's
Humorous Exhibition Dialogues, and Frost's Dialogues for Young Folks, combined in one volume. By getting this excellent book, the difficulty in procuring a good dialogue for a school exhibition will be entirely overcome. It contains sixty-one good dialogues of every shade and variety, and from its well-stored pages may be selected enough original matter to insure the success of a score of entertainments. Bound in cloth...............$1.50

Twenty-six Short and Amusing Plays for Private Theat-
ricals. Being Howard's Drawing-room Theatricals and Hudson's Private Theatricals combined in one volume. This book, as the title implies, contains twenty-six of the best plays that can be selected for a private theatrical entertainment. It contains several amusing plays for one sex only, and is thus adapted for the army, navy, and male or female boarding-schools. It contains plain directions for getting up a good amateur performance. Bound in cloth.... ....$1.50

Dr. Valentine's Comic Lectures; or, Morsels of Mirth for
the Melancholy. Comprising Comic Lectures on Heads, Faces, Noses, Mouths, Animal Magnetism, etc., with Specimens of Eloquence, Transactions of Learned Societies, Delineations of Eccentric Characters, Comic Songs, etc., etc. By Dr. W. Valentine. Illustrated with 12 portraits of Dr. Valentine in his most celebrated characters. Paper covers......75 cts

Broad Grins of the Laughing Philosopher. This book is full
of the drollest and queerest incidents imaginable, interspersed with jokes, quaint sayings and funny pictures. It also contains twenty-nine laughable engravings...13 cts

The American Boy's Book of Sports and Games. A Re-

pository of In and Out-Door Amusements for Boys and Youths. Containing 600 large 12mo pages. Illustrated with nearly 7,000 engravings, designed by White, Herrick, Weir and Harvey, and engraved by N. Orr. This is unquestionably the most attractive and valuable book of its kind ever issued in this or any other country. It was three years in preparation, and embraces all the sports and games that tend to develop the physical constitution, improve the mind and heart, and relieve the tedium of leisure hours, both in the parlor and the field. The engravings are in the first style of the art, and embrace eight full-page ornamental titles, and four large colored chromos, illustrating the several departments of the work, beautifully printed on tinted paper. The book is issued in the best style, being printed on fine sized paper, and handsomely bound. Extra cloth, gilt side and back, extra gold, beveled boards..$2.00

Mrs. Crowen's American Lady's Cookery Book. Giving

every variety of information for ordinary and holiday occasions, and containing over 1,200 Original Receipts for Preparing and Cooking Soups and Broths, Fish and Oysters, Clams, Mussels, Crabs and Terrapins, Meats of all kinds, Poultry and Game, Eggs and Cheese, Vegetables and Salads, Sauces of all kinds, fancy Desserts, Puddings and Custards, Pies and Tarts, Bread and Biscuit, Rolls and Cakes, Preserves and Jellies, Pickles and Catsups, Potted Meats, etc., etc.; with valuable hints on choosing and purchasing all kinds of provisions, on preparing ripe fruits for the table, Bills of Fare for the guidance of young housekeepers, the arrangement of the table for Dinner Parties, the Etiquette of the Dinner-table, Cookery for invalids, Carving made easy, etc., the whole being a complete system of American Cookery. By Mrs. T. J. Crowen. 480 pages, 12mo, cloth...........$1.50

The Reason Why of General Science. A careful collection

of some thousands of Reasons for things which, though generally known, are imperfectly understood. It is a complete Encyclopedia of Science; and persons who have never had the advantage of a liberal education may, by the aid of this volume, acquire knowledge which the study of years only would impart in the ordinary course. It explains everything in Science that can be thought of, and the whole is arranged with a full index. 346 pages, bound in cloth, gilt, and illustrated with numerous wood-cuts..$1.50

Biblical Reason Why. A Handsome Book for Biblical Stu-

dents, and a Guide to Family Scripture Readings. This work gives 1,494 Reasons, founded upon the Bible, and assigned by the most eminent Divines and Christian Philosophers, for the great and all-absorbing events recorded in the History of the Bible, the Life of our Saviour and the Acts of his Apostles. It will enable Sunday-school teachers to explain most of the obscure and difficult passages that occur in the Scriptures. Cloth, gilt..$1.50

The Reason Why of Natural History. An illustrated book

of popular information on all matters relating to Birds. Beasts. Fishes, Reptiles, etc. It gives the Reasons for hundreds of interesting facts in connection with Zoology, and affords an immense amount of instruction in the peculiar habits and instincts of the various orders of the Animal Kingdom. Bound in cloth, gilt...... ....$1.50

The Three Volumes of the REASON WHY SERIES are uniform in size and style, and form a valuable addition to every Library.

Souillard's Book of Practical Receipts. For the use of

Families, Druggists, Perfumers, Confectioners, and Dealers in Soaps and Fancy Articles for the Toilet. By F. A. Souillard. Paper covers...25 cts.

The Amateur Printer; *or, Type-Setting at Home.* A thorough

and complete instructor for the amateur in all the details of the Printer's Art, giving practical information in regard to type, ink, paper and all the implements requisite, with illustrated directions for using them in a proper manner. It teaches how to set type in the stick, transfer the matter to the galley and make it up in forms; also how to take proofs and correct them, showing all the signs used by practical proof-readers in correcting proofs; it illustrates the plan of the type-case, showing the relative positions of the compartments allotted to the type of each letter, etc., and the correct manner of replacing or distributing type in the case. The practical instructions given in this work are complete and so plainly described that any amateur can become a good printer by studying and applying the information it contains. Paper covers. Price.......25 cts.

Talk of Uncle George to his Nephew About Draw Poker.

Containing valuable suggestions in connection with this Great American Game; also instructions and directions to Clubs and Social Card Parties, whose members play only for recreation and pastime, with timely warnings to young players. Illustrated. In which Uncle George narrates to his nephew the experience he has gathered in the course of his travels West and East; showing him, in a chatty and familiar style, the devices, tricks, appliances, and advantages by which gentlemanly gamblers fleece the unsophisticated and unwary in the popular game of Draw Poker, and offering him plain and fatherly advice as to the best means for frustrating their efforts and avoiding their traps. Every one who takes a hand at "Draw" will be a gainer by perusing what Uncle George says about it, and become a wiser as well as a richer man. Quarto. Paper. Price..25 cts.

Proctor on Draw-Poker. A Critical Dissertation on "Poker

Principles and Chance Laws." By Prof. RICHARD A. PROCTOR. An interesting Treatise on the Laws and Usages which govern the Game of Draw-Poker, with Practical Remarks upon the Chances and Probabilities of the Game, and a Critical Analysis of the Theories and Statistics advanced by Blackbridge and other writers on the subject, and especially in regard to their doctrines relating to cumulative recurrences. Small quarto...15 cts.

Lander's Revised Work of Odd-Fellowship. Containing all

the Lectures, complete, with Regulations for Opening, Conducting, and Closing a Lodge; together with Forms of Initiation, Charges of the Various Officers, etc., with the Complete work in the following Degrees: Initiation; First, or Pink Degree; Second, or Royal Blue Degree; Third, or Scarlet Degree. By EDWIN F. LANDER. This hand-book of the Revised Work of the Independent Order of Odd-Fellowship has been prepared in conformity with the amendments and alterations adopted by the Sovereign Grand Lodge of Canada in September, 1880. 16mo; paper cover, 25 cts.

The Jolly Joker; or, a Laugh all Round. An Immense Col

lection of the Funniest Jokes, Drollest Anecdotes and most Side-Splitting Oddities in existence, profusely illustrated from beginning to end, in the most mirth-provoking style. The illustrations alone are sufficient for a constant and long-sustained series of good, square laughs for all time. 12mo, 144 pages, illustrated cover............... .. ..25 cts.

Some Comicalities. A Whole Volume of Jolly Jokes, Quaint

Anecdotes, Funny Stories, Brilliant Witticisms, and Crushing Conundrums, with as many droll illustrations to the page—and every page at that—as can be crowded into it. 144 pages. Illustrated cover.....25 cts.

Dick's Dutch, French and Yankee Dialect Recitations.

An unsurpassed Collection of Droll Dutch Blunders, Frenchmen's Funny Mistakes, and Ludicrous and Extravagant Yankee Yarns, each Recitation being in its own dialect.

DUTCH DIALECT.

Der Mule Shtood on der Steamboad Deck.
Go Vay, Becky Miller.
Der Drummer.
Mygel Snyder's Barty.
Snyder's Nose.
Dyin' Vords of Isaac.
Fritz und I.
Betsey und I Hafe Bust Ub.
Schneider sees Leah.
Dot Funny Leetle Baby.
Schnitzerl's Philosopede.
Der Dog und der Lobster.
Schlosser's Ride.
Mine Katrine.
Maud Muller.
Ein Deutsches Lied.
Hans and Fritz.
Schneider's Tomatoes.
Deitsche Advertisement.
Vas Bender Henshpecked.
Life, Liberty and Lager.
Der Goot Lookin' Shnow.
Mr. Schmidt's Mistake.
Home Again.
Dot Surprise Party.
Der Wreck of der Hezberus.
Isaac Rosenthal on the Chinese Question.
Hans Breitmann's Party.
Shoo Flies.
A Dutchman's Answer.
How Jake Schneider Went Blind.
I Vash so Glad I Vash Here.
The Dutchman and the Yankee.
How the Dutchman Killed the Woodchuck.

Der Nighd Pehind Grisdmas.
The Dutchman's Snake.
Yoppy's Varder und Hees Drubbles.
Dhree Shkaders.
Katrina Likes Me Poody Vell.
Hans in a Fix.
Leedle Yawcob Strauss.
How a Dutchman was Done.
Dot Lambs vot Mary Had Got.
The Yankee and the Dutchman's Dog.
Zwei Lager.
Schneider's Ride.
The Dutchman and the Small-pox.
Tiamonds on der Prain.
A Dutchman's Testimony in a Steamboad Case.
Hans Breitmann and the Turners.

FRENCH DIALECT.

The Frenchman's Dilemma; or, Number Five Collect Street.
The Frenchman's Revenge.
Noozell and the Organ Grinder.
How a Frenchman Entertained John Bull.
Mr. Rogers and Monsieur Denise.
The Frenchman and the Landlord.
The Frenchman and the Sheep's Trotters.

A Frenchman's Account of the Fall.
I Vant to Fly.
The Generous Frenchman.
The Frenchman and the Flea Powder.
The Frenchman and the Rats.
Mousieur Tonson.
Vat You Please.
The Frenchman and the Mosquitoes.
The Frenchman's Patent Screw.
The Frenchman's Mistake.
Monsieur Mocquard Between Two Fires.

YANKEE DIALECT.

Mrs. Bean's Courtship.
Hez and the Landlord.
Squire Billings' Pickerel.
Deacon Thrush in Meeting.
The Yankee Fireside.
Peter Sorghum in Love.
Mrs. Smart Learns how to Skate.
Capt. Hurricane Jones on the Miracles.
The Dutchman and the Yankee.
The Yankee Landlord.
The Bewitched Clock.
The Yankee and the Dutchman's Dog.
Aunt Hetty on Matrimony.
The Courtin'.
Ebenezer on a Bust.
Sut Lovingood's Shirt.

This Collection contains all the best dialect pieces that are incidentally scattered through a large number of volumes of "Recitations and Readings," besides new and excellent sketches never before published. 170 pages, paper cover..................30 cts.
Bound in boards, cloth back..50 cts.

Dick's Irish Dialect Recitations. A carefully compiled Collection of Rare Irish Stories, Comic, Poetical and Prose Recitations, Humorous Letters and Funny Recitals, all told with the irresistible Humor of the Irish dialect. Containing

Biddy's Troubles.
Birth of St. Patrick, The.
Bridget O'Hoolegoin's Letter.
Connor.
Dermot O'Dowd.
Dick Macnamura's Matrimonial Adventures.
Dying Confession of Paddy M'Cabe.
Father Molloy.
Father Phil Blake's Collection.
Father Roach.
Fight of Hell-Kettle, The.
Handy Andy's Little Mistakes.
How Dennis Took the Pledge.
How Pat Saved his Bacon.
Irish Astronomy.

Irish Coquetry.
Irish Drummer, The.
Irish Letter, An.
Irish Philosopher, The.
Irish Traveler, The.
Irishman's Panorama, The.
Jimmy McBride's Letter.
Jimmy Butler and the Owl.
King O'Toole and St. Kevin.
Kitty Malone.
Love in the Kitchen.
Micky Free and the Priest.
Miss Malony on the Chinese Question.
Mr. O'Hoolahan's Mistake.
Paddy Blake's Echo.
Paddy Fagan's Pedigree.
Paddy McGrath and the Bear.
Paddy O'Rafther.
Paddy the Piper.

Paddy's Dream.
Pat and the Fox.
Pat and the Gridiron.
Pat and his Musket.
Pat and the Oysters.
Pat's Criticism.
Pat's Letter.
Pat O'Flanigan's Colt.
Patrick O'Rouke and the Frogs.
Paudeen O'Rafferty's Say Voyage.
Peter Mulrooney and the Black Filly.
Phaidrig Crohoore.
Rory O'More's Present to the Priest.
St. Kevin.
Teddy O'Toole's Six Bulls.
Wake of Tim O'Hara, The.
Widow Cummiskey, The.

This Collection contains, in addition to new and original pieces, all the very best Recitations in the Irish dialect that can be gathered from a whole library of "Recitation" books. It is full of sparkling witticisms and it furnishes also a fund of entertaining matter for perusal in leisure moments. 170 pages, paper cover..............30 cts.
Bound in boards, cloth back..50 cts.

Beecher's Recitations and Readings. Humorous, Serious,

Dramatic. Designed for Public and Private Exhibitions. Contents :

Miss Maloney at the Dentist's	The Cry of the Children	Signor Billsmethi's Dancing Academy
Lost and Found	The Dutchman and the Small-pox	Der Goot Lookin Shnow
Mygel Snyder's Barty	Sculpin	The Jumping Frog
Magdalena	Pats—Descriptive Recitalon	The Lost Chord
Jim Wolfe and the Cats	A Reader Introduces Himself to an Audience	The Tale of a Leg
The Woolen Doll		That West-side Dog
The Charity Dinner	A Dutchman's Dolly Varden	How Dennis Took the Pledge
Go-Morrow; or, Lots Wife	"Rock of Ages"	The Fisherman's Summons
The Wind and the Moon	Feeding the Black Fillies	Badger's Debut as Hamlet
Dyin' Words of Isaac	The Hornet	Hezekiah Stole the Spoons
Maude Muller in Dutch	The Glove and the Lions	Paddy's Dream
Moses the Sassy	I Vant to Fly	Victuals and Drink
Yarn of the "Nancy Bell"	That Dog of Jim Smiley's	How Jake Schneider Went Blind
Paddy the Piper	The Faithful Soul	Aurelia's Young Man
Schneider sees "Leah"	"My New Pittayatees"	Mrs. Brown on Modern Houses
Caldwell of Springfield	Mary Ann's Wedding	Farm Yard Song
Artemus Ward's Panorama	An Inquiring Yankee	Murphy's Pork Barrel
Tale of a Servant Girl	The Three Bells	The Prayer Seeker
How a Frenchman Entertained John Bull	Love in a Balloon	An Extraordinary Phenomenon
Tiamondts on der Prain	Mrs. Brown on the Streets	The Case of Young Bangs
King Robert of Sicily	Shoo Flies	A Mule Ride in Florida
Gloverson the Mormon	Discourse by the Rev. Mr. Bosan	Dhree Shkaders
De Pint wid Ole Pete	Without the Children	
Pat and the Pig		
The Widow Bedott's Letter		

Paper covers. Price - - - - - - - - - - - - - - - - **30cts.**
Bound in boards, cloth back - - - - - - - - - - - - - **50cts.**

Dick's Ethiopian Scenes, Variety Sketches and Stump

Speeches. Containing the following Rich Collection of Negro Dialogues, Scenes, Farces, End-Men's Jokes, Gags, Rollicking Stories, Excruciating Conundrums, Questions and Answers for Bones, Tambo and Interlocutor, etc. Contents :

I's Gwine to Jine de Masons	Speech on Bolls	Brudder Bones in Clover
Jes' Nail dat Mink to de Stable Do'—Oration	How Bones Cured a Smoky Chimney	Artemus Ward's Advice to Husbands
But the Villain still Pursned Her—A Thrilling Tale	Sermon on Keards, Hosses, Fiddlers, etc.	Where the Lion Roareth, and the Wang-Doodle Mourneth
Bones at a Free-and-Easy	Huggin' Lamp-Posts	Romeo and Juliet in 1880
Buncombe Speech	Not Opposed to Matrimony	Artemus Ward's Panorama
Shakespeare Improved	How Pat Sold a Sermon	Brudder Benes as a Carpet-Bagger—Interlocutor and Bones
Lud Gag—Bones and Tambo	The Coopers—one Act Farce	
A Man of Nerve—Comic Sketch	Questions Easily Answered —Bones and Tambo	Major Jones' Fourth of July Oration
End Gag—Bones and Tambo	Examination in Natural History—Minstrel Dialogue	Curiosities for a Museum—Minstrel Dialogue
Uncle Pete—Darkey Sketch	O'Quirk's Sinecure	Burlesque Oration on Matrimony
The Rival Darkeys	The Widower's Speech	Brudder Bones on the Raging Canawl
The Stage-Struck Darkey	Bones at a Raffle	The Snackin'-Turtle Man—Ethiopian Sketch
Add Ryman's Fourth of July Oration	Uncle Pete's Sermon	
Absent-Mindedness—Bones and Tambo	Bones at a Soiree—Interlocutor and Bones	Bones' Dream—Ethiopian Sketch
Don't Call a Man a Liar	Speech on Woman's Rights	Come and Hug Me
The Mysterious Larkey	Bones' Discovery	Widow O'Brien's Toast
Rev. Uncle Jim's Sermon	Mark Twain Introduces Himself — Characteristic Speech	Scenes at the Police Court —Musical Minstrel Dialogue
The 'Possum-Run Debating Society		
Tim Murphy's Irish Stew	Speech on Happiness	Brudder Bones as a Log-Roller
Brudder Bones in Love—Interlocutor and Bones	Burnt Corkers—Minstrel Dialogue	De Pint Wid Old Pete—Negro Dialect Recitation
'Lixey; or, The Old Gum Game—Negro Scene	The Nervous Woman	A Touching Appeal—Dutch Dialect Recitation
Brudder Bones' Duel	The Five Senses—Minstrel Dialogue	Wounded in the Corners—Darkey Dialogue
Brudder Bones' Sweetheart	The Dutchman's Experience	
Brudder Bones in Hard Luck	Essay on the Wheelbarrow	End Gag—Interlocutor and Bones
Two Left-Bones and Tambo	Bones at a Pic-Nic	
	The Virginia Mummy—Negro Furce	

178 pages, paper covers - - - - - - - - - - - - - - **30cts.**
Bound in board, cloth back - - - - - - - - - - - - - **50cts.**

Tambo's End-Men's Minstrel Gags. Containing some of the

best Jokes and Repartees of the most celebrated "burnt cork" performers of our day. Tambo and Bones in all sorts and manner of scrapes. This Book is full of Burnt-Cork Drolleries, Funny Stories, Colored Conundrums, Gags and Witty Repartee, all the newest side-splitting conversations between Tambo, Bones, and the Interlocutor, and will be found useful alike to the professional and amateur performer.
Contents :

A Bird that can't be Plucked
Annihilating Time
At Last
Bashful
Bet, The
Big Fortune, A
Blackberrying
Black Swan, The
Bones and his little Game
Bones and the Monkey Tricks
Bones as a Fortune Teller
Bones as a Legitimate Actor
Bones as a Pilot
Bones as a Prize Fighter
Bones as a "Stugent"
Bones as a Traveler
Bones as a Victim to the Pen
Bones as a Walkist
Bones assists at the Performance of a New Piece
Bones attends a Seance
Bones finds Himself Famous
Bones gets Dunned
Bones gets Stuck
Bones has a Small Game with the Parson
Bones' Horse Race
Bones in an Affair of Honor
Bones in Love
Bones keeps a Boarding House
Bones on the War Path
Bones on George Washington
Bones on the Light Fantastic

Bones Opens a Spout Shop
Bones Plays O'Fella
Bones sees a Ghost
Bones Slopes with Sukey Sly
Bones tells a "Fly" Story
Brother will come home to-night
Bones as a Carpet Bagger
Bones as an Inkslinger
Bones in a New Character
Bones In Clover
Bones' Love Scrape
"Cullud" Ball, The
Conundrums
Curious Boy
Dancing Mad
Dat's What I'd Like to Know
Definitions
De Mudder of Invention
Difference, The
Don't Kiss every Puppy
"Far Away in Alabam' "
First White Man, The
Fishy Argument
Four-Eleven-Forty-Four
Four Meetings, The
From the Polks
Girl at the Sewing Machine
Hard Times
Hard to take a Hint
Heavy Spell, A
Highfalutin'
Horrible !
How Bones became a Minstrel
How Tambo took his Bitters
How to do it

Impulsive Oration
Inquisitive
Jealousest of her Sect
Legal Problem, A
Liberal Discount for Cash
Manager in a Fix, The
Mathematics
Merry Life, A
Momentous Question
Mosquitoes
Music
Notes
Ob Course
Our Shop Girls
Pomp and Ephy Green
Presidency on de Brain
Proposed Increase of Taxes
Railroad Catastrophe
Reality versus Romance
Rough on Tambo
Sassy Sam and Susie Long
School's In
Shakespeare with a Vengeance
Simple Sum in Arithmetic
Sleighing in the Park
Sliding Down the Hill
Style
Sublime
Swearing by Proxy
Tambo's Traveling Agent
That Dear Old Home
"The Pervisions, Josiar"
Thieves
Tonsorial
Toast, A
Uncle Eph's Lament
Waiting to See Him Off
You Bet
And 40 popular songs and dances.

Everything new and rich. Paper covers - - - - - - - - - 30cts.
Bound in boards, with cloth back - - - - - - - - - 50cts.

McBride's Comic Speeches and Recitations. Designed for

Schools, Literary and Social Circles. By H. Elliott McBride, Author of "McBride's Humorous Dialogues," etc., etc. This is one of the very best series of original speeches, in Yankee, Darkey, Spread-Eagle and village styles, with a number of diverting addresses and recitations, and funny stories, forming an excellent volume of selections for supplying the humorous element of an exhibition. Contents:

A Burst of Indignation
Disco'se by a Colored Man
A Trumpet Sarmon
Sarmon on Skilletvillers
Nancy Matilda Jones
Hezekiah's Proposal
About the Billikinses
Betsy and I are Out Once More
A Stump Speech
About Katharine
Deborah Doolittle's Speech on Women's Rights
A Salutatory
A Mournful Story

An Address to Schoolboys
Zachariah Popp's Courtship and Marriage
A Sad Story
How to Make Hasty Pudding
My Matilda Jane
Courtship, Marriage, Separation and Reunion
Lecture by a Yankee
A Colored Man's Disco'se on Different Subjects
A Girl's Address to Boys
McSwinger's Fate

Peter Peabody's Stump Speech
Mr. Styx Rejoices on Account of a New Well Spring
Victuals and Drink
Speech by Billy Higgins on the Destruction of His Rambo Apple Tree
A Boy's Address to Young Ladies
An Old Man's Address to Young Wives
Salu-ta-tat-u-a-ry Valedictory.

Paper covers, illuminated - - - - - - - - - 30cts.
Board covers, illuminated - - - - - - - - - 50cts.

Burton's Amateur Actor.

A Complete Guide to Private Theatricals; giving plain directions for arranging, decorating and lighting the Stage and its appurtenances, with rules and suggestions for mounting, rehearsing and performing all kinds of Plays, Parlor Pantomimes and Shadow Pantomimes. Illustrated with numerous engravings, and including a selection of original Plays, with Prologues, Epilogues, etc. By C. E. Burton.

CONTENTS.

How to form an Amateur Company.
Duties of the Manager and Prompter.
Theatrical Music.
Rules for an Amateur Company.
How to Arrange a Stage.
How to Make a Curtain.
How to Light the Stage.
Colored and Calcium Light Effects.
How to Make and Paint the Scenes.
How to Imitate Moonlight, Sunrise, Thunder, Rain, Wind and various other effects.
How to make all kinds of "Properties."
How to make up Dresses, Wigs, Beards, etc.
How to "make up" the Face to imitate Old Men and other characters.
General Directions for Acting.
Stage Business, Entrances and Exits.
Four Appropriate Prologues; Three Epilogues.

On the Selection of Plays.
A Family Fix. Comedy for Three Males and three Females.
The Philopena. Comedy for two Males and one Female.
Directions for Performing Parlor Pantomimes.
Love's Obstacles; or, Jack's Triumph. An Original Parlor Pantomime.
Complete Directions for Performing Shadow Pantomimes.
Detailed Instructions for producing all Shadow Illusions.
The Feejee Islanders at Home. An Original and unequaled Shadow Pantomime.
A list of Farces. Comedies, etc., specially adapted to Parlor Performances, with the Characters of Each Enumerated and Described.

16mo, illuminated paper covers. Price...................................30 cts.
Bound in Boards..50 cts.

Howard's Book of Drawing-Room Theatricals.

A collection of short and amusing plays in one act and one scene, especially adapted for private performances; with practical directions for their preparation and management. Some of the plays are adapted for performers of one sex only.

CONTENTS.	Males.	Females.	CONTENTS.	Males.	Females.
Explanations of stage directions.			His First Brief.................	3	2
Hints to Amateurs.			A Sudden Arrival.............	5	
The Student's Frolic..........	3	2	A Medical Man...............	2	1
A Household Fairy...........	1	1	A Terrible Secret.............	2	2
A Kiss in the Dark...........	2	3	Poisoned......................	4	
Mrs. Willis' Will............		5	An Eligible Situation.........	2	6
Jack of all Trades...........	6		"Wanted a Young Lady"....	2	1

Paper Covers. Price..30 cts.
Bound in boards, with cloth back.......................................50 cts.

Tambo's Erd-Men's Minstrel Gags.

Containing some of the best jokes and repartees of the most celebrated "burnt cork" performers of our day. Tambo and Bones in all sorts and manner of scrapes. Also containing a rich collection of Ballads, humorous and pathetic. Darkey Dialogues, Sketches, Plantation Scenes, Eccentric Doings, Humorous Lectures, Laughable Interludes, Huge Africanisms, Burlesque Stump Speeches, Mirth-provoking Witticisms, Conundrums, Yarns, Plantation Songs and Dances, etc., etc. In short, a complete Hand-Book of Burnt Cork Drollery, which will be found alike useful to the professional and amateur. Everything new and rich. Paper covers..............30 cts
Bound in boards, with cloth back...................................50 cts

Tony Denier's Parlor Tableaux, or Living Pictures.

Containing about eighty popular subjects, with plain and explicit directions for arranging the stage, dressing-rooms, lights, full description of costumes, duties of stage manager, properties and scenery required, and all the necessary directions for getting them up. Among the contents there are nine tableaux for *male* and an equal number for *female* characters only. A great number of them introduce groups of boys, and many more groups of girls only; others again introducing both; and still more in which entire classes can take part. Everything is stated in a plain, simple manner, so that it will be easily understood; everything like style or un necessary show has been avoided. For public or private entertainment, there is nothing which is so interesting as the tableau. Price....25 cts

Tony Denier's Secret of Performing Shadow Pantomimes.

Showing how to get them up and how to act in them; with full and concise instructions and numerous illustrations. Also full and complete descriptions of properties and costumes.

CONTENTS.

Introduction; Shadow Bluff, or, Who's Who? Tooth Drawing Extraordinary; Amputation like Winking; The Haunted House; We Won't Go Home till Morning; Jocko, or the Mischievous Monkey; The Madcap Barber; Cribbage, or, The Devil among the Cards; The Lover's Stratagem; The Game of Base Ball; Regular Hash, or, The Boarding-House Conspiracy; The Mechanical Statue; The African Serenaders; The Model Prize Fight; The Magic Cask, or, The Industrious and Idle Apprentice; The Tragical Duel, or, The Comical Rivals; Old Dame Trot and her Comical Cat.

Price.....................25 cts

Brudder Bones' Book of Stump Speeches and Burlesque Orations.

Also containing Humorous Lectures, Dialogues, Plantation Scenes, Negro Farces and Burlesques, Laughable Interludes and Comic Recitations, interspersed with Dutch, Irish, French and Yankee Stories. Compiled and edited by John F. Scott.

This book contains some of the best hits of the leading negro delineators of the present time, as well as mirth-provoking jokes and repartees of the most celebrated End-Men of the day, and specially designed for the introduction of fun in an evening's entertainment. Price...........30 cts.
Bound in boards............. ....50 cts.

Burton's Amateur Actor.

A complete guide to Private Theatricals; giving plain directions for arranging, decorating and lighting the Stage; with rules and suggestions for mounting, rehearsing and performing all kinds of Plays, Parlor Pantomimes and Shadow Pantomimes. Illustrated with numerous engravings, and including a selection of original Plays, with Prologues, Epilogues, etc. 16mo, illuminated paper cover...30 cts.
Bound in boards, with cloth back..............................50 cts.

READINGS AND RECITATIONS.

Kavanaugh's New Speeches and Dialogues for Young Children. This is an entirely new series of Recitations and short Dialogues, by Mrs. Russell Kavanaugh. Containing easy pieces in plain language, readily understood by little children, and expressly adapted for School Exhibitions and Christmas and other juvenile celebrations. Paper cover...80 cts.
Bound in boards, cloth back...50 cts.

Kavanaugh's Exhibition Reciter, for Very Little Children. A collection of entirely Original Recitations, Dialogues, Short Speeches and Speaking Tableaux, adapted for very little boys and girls; including also a variety of pieces, humorous, serious and dramatic, suitable for children from Three to Ten Years Old. Paper covers..............30 cts.
Bound in board covers...50 cts.

Kavanaugh's Juvenile Speaker. For Very Little Boys and and Girls. Containing short and easily-learned Speeches and Dialogues, expressly adapted for School Celebrations, May-Day Festivals and other Children's Entertainments. Embracing one hundred and twenty-three effective pieces. By Mrs. Russell Kavanaugh. Illuminated paper cover...30 cts.
Bound in boards, cloth back...50 cts.

Dick's Series of Recitations and Readings, Nos. 1 to 15. Comprising a carefully compiled selection of Humorous, Pathetic, Eloquent, Patriotic and Sentimental Pieces in Poetry and Prose, exclusively designed for Recitation or Reading. Edited by Wm. B. Dick. Each number of the Series contains about 180 pages. Illuminated paper cover, each...30 cts.
Bound in full cloth...50 cts.

Beecher's Recitations and Readings. Humorous, Serious, Dramatic, including Prose and Poetical Selections in Dutch, Yankee, Irish, Negro and other Dialects. 180 pages, paper covers.................30 cts.
Bound in boards, cloth back...50 cts.

Howard's Recitations. Comic, Serious and Pathetic. Being a collection of fresh Recitations in Prose and Poetry, suitable for Exhibitions and Evening Parties. 180 pages, paper covers..............30 cts.
Bound in boards, cloth back...50 cts.

Spencer's Book of Comic Speeches and Humorous Recitations. A collection of Comic Speeches, Humorous Prose and Poetical Recitations, Laughable Dramatic Scenes and Eccentric Dialect Stories. 192 pages, paper covers...30 cts.
Bound in boards, cloth back...50 cts.

Wilson's Book of Recitations and Dialogues. Containing a choice selection of Poetical and Prose Recitations. Designed as an Assistant to Teachers and Students in preparing Exhibitions. 188 pages, paper covers...30 cts.
Bound in boards, with cloth back.....................................50 cts.

Barton's Comic Recitations and Humorous Dialogues. A variety of Comic Recitations in Prose and Poetry, Eccentric Orations and Laughable Interludes. 180 pages, paper covers..............30 cts.
Bound in boards, with cloth back....................................50 cts.

Martine's Droll Dialogues and Laughable Recitations. A collection of Humorous Dialogues, Comic Recitations, Brilliant Burlesques and Spirited Stump Speeches. 188 pages, paper covers...........30 cts.
Bound in boards, with cloth back.....................................50 cts.

**** CATALOGUES SENT FREE.**

DIALOGUE BOOKS.

Graham's School Dialogues for Young People. Being a new and original collection of Dialogues intended for Anniversaries and Exhibitions, carefully prepared and well calculated to develop dramatic talent. 176 pages, illuminated paper cover.................................(0 c s. Bound in boards, cloth back....................................50 cts.

McBride's New Dialogues. Especially designed for School and Literary Amateur Entertainments; containing twenty-four entirely New and Original Dialogues, introducing Irish, Yankee, and other eccentric characters. By H. Elliott McBride. 178 pages, illuminated paper cover..30 cts. Bound in boards...50 cts.

McBride's Temperance Dialogues. Designed for the use of Schools, Temperance Societies, Bands of Hope, Divisions, Lodges and Literary Circles. Introducing Yankee, Dutch, Irish, Negro and other dialect characters. By H. Elliott McBride. 183 pages, paper cover 30 cts. Bound in boards, cloth back....................................50 cts.

McBride's Humorous Dialogues. A collection of New Dialogues, full of humor and witty repartee; some of them introducing Irish, Dutch, Yankee and other dialect characters. 192 pages, paper cover ....30 cts. Bound in boards, cloth back....................................50 cts.

McBride's Comic Dialogues. A collection of twenty-three Original Humorous Dialogues, especially designed for the display of Amateur dramatic talent, and introducing a variety of sentimental, sprightly, comic and genuine Yankee characters, and other ingeniously developed eccentricities. By H. Elliott McBride. 180 pages, illuminated paper covers..30 cts. Bound in boards, cloth back....................................50 cts.

McBride's All Kinds of Dialogues. A collection of twenty-five Original, Humorous and Domestic Dialogues, introducing Yankee, Irish, Dutch and other characters. Excellently adapted for Amateur Performances. 180 pages, illuminated paper covers..............30 cts. Bound in boards, cloth back....................................50 cts.

Holmes' Very Little Dialogues for Very Little Folks. Containing forty-seven New and Original Dialogues, with short and easy parts, almost entirely in words of one syllable, suited to the capacity and comprehension of very young children. Paper covers...........30 cts. Bound in boards, cloth back....................................50 cts.

Frost's Dialogues for Young Folks. A collection of thirty-six Original, Moral and Humorous Dialogues. Adapted for boys and girls between the ages of ten and fourteen years. Paper covers........30 cts. Bound in boards, cloth back....................................50 cts

Frost's New Book of Dialogues. Containing twenty-nine entirely New and Original Humorous Dialogues for boys and girls between the ages of twelve and fifteen years. 180 pages, paper covers......30 cts. Bound in boards, cloth back....................................50 cts.

Frost's Humorous and Exhibition Dialogues. This is a collection of twenty-five Sprightly Original Dialogues in Prose and Verse, intended to be spoken at School Exhibitions. 178 pages, paper covers 30 cts. Bound in boards..50 cts.

⁎ CATALOGUES SENT FREE.

AMATEUR THEATRICALS.

All the plays in the following excellent books are especially designed for Amateur performance. The majority of them are in one act and one scene, and may be represented in any moderate-sized parlor, without much preparation of costume or scenery.

Kavanagh's Humorous Dramas for School Exhibitions and Private Theatricals. This collection of Dramas are all original, and were written expressly for School and Parlor performance. Paper covers..30 cts
Bound in boards...50 cts

Barmby's Musical Plays for Young People. Suitable for Private Theatricals. These Plays are in Burlesque style and entirely in Rhyme; they are irresistably Comical in expression, and elegant in construction. Each Play includes the Vocal Score and Piano Accompaniment to all Songs, Duets and Choruses introduced, making it complete in itself, both in text and music. 201 pages, paper covers.............30 cts
Bound in boards...50 cts

Parlor Theatricals; or, Winter Evenings' Entertainment. Containing Acting Proverbs, Dramatic Charades, Drawing-Room Pantomimes, a Musical Burlesque and an amusing Farce, with instructions for Amateurs. Illustrated with engravings. Paper covers............30 cts
Bound in boards, with cloth back..50 cts

Howard's Book of Drawing-Room Theatricals. A collection of twelve short and amusing plays. Some of the plays are adapted for performers of one sex only. 180 pages, paper covers..........30 cts
Bound in boards, with cloth back..50 cts

Hudson's Private Theatricals. A collection of fourteen humorous plays. Four of these plays are adapted for performance by males only, and three are for females. 180 pages, paper covers...........30 cts
Bound in boards, with cloth back..50 cts

Nugent's Burlesque and Musical Acting Charades. Containing ten Charades, all in different styles, two of which are easy and effective Comic Parlor Operas, with Music and Piano-forte Accompaniments. 176 Pages, paper covers....................................80 cts
Bound in boards, with cloth back..50 cts

Frost's Dramatic Proverbs and Charades. Containing eleven Proverbs and fifteen Charades, some of which are for Dramatic Performance, and others arranged for Tableaux Vivants. 176 pages. paper covers..50 cts
Bound in boards, with cloth backs..50 cts

Frost's Parlor Acting Charades. These twelve excellent and original Charades are arranged as short parlor Comedies and Farces, full of brilliant repartee and amusing situations. 182 pages, paper covers..30 cts
Illuminated boards..50 cts

Frost's Book of Tableaux and Shadow Pantomimes. A collection of Tableaux Vivants and Shadow Pantomimes, with stage instructions for Costuming, Grouping, etc. 180 pages, paper covers......80 cts
Bound in boards, with cloth back..50 cts

Frost's Amateur Theatricals. A collection of eight original plays; all short, amusing and new. 180 pages, paper covers.......30 cts
Bound in boards, with cloth back..50 cts

Dick's Original Album Verses and Acrostics.

Containing Original Verses

For Autograph Albums,	For Album Dedications;
To Accompany Bouquets;	To Accompany Philopena Forfeits;
For Birthday Anniversaries;	For Congratulation;
For Wooden, Tin, Crystal, Silver and Golden Weddings;	For Valentines in General, and all Trades and Professions.

It contains also Two Hundred and Eighteen Original Acrostic Verses, the initial letters of each verse forming a different Lady's Christian name, the meaning and derivation of the name being appended to each. The primary object of this book is to furnish entirely fresh and unhackneyed matter for all who may be called upon to fill and adorn a page in a Lady's Album; but it contains also new and appropriate verses to suit Birthday, Wedding, and all other Anniversaries and Occasions to which verses of Compliment or Congratulation are applicable. Paper covers. Price..50 cts. Bound in full cloth.. " ..75 cts.

The Debater, Chairman's Assistant, and

Rules of Order. A manual for Instruction and Reference in all matters pertaining to the Management of Public Meetings according to Parliamentary usages. It comprises:

How to Form and Conduct all kinds of Associations and Clubs,	Rules of Order, and Order of Business, with Mode of Procedure in all Cases.
How to Organize and Arrange Public Meetings, Celebrations, Dinners, Picnics and Conventions;	How to draft Resolutions and other Written Business;
Forms for Constitutions of Lyceums or Institutes, Literary and other Societies;	A Model Debate, introducing the greatest possible variety of points of order, with correct Decisions by the Chairman;
The Powers and Duties of Officers, with Forms for Treasurers', Secretaries', and other Official Reports;	The Rules of Order, in Tabular Form, for instant reference in all Cases of Doubt that may arise, enabling a Chairman to decide on all points at a glance.
The Formation and Duties of Committees;	

The Work is divided into different Sections, for the purpose of Consecutive Instruction as well as Ready Reference, and includes all Decisions and Rulings up to the present day. Paper covers......................30 cts. Bound in boards, cloth back...50 cts.

Dick's Ethiopian Scenes, Variety Sketches

and Stump Speeches. Containing End-Men's Jokes,

Negro Interludes and Farces;	Dialect Sketches and Eccentricities;
Fresh Dialogues for Interlocutor and Banjo;	Dialogues and Repartee for Interlocutor and Bones;
New Stump Speeches;	Quaint Burlesque Sermons;
Humorous Lectures;	Jokes, Quips and Gags.

It includes a number of Amusing Scenes and Negro Acts, and is full of the side-splitting vagaries of the best Minstrel Troupes in existence, besides a number of Original Recitations and Sketches in the Negro Dialect. 178 pages, paper covers..30 cts. Bound in boards, cloth back............... ....50 cts.

Dick's Dutch, French and Yankee Dialect Recitations. An
unsurpassed Collection of Droll Dutch Blunders, Frenchmen's Funny
Mistakes, and Ludicrous and Extravagant Yankee Yarns, each Recitation
being in its own peculiar dialect. To those who make Dialect Recitations
a speciality, this Collection will be of particular service, as it contains all
the best pieces that are incidently scattered through a large number of volumes of "Recitations and Readings," besides several new and excellent
sketches never before published.
170 pages, paper cover..30 cts.
Bound in boards, cloth back.......................................50 cts.

Dick's Irish Dialect Recitations. A carefully compiled
Collection of Rare Irish Stories, Comic, Poetical and Prose Recitations,
Humorous Letters and Funny Recitals, all told with the irresistible Humor
of the Irish Dialect. This Collection contains, in addition to new and original pieces, all the very best Recitations in the Irish Dialect that can be
gathered from a whole library of "Recitation" books.
It is full of the sparkling witticisms and queer conceits of the wittiest
nation on earth, and apart from its special object, it furnishes a fund of
the most entertaining matter for perusal in leisure moments.
170 pages, paper cover..30 cts.
Bound in boards, cloth back.......................................50 cts.

Worcester's Letter-Writer and Book of Business Forms for
Ladies and Gentlemen. Containing Accurate Directions for Conducting
Epistolary Correspondence, with 270 Specimen Letters, adapted to every
Age and Situation in Life, and to Business Pursuits in General; with an
Appendix comprising Forms for Wills, Petitions, Bills, Receipts, Drafts,
Bills of Exchange, Promissory Notes, Executors' and Administrators'
Accounts, etc., etc. The Orthography of the entire work is based on
Worcester's method, which is coming more and more into general use.
This work is divided into two parts, the portion applicable to Ladies being
kept distinct from the rest of the book, in order to provide better facilities
for ready reference.
216 pages. Bound in boards, cloth back...........................50 cts.

Dick's Hand-Book of Cribbage. Containing full directions
for playing all the Varieties of the Game, and the Laws which govern
them. This work is ENTIRELY NEW, and gives the correct method of playing the Six-Card, Five-Card, Two-Handed, Three-Handed, and Four-Handed
Varieties of the Game, with instructive examples, showing clearly all the
combinations of Hand, Crib, and Play, with a thorough investigation of
long sequences in play, and the value of Hands. The Laws of the game
have been carefully revised in accordance with the recognized usages of
the present time, and constitute a reliable authority on all points of the
Game. 18 mo. Cloth, Flexible....................................50 cts.

Dick's Art of Gymnastics. Containing practical and pro-
gressive exercises applicable to all the principal apparatus of a well-ap-
pointed Gymnasium. Profusely illustrated. This work conveys plain and
thorough instruction in the exercises and evolutions taught by the leading
Professors of Gymnastics; so that proficiency may be attained, even
without the aid of a Teacher. It also offers to Teachers a ready-arranged
systematic course for their guidance.
Artistically bound in cloth, 4to..................................$1 00

Dick's Dialogues and Monologues. Containing entirely or-
iginal Dialogues, Monologues, Farces, etc., etc., expressly designed for
parlor performance, full of humor and telling "situations," and requiring
the least possible preparation of Costumes and Scenery to make them
thoroughly effective.
180 pages. 16 mo., paper cover...................................30 cts.
Bound in boards, cloth back......................................50 cts.

Dr. Valentine's Comic Lectures; or, Morsels of Mirth for

the Melancholy. A certain cure for the "blues" and all other serious complaints. Containing Comic Lectures on Heads, Faces, Noses and Mouths; Comic Lectures on Animal Magnetism; Humorous Specimens of Stump Eloquence; Burlesque Specimens of Eloquence; Transactions of Learned Societies; Comical Delineation of Eccentric Characters; Amusing Colloquies and Monologues; Laughable Duologues and Characteristic Drolleries. Illustrated with twelve portraits of Dr. Valentine in his most celebrated characters. 192 pages. Paper cover. Price..30 cts.

Mrs. Partington's Carpet-Bag of Fun. Containing the Queer,

Sayings of Mrs. Partington, and the Funny Doings of her remarkable Son Isaac. Also the most amusing collection extant of Playful Puns, Phunny Poems, Pleasing Prose. Popular Parodies, and Political Pasquinades, Rhymes Without Reason and Reason Without Rhymes, Anecdotes, Conundrums, Anagrams, and, in fact, all other kinds of Grams. Illustrated with 100 most amusing engravings, prepared expressly for this work from designs by the most eminent Comic Artists. Ornamented paper cover..30 cts.

The Comical Doings of a Funny Man. Being the Scrapes

and Adventures of a Practical Joker. Illustrated with Laughable Engravings. Octavo. Price..10 cts.

Chips from Uncle Sam's Jack-Knife. Illustrated with over

100 Comical Engravings, and comprising a collection of over 500 Laughable Stories, Funny Adventures, Comic Poetry, Queer Conundrums. Terrific Puns and Sentimental Sentences. Large octavo..............25 cts.

Fox's Ethiopian Comicalities. Containing Strange Sayings,

Eccentric Doings, Burlesque Speeches. Laughable Drolleries and Funny Stories, as recited by the celebrated Ethiopian Comedian..........10 cts.

Ned Turner's Circus Joke Book. A collection of the best Jokes,

Bon Mots, Repartees, Gems of Wit and Funny Sayings and Doings of the celebrated Equestrian Clown and Ethiopian Comedian, Ned Turner.10 cts.

Ned Turner's Black Jokes. A collection of Funny Stories,

Jokes and Conundrums, interspersed with Witty Sayings and Humorous Dialogues, as given by Ned Turner, the celebrated Ethiopian Delineator..10 cts.

Ned Turner's Clown Joke Book. Containing the best Jokes

and Gems of Wit, composed and delivered by the favorite Equestrian Clown, Ned Turner. Selected and arranged by G. E. G............10 cts.

Charley White's Joke Book. Containing a full exposé of all

the most Laughable Jokes, Witticisms, etc., as told by the celebrated Ethiopian Comedian, Charles White.........................10 cts.

Black Wit and Darky Conversations. By Charles White.

Containing a large collection of laughable Anecdotes, Jokes, Stories, Witticisms and Darky Conversations....................................10 cts.

Yale College Scrapes; or, How the Boys Go it at New

Haven. This is a book of 114 pages, containing accounts of all the famous "Scrapes" and "Sprees" of which Students of Old Yale have been guilty for the last quarter of a century.........................25 cts.

How to Conduct a Debate. A Series of Complete Debates,
Outlines of Debates and Questions for Discussion. In the complete debates, the questions for discussion are defined, the debate formally opened, an array of brilliant arguments adduced on either side, and the debate closed according to parliamentary usages. The second part consists of questions for debate, with heads of arguments, for and against, given in a condensed form, for the speakers to enlarge upon to suit their own fancy. In addition to these are a large collection of debatable questions. The authorities to be referred to for information being given at the close of every debate throughout the work. By F. Rowton. 232 pages.
Paper covers...50 cts
Bound in boards, cloth back................................75 ct

The Amateur Trapper and Trap-Maker's Guide. A complete and carefully prepared treatise on the art of Trapping, Snaring and Netting. This comprehensive work is embellished with fifty engraved illustrations; and these, together with the clear explanations which accompany them, will enable anybody of moderate comprehension to make and set any of the traps described. It also gives the baits usually employed by the most successful Hunters and Trappers, and exposes their secret methods of attracting and catching animals, birds, etc., with scarcely a possibility of failure. Large 16mo, paper covers..................50 cts
Bound in boards, cloth back................................75 cts

How to Write a Composition. The use of this excellent handbook will save the student the many hours of labor too often wasted in trying to write a plain composition. It affords a perfect skeleton of one hundred and seventeen different subjects, with their headings or divisions clearly defined, and each heading filled in with the ideas which the subject suggests; so that all the writer has to do, in order to produce a good composition, is to enlarge on them to suit his taste and inclination.
178 pages, paper covers....................................30 cts
Bound in boards, cloth back................................50 cts

Duncan's Masonic Ritual and Monitor; or, Guide to the
Three Symbolic Degrees of the Ancient York Rite, Entered Apprentice, Fellow Craft and Master Mason. And to the Degrees of Mark Master, Past Master, Most Excellent Master, and the Royal Arch. By Malcom C. Duncan. Explained and Interpreted by copious Notes and numerous Engravings. This is a valuable book for the Fraternity, containing, as it does, the Modern "Work" of the order. No Mason should be without it.
Bound in cloth...$2 50
Leather tucks (pocket-book style), with gilt edges..........3 00

The Laws of Athletics. How to Preserve and Improve
Health, Strength, and Beauty; and to Correct Personal Defects caused by Want of Physical Exercise. How to Train for Walking, Running, Rowing, etc., with the Systems of the Champion Athletes of the World. Including the Latest Laws of all Athletic Games and How to Play Them. By William Wood, Professor of Gymnastics. Paper cover....... 25 cts.
Flexible cloth cover..50 cts.

The Bartender's Guide; or, How to Mix all Kinds of Fancy
Drinks. Containing clear and reliable directions for mixing all the beverages used in the United States. Embracing Punches, Juleps, Cobblers, Cocktails, etc., etc., in endless variety. By Jerry Thomas.
Illuminated paper covers...................................50 cts
Bound in full cloth..75 cts

Spayth's Draughts or Checkers for Beginners. This treatise was written by Henry Spayth, the celebrated player, and is by far the most complete and instructive elementary work on Draughts ever published. Cloth, gilt side..75 cts

Dick's Society Letter Writer for Ladies. Containing

MORE THAN FIVE HUNDRED entirely Original Letters and Notes, with appropriate answers, on all subjects and occasions incident to life in Good Society; including specific instructions in all the details of a well-written letter, and General Hints for Conducting Polite Correspondence. Edited by Wm. B. Dick.

THE CONTENTS EMBRACE THE FOLLOWING SUBJECTS:

Hints on Letter Writing
Letters of Introduction
Answers to Letters of Introduction
Letters and Notes of Invitation
Forms of Cards
Notes of Postponement
Letters and Notes Accepting and
  Declining Invitations
Letters of Apology
Letters of Announcement
Notes and Letters Accompanying Gifts
Notes and Letters of Acknowledgment
Notes and Letters Soliciting Favors
Notes and Letters Offering Favors
Notes and Letters Granting or Declining Favors

Notes Soliciting Donations
Notes and Letters Granting or
  Refusing Donations
Letters of Congratulation
Letters of Condolence
Answers to Letters of Condolence
Household Letters and Notes
Forms of Household Orders
Answers to Household Letters
Business Letters and Notes
Shopping by Mail
Forms of Orders
Miscellaneous Business Letters
Family Letters
Miscellaneous Notes and Letters

These new and Original Letters have been written expressly for this work in an easy and elegant style, furnishing excellent models which fulfill all the social, formal and business conditions that occur in the Correspondence of Ladies who move in refined society. There are many otherwise highly accomplished ladies who experience considerable difficulty in inditing a good letter, and frequently find themselves embarrassed from a want of facility in method of expression and proper form; to them this work is especially adapted, and will afford them valuable aid in rendering the task of correspondence easy and light. 12mo., Cloth, Price.........$1.25

Dick's Mysteries of the Hand; or, Palmistry made Easy.

Translated, Abridged and Arranged from the French Works of Desbarrolles, D'Arpentigny and De Para d'Hermes. This book is a concise summary of the elaborate works of the above-named authorities on Palmistry.

The various lines and mounts on the palm of the hand, and the typical formation of the hand and fingers are all clearly explained and illustrated by diagrams. The meaning to be deduced from the greater or less development of these mounts and lines (each of which has its own signification), also from the length, thickness and shape of the thumb and fingers, and from the mutual bearing they exercise on each other, is all distinctly explained.

Complete facility for instant reference is insured by means of marginal notes by which any point of detail may be found and consulted at a glance.

By means of this book the hitherto occult mystery of Palmistry is made simple and easy, and the whole Art may be acquired without difficulty or delay. It is emphatically Palmistry in a nutshell, and by its use, character and disposition can be discerned and probable future destiny foretold with surprising accuracy. Illuminated paper cover...........50 cts.

Dick's Hand-Book of Whist. Containing Pole's and Clay's

Rules for playing the modern scientific game; the Club Rules of Whist, and two interesting Double Dummy Problems. This is a thorough treatise on the game of Whist, taken from "The American Hoyle" which is the standard authority. It covers all the points and intricacies which arise in the game; including the acknowledged code of etiquette observed by the players, with Drayson's remarks on Trumps, their use and abuse, and all the modern methods of signalling between partners. Price.......25 cts.

The Amateur Printer; or, Type-Setting at Home.

A thorough and complete instructor for the amateur in all the details of the Printer's Art, giving practical information in regard to type, ink, paper and all the implements requisite, with illustrated directions for using them in a proper manner. It teaches how to set type in the stick, transfer the matter to the galley and make it up in forms; also how to take proofs and correct them, showing all the signs used by practical proof-readers in correcting proofs; it illustrates the plan of the type-case, showing the relative positions of the compartments allotted to the type of each letter, etc., and the correct manner of replacing or distributing type in the case. The practical instructions given in this work are complete and so plainly described that any amateur can become a good printer by studying and applying the information it contains. Paper covers. Price.......25 cts.

Talk of Uncle George to his Nephew About Draw Poker.

Containing valuable suggestions in connection with this Great American Game; also instructions and directions to Clubs and Social Card Parties, whose members play only for recreation and pastime, with timely warnings to young players. Illustrated. In which Uncle George narrates to his nephew the experience he has gathered in the course of his travels West and East; showing him, in a chatty and familiar style, the devices, tricks, appliances, and advantages by which gentlemanly gamblers fleece the unsophisticated and unwary in the popular game of Draw Poker, and offering him plain and fatherly advice as to the best means for frustrating their efforts and avoiding their traps. Every one who takes a hand at "Draw" will be a gainer by perusing what Uncle George says about it, and become a wiser as well as a richer man. Quarto. Paper. Price..25 cts.

Proctor on Draw-Poker.

A Critical Dissertation on " Poker Principles and Chance Laws." By Prof. RICHARD A. PROCTOR. An interesting Treatise on the Laws and Usages which govern the Game of Draw-Poker, with Practical Remarks upon the Chances and Probabilities of the Game, and a Critical Analysis of the Theories and Statistics advanced by Blackbridge and other writers on the subject, and especially in regard to their doctrines relating to cumulative recurrences. Small quarto...15 cts.

Lander's Revised Work of Odd-Fellowship.

Containing all the Lectures, complete, with Regulations for Opening, Conducting, and Closing a Lodge; together with Forms of Initiation, Charges of the Various Officers, etc., with the Complete work in the following Degrees: Initiation; First, or Pink Degree; Second, or Royal Blue Degree; Third, or Scarlet Degree. By EDWIN F. LANDER. This hand-book of the Revised Work of the Independent Order of Odd-Fellowship has been prepared in conformity with the amendments and alterations adopted by the Sovereign Grand Lodge of Canada in September, 1880. 16mo, paper cover, 25 cts.

The Jolly Joker; or, a Laugh all Round.

An Immense Collection of the Funniest Jokes, Drollest Anecdotes and most Side-Splitting Oddities in existence, profusely illustrated from beginning to end, in the most mirth-provoking style. The illustrations alone are sufficient for a constant and long-sustained series of good, square laughs for all time. 12mo, 144 pages, illustrated cover...................................25 cts.

Some Comicalities.

A Whole Volume of Jolly Jokes, Quaint Anecdotes, Funny Stories, Brilliant Witticisms, and Crushing Conundrums, with as many droll illustrations to the page—and every page at that—as can be crowded into it. 144 pages Illustrated cover.....25 cts.

McBride's New Dialogues. Especially designed for School

and Literary Amateur Entertainments; containing entirely New and Original Dialogues, introducing Irish, Yankee, and other eccentric characters. By H. ELLIOTT McBRIDE.

CONTENTS.

A Happy Woman.	*An Uncomfortable Predicament.*
The Somnambulist.	*The Opening Speech.*
Those Thompsons.	*The Cucumber Hill Debating Club.*
Playing School.	*Married by the New Justice.*
Tom and Sally.	*Bread on the Waters.*
Assisting Hezekiah.	*An Unsuccessful Advance.*
A Visit to the Oil Regions.	*When Women Have Their Rights.*
Breaking up the Exhibition.	*Only Another Footprint.*
Turning Around.	*Rosabella's Lovers.*
A Little Boy's Debate.	*A Smart Boy.*
The Silver Lining.	*A Heavy Shower.*
Restraining Jotham.	*Master of the Situation.*
A Shoemaker's Troubles.	

The marked favor with which the four preceding volumes have been received suggested the necessity for an increased variety of new eccentric and characteristic pieces, to form an addition to the repertoire contained in " McBride's Comic Dialogues," " McBride's All Kinds of Dialogues," " McBride's Humorous Dialogues," and " McBride's Temperance Dialogues." They are all written with a view to develop dramatic talent, and abound in quaint humor, Dialect Drolleries, and telling 'tage " situations." 16mo, 178 pages, illuminated paper cover..................30 cts.
Bound in boards...50 cts.

Dick's Book of Toasts, Speeches and Responses. Contain-

ing Toasts and Sentiments for Public and Social Occasions, and specimen Speeches with appropriate replies suitable for the following occasions :

Public Dinners,	*Friendly Meetings,*
Social Dinners,	*Weddings and their Anniversaries,*
Convivial Gatherings,	*Army and Navy Banquets,*
Art and Professional Banquets,	*Patriotic and Political Occasions,*
Manufacturers' Meetings,	*Trades' Unions and Dinners,*
Agricultural and Commercial Festivals,	*Benedicts' and Bachelors' Banquets,*
Special Toasts for Ladies,	*Masonic Celebrations,*
Christmas, Thanksgiving and other Festivals,	*Sporting Coteries,*
	All Kinds of Occasions.

This work includes an instructive dissertation on the Art of making amusing After-dinner Speeches, giving hints and directions by the aid of which persons with only ordinary intelligence can make an entertaining and telling speech. Also, Correct Rules and Advice for Presiding at Table.
The use of this work will render a poor and diffident speaker fluent and witty—and a good speaker better and wittier, besides affording an immense fund of anecdotes, wit and wisdom, and other serviceable matter to draw upon at will. Paper covers. Price......................30 cts.

How Boggins Was Cured. An intensely ludicrous sketch,

pictorially expressed; showing how Mr. Boggins, who had been reduced to a despairingly crippled state by rheumatism and a complication of other causes, was induced to submit to the wonderful effects of a course of dynamo-electro magnetic therapeutics, tracing the magical and potent effects of the treatment, and the heroic efforts he made while submitting to the doctor's system of pathology ; until, crowned with complete success, he is able to throw aside his crutches and is restored to perfect health and pristine agility. An entirely new and original series of sketches. Funny ! is no name for it. Small quarto. Illustrated............10 cts.

Dick's Games of Patience; or Solitaire with Cards. New and

Revised Edition. Containing Sixty-four Games. Illustrated with Fifty explanatory full-page Tableaux. This treatise on Solitaire, a pastime which is steadily gaining in popularity, embraces a number of new and original Games, and all the Games of Patience at present in favor with the most experienced players. This comprehensive work contains the following Games :

Auld Lang-Syne.	The Beleaguered Castle.	The Fourteens.
Tam O'Shanter.	The Citadel.	Napoleon's Favorite.
The Four Seasons.	The Exiled Kings.	The Fifteen Puzzle.
Simplicity.	Penelope's Web.	The Contra-Dance.
The Gathering of the	Napoleon's Square.	The Betrothal.
Clans.	The Court Yard.	The Reinforcements.
Napoleon at St. Helena.	The Windmill.	The Reserve.
The Calculation.	Leoni's Own.	The Frog.
The Surprise Party.	La Nivernaise.	The Pyramid.
The Four Kings.	The Four Corners.	The Quadrille.
The Clock.	The Baker's Dozen.	The Chatelaine.
The Garden.	The Salic Law.	The Order of Precedence.
The Queen's Audience.	The Sultan of Turkey.	The Congress.
The Phalanx.	The Fortress.	Thirteen Down.
The Idle Year.	The Hemispheres.	The Octagon.
The Chameleon.	The Elevens.	Light and Shade.
La Belle Lucie.	The Chester Game.	St. Louis.
The Shamrocks.	The Shah of Persia.	Rouge et Noir.
The House in the Wood.	The Empress of India.	The Blondes and Bru-
The House on the Hill.	The Zodiac.	nettes.
The Grand Duchess.	The Blockade.	The Royal Cotillion.
The Constitution.	The Besieged City.	Nestor.

Each game is carefully and lucidly described, with the distinctive rules to be observed and hints as to the best means of success in play. The Tableaux furnish efficient aid in rendering the disposition of the cards necessary to each game plain and easily comprehensible. The difficulty usually attending descriptions of intricate games is reduced, as far as possible, by precision in method and terseness of expression in the text. and the illustrations serve to dispel any possible ambiguity that might be unavoidable without their aid. The work is attractive in style and elegant in execution, and will prove an interesting companion for many a solitary hour. Quarto. 143 pages. Board cover . . . . 75 cts.
Cloth . . . . $1 00.

Dick's Parlor Exhibitions, and How to Make them Suc-

cessful. Containing complete and detailed directions for preparing and arranging Parlor Exhibitions and Amateur Performances. It includes :

Tableaux Vivants.	Popular Ballads illustrated by appro-
Living Portraits.	priate action.
Living Statuary.	Charades of all kinds.
Dame History's Peep Show.	Parlor Pantomimes.
Shadow Pantomimes.	Punch and Judy.

AND FIFTY OTHER DIVERTING PARLOR PASTIMES AND AMUSEMENTS.

It contains also a full Catalogue of the celebrated "ART EXHIBITION," and a practical treatise on the wonderful SCIENCE OF SECOND-SIGHT, by the aid of which all the startling effects and achievements of second-sight may be performed by any one possessing a tolerable retentive memory.

This work is thoroughly practical and gives the fullest instructions for preparing and lighting the stage, the construction of the FRAMES FOR LIVING PORTRAITS, and shows how each performance can be presented with complete success. It is illustrated with numerous engravings explaining the text. 150 pages, paper cover . . . . 30 cts
Bound in boards, cloth back . . . . 50 cts

Barber's American Book of Ready-Made Speeches.

Containing 159 original examples of Humorous and Serious Speeches, suitable for every possible occasion where a speech may be called for, together with appropriate replies to each. Including:

Presentation Speeches.	Off-Hand Speeches on a Variety of
Convivial Speeches.	Subjects.
Festival Speeches.	Miscellaneous Speeches.
Addresses of Congratulation.	Toasts and Sentiments for Public and
Addresses of Welcome.	Private Entertainments.
Addresses of Compliment.	Preambles and Resolutions of Con-
Political Speeches.	gratulation, Compliment and Con-
Dinner and Supper Speeches for Clubs.	dolence.
etc.	

With this book any person may prepare himself to make a neat little speech, or reply to one when called upon to do so. They are all short, appropriate and witty, and even ready speakers may profit by them. Paper....**50 cts.**
Bound in boards, cloth back................................. ....**75 cts.**

Day's American Ready-Reckoner. By B. H. Day.

This Ready-Reckoner is composed of Original Tables, which are positively correct, having been revised in the most careful manner. It is a book of 192 pages, and embraces more matter than 500 pages of any other Reckoner. It contains: Tables for Rapid Calculations of Aggregate Values, Wages, Salaries, Board, Interest Money, etc.; Tables of Timber and Plank Measurement; Tables of Board and Log Measurement, and a great variety of Tables and useful calculations which it would be impossible to enumerate in an advertisement of this limited space. All the information in this valuable book is given in a simple manner, and is made so plain, that any person can use it at once without any previous study or loss of time.
Bound in boards, with cloth back....... ....**50 cts.**
Bound in cloth, gilt back............................ ....**75 cts.**

The Art and Etiquette of Making Love. A Manual of Love,

Courtship and Matrimony. It tells

How to cure bashfulness,	How to break off an engagement,
How to commence a courtship,	How to act after an engagement,
How to please a sweetheart or lover,	How to act as bridesmaid or grooms
How to write a love-letter,	man,
How to "pop the question,"	How the etiquette of a wedding and the
How to act before and after a proposal,	after reception should be observed,
How to accept or reject a proposal,	

And, in fact, how to fulfill every duty and meet every contingency con nected with courtship and matrimony. 176 pages. Paper covers ....**30 cts.**
Bound in boards, cloth back......, ...**50 cts.**

Frank Converse's Complete Banjo Instructor Without a

Master. Containing a choice collection of Banjo Solos and Hornpipes, Walk Arounds, Reels and Jigs, Songs and Banjo Stories, progressively arranged and plainly explained, enabling the learner to become a proficient banjoist without the aid of a teacher. The necessary explanations accompany each tune, and are placed under the notes on each page, plainly showing the string required, the finger to be used for stopping it, the manner of striking, and the number of times it must be sounded. The Instructor is illustrated with diagrams and explanatory symbols. 100 pages. Bound in boards, cloth back............................... ....**50 cts.**

Hard Words Made Easy. Rules for Pronunciation and Accent;

with instructions how to pronounce French, Italian, German, Spanish, and other foreign names.................................... ....**12 cts**

Rarey & Knowlson's Complete Horse Tamer and Farrier.

A New and Improved Edition, containing: Mr. Rarey's Whole Secret of Subduing and Breaking Vicious Horses; His Improved Plan of Managing Young Colts, and Breaking them to the Saddle, to Harness and the Sulky. Rules for Selecting a Good Horse, and for Feeding Horses. Also the Complete Farrier or Horse Doctor; being the result of fifty years' extensive practice of the author, John C. Knowlson, during his life an English Farrier of high popularity; containing the latest discoveries in the cure of Spavin. Illustrated with descriptive engravings. Bound in boards, cloth back.**50 cts.**

How to Amuse an Evening Party. A Complete collection of

Home Recreations. Profusely Illustrated with over Two Hundred fine wood-cuts, containing Round Games and Forfeit Games, Parlor Magic and Curious Puzzles, Comic Diversions and Parlor Tricks, Scientific Recreations and Evening Amusements. A young man with this volume may render himself the *beau ideal* of a delightful companion at every party, and win the hearts of all the ladies, by his powers of entertainment. Bound in ornamental paper covers...**30 cts.**
Bound in boards, with cloth back..................................**50 cts.**

Frost's Laws and By-Laws of American Society. A Com-

plete Treatise on Etiquette. Containing plain and Reliable Directions for Deportment in every Situation in Life, by S. A. Frost, author of "Frost's Letter-Writer." etc. This is a book of ready reference on the usages of Society at all times and on all occasions, and also a reliable guide in the details of deportment and polite behavior. Paper covers...................**30 cts.**
Bound in boards, with cloth back..................................**50 cts.**

Frost's Original Letter-Writer. A complete collection of Orig-

inal Letters and Notes, upon every imaginable subject of Every-Day Life, with plain directions about everything connected with writing a letter. By S. A. Frost. To which is added a comprehensive Table of Synonyms, alone worth double the price asked for the book. We assure our readers that it is the best collection of letters ever published in this country; they are written in plain and natural language, and elegant in style without being high-flown. Bound in boards, cloth back, with illuminated sides................**50 cts.**

North's Book of Love-Letters. With directions how to write

and when to use them, and 120 Specimen Letters, suitable for Lovers of any age and condition. and under all circumstances. Interspersed with the author's comments thereon. The whole forming a convenient Hand-book of valuable information and counsel for the use of those who need friendly guidance and advice in matters of Love, Courtship and Marriage. By Ingoldsby North. Bound in boards...... ....**50 cts.**
Bound in cloth...**75 cts.**

How to Shine in Society; or, The Science of Conversation.

Containing the principles, laws and general usages of polite society, including easily applied hints and directions for commencing and sustaining an agreeable conversation, and for choosing topics appropriate to the time, place and company, thus affording immense assistance to the bashful and diffident. 16mo. Paper covers...................................**25 cts.**

The Poet's Companion. A Dictionary of all Allowable Rhymes

in the English Language. This gives the Perfect, the Imperfect and Allowable Rhymes, and will enable you to ascertain to a certainty whether any word can be mated. It is invaluable to any one who desires to court the Muses, and is used by some of the best writers in the country.......**25 cts.**

Mind Your Stops. Punctuation made plain, and Composition

simplified for Readers, Writers and Talkers.....................**12 cts.**

Five Hundred French Phrases. A book giving all the French

words and maxims in general use in writing the English language...**12 cts**

Steele's Exhibition Dialogues.

A Collection of Dramatic Dialogues and easy Plays, excellently adapted for Amateurs in Parlor and Exhibition Performances ; with Hints and instructions relative to management, arrangements and other details necessary to render them successful. By Silas S. Steele.

CONTENTS.

The Stage-Struck Clerk. For 6 *Males and 3 Females.*	*The Hypochondriac.* For 4 *Males and 1 Female.*
The Tailor of Tipperary. For 7 *Males and 4 Females.*	*Two Families in One Room.* For 4 *Males and 2 Females.*
Opera Mad. For 7 *Males and 1 Female.*	*The Country Cousin.* For 4 *Males and 2 Females.*
The Painter's Studio. Portrait Sketch. For 2 *Males.*	*The Carpenter and his Apprentice.* For 8 *Males.*
The Well of Death. For 2 males.	*The Yankee Tar's Return.* For 5 *Males and 1 Female.*
Blanche of Devan. For 3 *Males and 1 Female.*	*The Lawyer, Doctor, Soldier and Actor.* For 3 *Males.*
The Youth Who Never Saw a Woman. For 3 *Males and 1 Female.*	*The Children in the Wood.* For 6 *Males and 4 Females.*
The Masked Ball. For 3 *Males and 2 Females.*	*The Wizard's Warning.* For 2 *Males.*

Paper covers. Price.. **30 cts.**
Bound in boards, cloth back.. **50 cts.**

Kavanaugh's Humorous Dramas for School Exhibitions and Private Theatricals.

Consisting of short and easy Dramatic Pieces, suitable for Amateur Exhibitions. By Mrs. Russell Kavanaugh, author of "The Juvenile Speaker."

CONTENTS.	Boys.	Girls.	CONTENTS.	Boys.	Girls.
Eh! What is it ?..............	3	2	A Fair Fight..............	4	4
That Awful Girl..............	5	5	Between Two Stools..........	2	3
The Lady Killer..............	2	1	The Pet of the School........	8	3
How I Made My Fortune......	6		Maud May's Lovers..........	8	2
A Cure for Obstinancy........	3	9	The Heiress' Ruse..........	4	4
Aunt Jerusha's Mistake......	2	2	The Cardinal's Godson.......	6	1

The foregoing collection of Dramas are all original, and were written expressly for School and Parlor performance.
Bound in boards ....**50 cts.**
Paper covers..**30 cts.**

Dick's One Hundred Amusements for Evening Parties,

Picnics and Social Gatherings. This book is full of Original Novelties. It contains :

New and Attractive Games, clearly illustrated by means of Witty Examples, showing how each may be most successfully played.
Surpassing Tricks, easy of performance.
Musical and other innocent sells.

A variety of new and ingenious puzzles.
Comical illusions, fully described.
These surprising and grotesque illusions are very startling in their effects, and present little or no difficulty in their preparation.

ALSO AN ENTIRELY NEW VERSION OF THE CELEBRATED "MRS. JARLEY'S WAX WORKS."

The whole being illustrated by sixty fine wood engravings.
Illuminated paper covers.. **30 cts.**
Bound in boards, with cloth back.................................... **50 cts.**

Popular Books sent Free of Postage at the Prices annexed.

Madame Le Normand's Fortune Teller.

An entertaining book, said to have been written by Madame Le Normand, the celebrated French Fortune Teller, who was frequently consulted by the Emperor Napoleon. A party of ladies and gentlemen may amuse themselves for hours with this curious book. It tells fortunes by "The Chart of Fate" (a large lithographic chart), and gives 624 answers to questions on every imaginable subject that may happen in the future. It explains a variety of ways for telling fortunes by Cards and Dice; gives a list of 79 curious old superstitions and omens, and 187 weather omens, and winds up with the celebrated Oraculum of Napoleon. We will not endorse this book as infallible; but we assure our readers that it is the source of much mirth whenever introduced at a gathering of ladies and gentlemen. Bound in boards. 40 cts.

The Fireside Magician; or, The Art of Natural Magic

Made Easy. Being a scientific explanation of Legerdemain, Physical Amusement, Recreative Chemistry, Diversion with Cards, and of all the mysteries of Mechanical Magic, with feats as performed by Herr Alexander, Robert Heller, Robert Houdin, "The Wizard of the North," and distinguished conjurors—comprising two hundred and fifty interesting mental and physical recreations, with explanatory engravings. 132 pages, paper. 20 cts. Bound in boards, cloth back..50 cts.

Howard's Book of Conundrums and Riddles.

Containing over 1,200 of the best Conundrums, Riddles, Enigmas, Ingenious Catches and Amusing Sells ever invented. This splendid collection of curious paradoxes will afford the material for a never-ending feast of fun and amusement. Any person, with the assistance of this book, may take the lead in entertaining a company, and keep them in roars of laughter for hours together. Paper covers...... ....30 cts. Bound in boards, cloth back...............................50 cts.

The Parlor Magician; or, One Hundred Tricks for the

Drawing-Room. Containing an extensive and miscellaneous collection of Conjuring and Legerdemain, embracing: Tricks with Dice, Dominoes and Cards; Tricks with Ribbons, Rings and Fruit; Tricks with Coin, Handkerchiefs and Balls, etc. The whole illustrated and clearly explained with 121 engravings. Paper covers............................30 cts. Bound in boards, with cloth back...........................50 cts.

Book of Riddles and 500 Home Amusements.

Containing a curious collection of Riddles, Charades and Enigmas; Rebuses, Anagrams and Transpositions; Conundrums and Amusing Puzzles; Recreations in Arithmetic, and Queer Sleights, and numerous other Entertaining Amusements. Illustrated with 60 engravings. Paper covers............30 cts. Bound in boards, with cloth back...... ....50 cts.

The Book of Fireside Games.

Containing an explanation of a variety of Witty, Rollicking, Entertaining and Innocent Games and Amusing Forfeits, suited to the Family Circle as a Recreation. This book is just the thing for social gatherings, parties and pic-nics. Paper covers. . 30 cts. Bound in boards, cloth back...................................50 cts.

The Book of 500 Curious Puzzles.

Containing a large collection of Curious Puzzles, Entertaining Paradoxes, Perplexing Deceptions in Numbers, Amusing Tricks in Geometry; illustrated with a great variety of Engravings. Paper covers.................................20 cts. Bound in boards, with cloth back...........................50 cts.

Parlor Tricks with Cards.

Containing explanations of all the Tricks and Deceptions with Playing Cards ever invented.. The whole illustrated and made plain and easy with 70 engravings. Paper covers.. 30 cts. Bound in boards, with cloth back...............................50 cts.

Day's Book-Keeping Without a Master.

Containing the Rudiments of Book-keeping in Single and Double Entry, together with the proper Forms and Rules for opening and keeping condensed and general Book Accounts. This work is printed in a beautiful script type, and hence combines the advantages of a handsome style of writing with its very simple and easily understood lessons in Book-keeping. The several pages have explanations at the bottom to assist the learner, in small type. As a pattern for opening book accounts it is especially valuable—particularly for those who are not well posted in the art. DAY'S BOOK-KEEPING is the size of a regular quarto Account Book, and is made to lie flat open for convenience in use...50 cts.

The Young Reporter; or, how to Write Shorthand.

A Complete Phonographic Teacher, intended as a School-book, to afford thorough instructions to those who have not the assistance of an Oral Teacher. By the aid of this work, and the explanatory examples which are given as practical exercises, any person of the most ordinary intelligence may learn to write Shorthand, and report Speeches and Sermons in a short time. Bound in boards. with cloth back..............50 cts.

How to Learn the Sense of 3,000 French Words in one

Hour. This ingenious little book actually accomplishes all that its title claims. It is a fact that there are at least three thousand words in the French language, forming a large proportion of those used in ordinary conversation, which are spelled exactly the same as in English, or become the same by very slight and easily understood changes in their termination. 16mo, illuminated paper covers...................................25 cts.

How to Speak in Public; or, The Art of Extempore Oratory.

A valuable manual for those who desire to become ready off-hand speakers; containing clear directions how to arrange ideas logically and quickly, including illustrations. by the analysis of speeches delivered by some of the greatest orators, exemplifying the importance of correct emphasis, clearness of articulation, and appropriate gesture. Paper covers................25 cts.

Live and Learn.

A guide for all those who wish to speak and write correctly; particularly intended as a Book of Reference for the solution of difficulties connected with Grammar, Composition, Punctuation, &c., &c., containing examples of 1,000 mistakes of daily occurrence in speaking, writing and pronunciation. Paper, 16mo, 216 pages..............30 cts.

The Art of Dressing Well.

By Miss S. A. Frost. This book is designed for ladies and gentlemen who desire to make a favorable impression upon society. Paper covers.....................................30 cts.
Bound in boards, cloth back......................................50 cts.

Thimm's French Self-Taught.

A new system, on the most simple principles. for Universal Self-Tuition, with English pronunciation of every word. By this system the acquirement of the French Language is rendered less laborious and more thorough than by any of the old methods. By Franz Thimm ....25 cts.

Thimm's German Self-Taught.

Uniform with "French Self-Taught," and arranged in accordance with the same principles of thoroughness and simplicity. By Franz Thimm..........................25 cts.

Thimm's Spanish Self-Taught.

A book of self-instruction in the Spanish Language, arranged according to the same method as the "French" and "German," by the same author, and uniform with them in size. By Franz Thimm......................................25 cts.

Thimm's Italian Self-Taught.

Uniform in style and size with the three foregoing books. By Franz Thimm.....................25 cts.

Martine's Sensible Letter-Writer.

Being a comprehensive and complete Guide and Assistant for those who desire to carry on Epistolary Correspondence; containing a large collection of model letters on the simplest matters of life, adapted to all ages and conditions—

EMBRACING,

Business Letters;
Applications for Employment, with Letters of Recommendation and Answers to Advertisements;
Letters between Parents and Children;
Letters of Friendly Counsel and Remonstrance;
Letters soliciting Advice, Assistance and Friendly Favors;

Letters of Courtesy, Friendship and Affection;
Letters of Condolence and Sympathy;
A Choice Collection of Love-Letters, for Every Situation in a Courtship;
Notes of Ceremony, Familiar Invitations, etc., together with Notes of Acceptance and Regret.

The whole containing 300 Sensible Letters and Notes. This is an invaluable book for those persons who have not had sufficient practice to enable them to write letters without great effort. It contains such a variety of letters, that models may be found to suit every subject.
207 pages, bound in boards, cloth back.............................50 cts.
Bound in cloth..75 cts.

Martine's Hand-Book of Etiquette and Guide to True Politeness.

A complete Manual for all those who desire to understand good breeding, the customs of good society, and to avoid incorrect and vulgar habits. Containing clear and comprehensive directions for correct manners, conversation, dress, introductions, rules for good behavior at Dinner Parties and the Table, with hints on carving and wine at table; together with the Etiquette of the Ball and Assembly Room, Evening Parties, and the usages to be observed when visiting or receiving calls; Deportment in the street and when traveling. To which is added the Etiquette of Courtship, Marriage, Domestic Duties and fifty-six rules to be observed in general society. By Arthur Martine. Bound in boards ..50 cts.
Bound in cloth, gilt sides...................................75 cts.

Dick's Quadrille Call-Book and Ball-Room Prompter.

Containing clear directions how to call out the figures of every dance, with the quantity of music necessary for each figure, and simple explanations of all the figures which occur in Plain and Fancy Quadrilles. This book gives plain and comprehensive instructions how to dance all the new and popular dances, fully describing

The Opening March or Polonaise,
Various Plain and Fancy Quadrilles,
Waltz and Glide Quadrilles,
Plain Lancers and Caledonians,
Glide Lancers and Caledonians,
Saratoga Lancers,
The Parisian Varieties,
The Prince Imperial Set,
Social and Basket Quadrilles,
Nine-Pin and Star Quadrilles,
Gavotte and Minuet Quadrilles,

March and Cheat Quadrilles,
Favorite Jigs and Contra-Dances,
Polka and Polka Redowa,
Redowa and Redowa Waltz,
Polka Mazourka and Old Style Waltz,
Modern Plain Waltz and Glide,
Boston Dip and Hop Waltz,
Five-Step Waltz and Schottische,
Varsovienne and Zulma L'Orientale,
Galop and Deux Temps,
Esmeralda, Sicilienne, Danish Dance,

AND OVER ONE HUNDRED FIGURES FOR THE "GERMAN;"

To which is added a Sensible Guide to Etiquette and Proper Deportment in the Ball and Assembly Room, besides seventy pages of dance music for the piano.
Paper covers...50 cts.
Bound in boards..75 cts.

Odell's System of Short-Hand. (Taylor Improved.) By

which the method of taking down sermons, lectures, trials, speeches, etc., may be easily acquired, without the aid of a master. With a supplement containing exercises and other useful information for the use of those who wish to perfect themselves in the art of stenography. The instructions given in this book are on the inductive principle: first showing the learner how to get accustomed to the contracted form of spelling words, and then substituting the stenographic characters for the contractions. By this plan the difficulties of mastering this useful art are very much lessened, and the time required to attain proficiency reduced to the least possible limits. Small quarto, paper cover.........................25 cts.

Alice in Wonderland, and other Fairy Plays for Children.

Consisting of Four Juvenile Dramas, the first of which is a faithful Dramatic Version of Mr. Lewis Carroll's well-known "Alice in Wonderland;" and all combining, in the happiest manner, light comedy, burlesque, and extravaganza. By Kate Freiligrath-Kroeker. These plays are written in a style of quaint, childish simplicity, but embody a brilliant vein of wit and humor. The music of all the songs introduced is given, thus rendering each drama complete in all respects. 143 pages, illuminated paper cover... ....30 cts.
Bound in boards...50 cts.

The American Housewife and Kitchen Directory. This val-

uable book embraces three hundred and seventy-eight recipes for cooking all sorts of American dishes in the most economical manner; it also contains a variety of important secrets for washing, cleaning, scouring and extracting grease, paint, stains and iron-mould from cloth, muslin and linen. Bound in ornamental paper covers.........................30 cts.
Bound in boards, with cloth back..............................50 cts.

The American Card Player. An entirely new edition, con-

taining all the improvements, latest decisions, and modern methods of playing the games of Whist, Euchre, Cribbage, Bézique, Sixty-six, Penuchle, Cassino, Draw Poker, and All Fours, in exact accordance with the best authorities, with all the accepted varieties of these popular games. 150 pages, bound in boards, cloth back..........................50 cts.

Draiper's Six Hundred Ways to Make Money. A reliable

Compendium of valuable Receipts for making articles in constant demand and of ready sale, carefully selected from private sources and the best established authorities. By Edmund S. Draiper, Professor of Analytical Chemistry, etc. This Collection of Receipts is undoubtedly the most valuable and comprehensive that has ever been offered to the public in so cheap a form. 144 pages, paper cover....................20 cts.

The Language of Flowers. A complete dictionary of the

Language of Flowers, and the sentiments which they express. Well arranged and comprehensive in every detail. All unnecessary matter has been omitted. This little volume is destined to fill a want long felt for a reliable book at a price within the reach of all. Paper.............15 cts.

Chilton's One Thousand Secrets and Wrinkles. A book of

hints and helps for every-day emergencies. Containing 1 000 useful hints and receipts. No family should be without this little storehouse of valuable information. Paper covers..............................30 cts.

The Ladies' Love Oracle. A Complete Fortune Teller of

all questions upon Love, Courtship and Matrimony..............30 cts.

Trumps' American Hoyle; or, Gentleman's Handbook of

Games. Containing all the games played in the United States, with rules, descriptions and technicalities, adapted to the American method of playing. By TRUMPS. Thirteenth edition ; illustrated with numerous diagrams. This work is designed and acknowledged as an authority on all games as played in America, being a guide to the correct methods of playing and an arbiter on all disputed points. In each of the previous editions the work was subjected to careful revision and correction; but this, the THIRTEENTH EDITION, IS ENTIRELY NEW, and re-written from the latest reliable sources. It includes an exhaustive treatise on Whist, with all the latest essays on the modern game, by Clay, Pole, Drayson, &c.. &c. Also, a lucid description of all the games now in vogue in America, with the laws that govern them, revised and corrected to conform to present usages, and embraces an elaborate and practical analysis of the Doctrine of Chances. 12mo., cloth, 536 pages. Price....................$2.00

Dick's Games of Patience; or, Solitaire with Cards. Contain-

ing Forty-three Games. Illustrated with Thirty-three explanatory full-page Tableaux. This treatise on Solitaire, a pastime which is steadily gaining in popularity, embraces a number of new and original Games, and all the Games of Patience at present in favor with the most experienced players. Each game is carefully and lucidly described, with the distinctive rules to be observed and hints as to the best means of success in play. The Tableaux furnish efficient aid in rendering the disposition of the cards necessary to each game plain and easily comprehensible. The difficulty usually attending descriptions of intricate games is reduced, as far as possible, by precision in method and terseness of expression in the text, and the illustrations serve to dispel any possible ambiguity that might be unavoidable without their aid. The work is attractive in style and will prove an interesting companion for many a solitary hour. Quarto. Illustrated. Paper cover..75 cts.
Cloth $1.00

Blackbridge's Complete Poker Player. A Practical Guide-

book to the American National Game ; containing mathematical and experimental analyses of the probabilities of Draw Poker. By JOHN BLACKBRIDGE, Actuary. This, as its title implies, is an exhaustive treatise on Draw Poker, giving minute and detailed information on the various chances, expectations, possibilities and probabilities that can occur in all stages of the game, with directions and advice for successful play, deduced from actual practice and experience, and founded on precise mathematical data. Small quarto, 142 pages, paper............................50 cts.
Bound in full cloth.. ....$1.00

The Modern Pocket Hoyle. By "Trumps." Containing all

the games of skill and chance, as played in this country at the present time, being an "authority on all disputed points." This valuable manual is all original, or thoroughly revised from the best and latest authorities, and includes the laws and complete directions for playing one hundred and eleven different games. 388 pages, paper covers..............50 cts.
Bound in boards, with cloth backs.............................75 cts.

Hoyle's Games. A complete Manual of the laws that govern all

games of skill and chance, including Card Games, Chess, Checkers, Dominoes, Backgammon. Dice, Billiards, as played in this country at the present time, and all Field Games. Entirely original, or thoroughly revised from the latest and best American authorities. Paper covers..50 cts.
Boards...75 cts.

CHECKERS AND CHESS.

Spayth's American Draught Player; or, The Theory and Practice of the Scientific Game of Checkers. Simplified and Illustrated with Practical Diagrams. Containing upwards of 1,700 Games and Positions. By Henry Spayth. Sixth edition, with over three hundred Corrections and Improvements. Containing: The Standard Laws of the Game—Full instructions—Draught Board Numbered—Names of the Games, and how formed—The "Theory of the Move and its Changes" practically explained and illustrated with Diagrams—Playing Tables for Draught Clubs—New Systems of numbering the Board—Prefixing signs to the Variations—List of Draught Treatises and Publications chronologically arranged. Bound in cloth, gilt side and back...$3.00

Spayth's Game of Draughts. By Henry Spayth. This book is designed as a supplement to the author's first work, "The American Draught Player"; but it is complete in itself. It contains lucid instructions for beginners, laws of the game, diagrams, the score of 364 games, together with 34 novel, instructive and ingenious "critical positions." Cloth, gilt back and side...$1.50

Spayth's Draughts or Checkers for Beginners. This treatise was written by Henry Spayth, the celebrated player, and is by far the most complete and instructive elementary work on Draughts ever published. It is profusely illustrated with diagrams of ingenious stratagems, curious positions and perplexing problems, and contains a great variety of interesting and instructive Games, progressively arranged and clearly explained with notes, so that the learner may easily comprehend them. With the aid of this Manual a beginner may soon become a proficient in the game. Cloth, gilt side..75 cts.

Scattergood's Game of Draughts, or Checkers, Simplified and Explained. With practical Diagrams and Illustrations, together with a Checker-Board, numbered and printed in red. Containing the Eighteen Standard Games, with over 200 of the best variations, selected from various authors, with some never before published. By D. Scattergood. Bound in cloth, with flexible covers..............................50 cts.

Marache's Manual of Chess. Containing a description of the Board and Pieces, Chess Notation, Technical Terms, with diagrams illustrating them, Laws of the Game, Relative Value of Pieces. Preliminary Games for Beginners, Fifty Openings of Games, giving all the latest discoveries of Modern Masters, with the best games and copious notes, Twenty Endings of Games, showing easiest ways of effecting Checkmate, Thirty-six ingenious Diagram Problems, and sixteen curious Chess Stratagems, being one of the best Books for Beginners ever published. By N. Marache. Bound in boards, cloth back...................................50 cts. Bound in cloth, gilt side..75 cts.

DICK & FITZGERALD, Publishers,

Box 2975.   NEW YORK.

Lola Montez' Arts of Beauty; or, Secrets of a Lady's Toilet.
With hints to Gentlemen on the Art of Fascinating. Lola Montez here explains all the Arts employed by the celebrated beauties and fashionable ladies in Paris and other cities of Europe, for the purpose of preserving their beauty and improving and developing their charms. The recipes are all clearly given, so that any person can understand them, and the work embraces the following subjects:

How to obtain such desirable and indispensable attractions as A Handsome Form; A Bright and Smooth Skin; A Beautiful Complexion; Attractive Eyes, Mouth and Lips; A Beautiful Hand, Foot and Ankle; A Well-trained Voice;

A Soft and Abundant Head of Hair; Also, How to Remedy Gray Hair; And harmless but effectual methods of removing Superfluous Hair and other blemishes, with interesting information on these and kindred matters.

Illuminated paper cover.......................................**25 cts.**

Hillgrove's Ball-Room Guide and Complete Dancing-Master.
Containing a plain treatise on Etiquette and Deportment at Balls and Parties, with valuable hints on Dress and the Toilet, together with

Full Explanations of the Rudiments, Terms, Figures and Steps used in Dancing; Including Clear and Precise Instructions how to dance all kinds of Quadrilles, Waltzes, Polkas, Redowas,

Reels, Round, Plain and Fancy Dances, so that any person may learn them without the aid of a Teacher; To which is added easy directions how to call out the Figures

of every dance, and the amount of music required for each. Illustrated with 176 descriptive engravings. By T. Hillgrove, Professor of Dancing.
Bound in cloth, with gilt side and back............................**$1.00**
Bound in boards, with cloth back..................................**75 cts.**

The Banjo, and How to Play it.
Containing, in addition to the elementary studies, a choice collection of Polkas, Solos, Schottisches. Songs, Hornpipes, Jigs, Reels, etc., with full explanations of both the "Banjo" and "Guitar" styles of execution, and designed to impart a complete knowledge of the art of playing the Banjo practically, without the aid of a teacher. This work is arranged on the progressive system, showing the learner how to play the first few notes of a tune, then the next notes, and so on, a small portion at a time, until he has mastered the entire piece, every detail being as clearly and thoroughly explained as if he had a teacher at his elbow all the time. By Frank B. Converse. author of the "Banjo without a Master." 16mo, bound in boards, cloth back..**50 cts.**

Ned Donnelly's Art of Boxing.
A thorough Manual of Sparring and Self-Defence, illustrated with Forty Engravings, showing the various Blows, Stops and Guards; by Ned Donnelly. Professor of Boxing to the London Athletic Club, etc., etc. This work explains in detail every movement of attack and defence in the clearest language, and in accordance with the most approved and modern methods; the engravings are very distinctly drawn, and show each position and motion as plainly as the personal instruction of a professor could convey it. It teaches all the feints and dodges practised by experienced boxers, and gives advice to those who desire to perfect themselves in the Manly Art. 121 pages.
Price.. **25 cts.**

Athletic Sports for Boys.
Containing clear and complete instructions in Gymnastics. and the manly accomplishments of Skating, Swimming, Rowing, Sailing, Horsemanship, Riding, Driving, Angling, Fencing and Broadsword Illustrated with 194 wood cuts.
Bound in boards...**75 cts.**

Sut Lovingood. Yarns spun by "A Nat'ral Born Durn'd Fool."

Warped and Wove for Public Wear, by George W. Harris. Illustrated with eight fine full page engravings, from designs by Howard. It would be difficult, we think, to cram a larger amount of pungent humor into 300 pages than will be found in this really funny book. The Preface and Dedication are models of sly simplicity, and the 24 Sketches which follow are among the best specimens of broad burlesque to which the genius of the ludicrous, for which the Southwest is so distinguished, has yet given birth. 12mo, tinted paper, cloth, gilt edges..$1.50

Uncle Josh's Trunkful of Fun. Containing a rich collection of

Comical Stories, Cruel Sells,	*New Conundrums, Mirth-Provoking*
Side-Splitting Jokes, Humorous Poet-	*Speeches,*
ry,	*Curious Puzzles, Amusing Card*
Quaint Parodies, Burlesque Ser-	*Tricks, and*
mons,	*Astonishing Feats of Parlor-Magic.*

This book is illustrated with nearly 200 funny engravings, and contains, in 64 large octavo double-column pages, at least three times as much reading matter and real fun as any other book of the price................... 15 cts.

The Strange and Wonderful Adventures of Bachelor

Butterfly. Showing how his passion for Natural History completely eradicated the tender passion implanted in his breast—also detailing his Extraordinary Travels, both by sea and land—his Hair-breadth Escapes from fire and cold—his being come over by a Widow with nine small children—his wonderful Adventures with the Doctor and the Fiddler and other Perils of a most extraordinary nature. The whole illustrated by about 200 engravings...30 cts.

The Laughable Adventures of Messrs. Brown, Jones and

Robinson. Showing where they went, and how they went, what they did. and how they did it. Here is a book which will make you split your sides laughing. It shows the comical adventures of three jolly young greenhorns, who went traveling, and got into all manner of scrapes and funny adventures. Illustrated with nearly 200 thrillingly-comic engravings.....30 cts.

The Mishaps and Adventures of Obadiah Oldbuck. This

humorous and curious book sets forth, with 188 comic drawings, the misfortunes which befell Mr. Oldbuck ; and also his five unsuccessful attempts to commit suicide—his hair-breadth escapes from fire, water and famine—his affection for his poor dog, etc. To look over this book will make you laugh, and you can't help it...... ....30 cts.

Jack Johnson's Jokes for the Jolly. A collection of Funny

Stories, Droll Incidents, Queer Conceits and Apt Repartees. Illustrating the Drolleries of Border Life in the West, Yankee Peculiarities, Dutch Blunders, French Sarcasms. Irish Wit and Humor. etc.. with short Ludicrous Narratives ; making altogether a Medley of Mirthful Morsels for the Melancholy that will drive away the blues, and cause the most misanthropic mortal to laugh. Illustrated paper covers......................25 cts.

Snipsnaps and Snickerings of Simon Snodgrass. A collec-

tion of Droll and Laughable Stories, illustrative of Irish Drolleries and Blarney, Ludicrous Dutch Blunders, Queer Yankee Tricks and Dodges, Backwoods Boasting. Humors of Horse-trading. Negro Comicalities, Perilous Pranks of Fighting Men, Frenchmen's Queer Mistakes. Scotch Shrewdness, and other phases of eccentric character, that go to make up a perfect and complete Medley of Wit and Humor. It is also full of funny engravings..25 cts.

Day's Cards of Courtship. Arranged with such apt conversations, that you will be enabled to ask the momentous question categorically, in such a delicate manner that the young lady will not suspect what you are at. These cards may be used either by two persons, or they will make lots of fun for an evening party of young people. When used in a party, the question is read aloud by the lady receiving it—she shuffles and hands out an answer—and that also must be read aloud by the gentleman receiving it. The fun thus caused is intense. Put up in handsome card cases, on which are printed directions..30 cts.

Day's Love-Letter Cards; or, Love-Making Made Easy. We have just printed a novel Set of Cards which will delight the hearts of young people susceptible of the tender passion. Both letters and answers are either humorous or humorously sentimental—thus creating lots of fun when used at a party of young people—and special pains has been taken with them to avoid that silly, sentimental formality so common in printed letters of this kind. Put up in handsome cases, on which are printed directions...30 cts.

Day's Conversation Cards. A New and Original Set, comprising Eighteen Questions and Twenty-four Answers, so arranged that the whole of the answers are apt replies to each one of the eighteen questions. The plan of these Cards is very simple, and easily understood. Used by a party of young people, they will make a good deal of fun. The set comprises forty-two Cards in the aggregate, which are put up in a handsome case, with printed directions for use.............................30 cts.

Day's Fortune-Telling Cards. We have just printed an original set of Cards for telling fortunes, which are an improvement on any hitherto made. They are so arranged that each answer will respond to every one of the questions which may be put. These cards will also afford a fund of amusement in a party of young people. Each pack is enclosed in a card case, on which are printed directions........................30 cts.

Day's Cards for Popping the Question. An Original Game for Lovers and Sweethearts, or for Merry-Making in a Party of Young People. As soon as these cards become known, we feel sure that they will have an endless sale. Put up in cases, with directions for playing...30 cts.

Day's Leap-Year Cards. To enable any lady to pop the question to the chosen one of her heart. This set of Cards is intended more to make fun among young people than for any practical utility. Put up in handsome cases, with printed directions.........................30 cts.

Chesterfield's Letter-Writer and Complete Book of Etiquette. Containing the Art of Letter-Writing simplified, a guide to friendly. affectionate. polite and business correspondence, and rules for punctuation and spelling, with complete rules of Etiquette and the usages of Society. An excellent hand-book for reference. 16mo, bound in boards.40 cts.

How to Behave; or, The Spirit of Etiquette. A Guide to Polite Society, for Ladies and Gentlemen ; containing rules for good behavior at the dinner table, in the parlor, and in the street; with important hints on introduction, conversation, etc..12 cts.

How to Win and How to Woo. Containing Rules for the Etiquette of Courtship, with directions showing how to win the favor of the Ladies, how to begin and end a Courtship, and how Love-Letters should be written...15 cts.

Allyn's Ritual of Freemasonry. Containing a complete Key

to the following Degrees: Degree of Entered Apprentice; Degree of Fellow Craft; Degree of Master Mason; Degree of Mark Master; Degree of Past Master; Degree of Excellent Master; Degree of Royal Arch; Royal Arch Chapter; Degree of Royal Master; Degree of Select Master; Degree of Super-Excellent Master; Degree of Ark and Dove; Degree of Knights of Constantinople; Degree of Secret Monitor; Degree of Heroine of Jericho; Degree of Knights of Three Kings; Mediterranean Pass; Order of Knights of the Red Cross; Order of Knights Templar and Knights of Malta; Knights of the Christian Mark, and Guards of the Conclave; Knights of the Holy Sepulchre; The Holy and Thrice Illustrious Order of the Cross; Secret Master; Perfect Master; Intimate Secretary; Provost and Judge; Intendant of the Buildings, or Master in Israel; Elected Knights of Nine; Elected Grand Master; Sublime Knights Elected; Grand Master Architect; Knights of the Ninth Arch; Grand Elect; Perfect and Sublime Mason. Illustrated with 38 copper-plate engravings. By Avery Allyn, K. R. C. K. T. K. M., etc. 12mo, cloth............**$5.00**.

Lester's "Look to the East." (Webb Work.) A Ritual of

the First Three Degrees of Masonry. Containing the complete work of the Entered Apprentice, Fellow Craft and Master Mason's Degrees, and their Ceremonies, Lectures, etc. Edited by Ralph P. Lester. This complete and beautiful Pocket Manual of the First Three Degrees of Masonry is printed in clear, legible type and not obscured by any attempts at cypher or other perplexing contractions. It differs entirely from all other Manuals, from the fact that it contains neither the passwords, grips, nor any other purely esoteric matter, with which Masons, and Masons only, are necessarily entirely familiar. It affords, therefore, a thorough guide to the regular "work" in the above degrees, divested of everything that any member of the Fraternity would object to see in print, or hesitate to carry in his pocket. Bound in cloth......................**$2.00**.
Leather tucks (pocket book style), gilt edges....................**$2.50**.

Courtship Made Easy; or, The Art of Making Love Fully

Explained. Containing full directions for Conducting a Courtship with Ladies of every age and position in society, and valuable information for persons who desire to enter the marriage state. Also, forms of Love-letters to be used on certain occasions. 64 pages....................**15 cts.**

How Gamblers Win; or the Secrets of Advantage Play-

ing Exposed. Being a complete and scientific exposé of the manner of playing all the numerous advantages in the various Card Games, as practised by professional gamblers. This work is designed as a warning to self confident card-players. Bound in boards, with cloth back....**50 cts.**

Row's Complete Fractional Ready Reckoner. For buying

and selling any kind of merchandise, giving the fractional parts of a pound, yard, etc., from one-quarter to one thousand, at any price from one-quarter of a cent to five dollars. By Nelson Row. 36mo, 232 pages, Boards...................... ....**50 cts.**

How to Talk and Debate; or, Fluency of Speech Attained

without the Sacrifice of Elegance and Sense. A useful hand-book on Conversation and Debate....................................**12 cts.**

Boxing Made Easy; or, The Complete Manual of Self-

Defense. Clearly Explained and Illustrated in a Series of Easy Lessons, with some Important Hints to Wrestlers...........................**15 cts.**

What Shall We Do To-Night? or, Social Amusements for

Evening Parties. This elegant book affords an almost inexhaustible fund of amusement for evening parties, social gatherings and all festive occasions, ingeniously grouped together so as to furnish complete and ever-varying entertainment for Twenty-six evenings. Its repertoire embraces all the best round and forfeit games, clearly described and rendered perfectly plain by original and amusing examples, interspersed with a great variety of ingenious puzzles, entertaining tricks and innocent sells; new and original Musical and Poetical pastimes, startling illusions and mirth-provoking exhibitions; including complete directions and text for performing Charades, Tableaux, Parlor Pantomimes, the world-renowned Punch and Judy, Galanty Shows and original Shadow-pantomimes; also, full information for the successful performance of Dramatic Dialogues and Parlor Theatricals, with a selection of Original Plays, etc., written expressly for this work. It is embellished with over one hundred descriptive and explanatory engravings, and contains 366 pages, printed on fine toned paper. Extra cloth...$2.00

The Secret Out; or, 1,000 Tricks with Cards, and Other

Recreations. Illustrated with over 300 engravings. A book which explains all the Tricks and Deceptions with Playing Cards ever known, and gives, besides, a great many new ones. The whole being described so carefully, with engravings to illustrate them, that anybody can easily learn how to perform them. This work also contains 240 of the best Tricks of Legerdemain, in addition to the Card Tricks. Such is the unerring process of instruction adopted in this volume, that no reader can fail to succeed in executing every Trick, Experiment, Game, etc., set down, if he will at all devote his attention, in his leisure hours, to the subject; and, as almost every trick with cards known will be found in this collection, it may be considered the only complete work on the subject ever published.
12mo, 400 pages, bound in cloth, gilt side and back.................$1.50

The Magician's Own Book; or, The Whole Art of Con-

juring. A complete hand-book of Parlor Magic, containing over a thousand Optical, Chemical, Mechanical, Magnetic and Magical Experiments, Amusing Transmutations, Astonishing Sleights and Subtleties, Celebrated Card Deceptions, Ingenious Tricks with Numbers, curious and entertaining Puzzles, the Art of Secret Writing, together with all the most noted tricks of modern performers. Illustrated with over 500 wood-cuts, the whole forming a comprehensive guide for amateurs. 12mo, cloth, gilt... ..$1.50

The Sociable; or, One Thousand and One Home Amuse-

ments. Containing Acting Proverbs, Dramatic Charades, Acting Charades or Drawing-room Pantomimes, Musical Burlesques, Tableaux Vivants, Parlor Games, Games of Action, Forfeits, Science in Sport and Parlor Magic, and a choice collection of curious Mental and Mechanical Puzzles etc. Illustrated with numerous engravings and diagrams. The whole being a fund of never-ending entertainment. 376 pages, cloth, gilt......$1.50

Confectioner's Hand Book. Giving plain and practical

directions for making Confectionery. Containing upwards of three hundred Recipes, consisting of directions for making all sorts of Candies, Jellies, Comfits, Preserves, Sugar Boiling, Iced Liquors, Waters, Gum, Paste and Candy Ornaments, Syrups, Marmalades, Essences, Fruit Pastes, Ice Creams, Icings, Meringues, Chocolates, etc., etc. A complete Hand-Book of the Confectioner's Art. Price.................... 25cts.

Howard's Book of Love-Poetry. A Curious and Beautiful

Collection of Tenderly Delicate, Sweetly Pathetic and Amusingly Quizzical Poetical Love-Addresses · containing a large number of the most admired selections from the leading Poets, suitable for quotations in Love Letters, and applicable to all phases and contingencies incident to the tender passion. 141 pages. Price.................... 25cts.

Brisbane's Golden Ready-Reckoner. Calculated in Dollars

and Cents. Showing at once the amount or value of any number of articles or quantity of goods, or any merchandise, either by gallon, quart, pint, ounce, pound, quarter, hundred, yard, foot, inch, bushel, etc., in an easy and plain manner. To which are added Interest Tables, calculated in dollars and cents, for days and for months, at six per cent. and at seven per cent. per annum, alternately; and a great number of other Tables and Rules for calculation never before in print. Bound in boards.35 cts.

How to Cook Potatoes, Apples, Eggs and Fish, Four

Hundred Different Ways. Our lady friends will be surprised when they examine this book, and find the great variety of ways that the same article may be prepared and cooked. The work especially recommends itself to those who are often embarrassed for want of variety in dishes suitable for the breakfast-table, or on occasions where the necessity arises for preparing a meal at short notice. Paper covers..............30 cts. Bound in boards, with cloth back.................................50 cts.

The Science of Self-Defense. Illustrated with explanatory

engravings. This book was written by Ned Price, the celebrated boxer, and is the best work that was ever written upon the subject of Sparring and Wrestling. It contains all the tricks and stratagems resorted to by professional boxers, and the descriptions of the passes, blows and parries are all clearly explained by the aid of numerous diagrams and engravings. That portion of the work which treats on wrestling is particularly thorough, and is well illustrated with engravings. Bound in boards..75 cts.

Richardson's Monitor of Freemasonry. A complete Guide

to the various Ceremonies and Routine in Freemasons' Lodges, Chapters, Encampments, Hierarchies, etc., in all the Degrees, whether Modern, Ancient, Ineffable, Philosophical or Historical. Containing, also, the Lectures, Addresses, Charges, Signs, Tokens, Grips, Passwords, Regalias and Jewels in each Degree. Profusely illustrated with Explanatory Engravings, Plans of the interior of Lodges, etc. 185 pages, paper covers..75 cts. Bound in gilt...$1.25. Bound in leather tucks (pocket-book style).....................$2.00.

How to Cook and How to Carve. Giving plain and easily

understood directions for preparing and cooking, with the greatest economy, every kind of dish, with complete instructions for serving the same. This book is just the thing for a young Housekeeper. It is worth a dozen of expensive French books. Paper covers.......................30 cts. Bound in boards, with cloth back........................50 cts.

The American Home Cook Book. Containing several hun-

dred excellent recipes. The whole based on many years' experience of an American Housewife, Illustrated with engravings. All the recipes in this book are written from actual experience in Cooking. Paper..30 cts. Bound in boards, cloth back....................................50 cts.

The Yankee Cook Book. A new system of Cookery. Con-

taining hundreds of excellent recipes from actual experience in Cooking; also, full explanations in the art of Carving. 126 pages, paper covers.30 cts. Bound in boards, with cloth back................................50 cts.

Morgan's Freemasonry Exposed and Explained. Showing

the Origin, History and Nature of Masonry, and containing a Key to all the Degrees of Freemasonry. Giving a clear and correct view of the manner of conferring the different degrees, as practised in all Lodges..25 cts.

'Popular Books sent Free of Postage at the Prices annexed.

DICK'S
ENCYCLOPEDIA
OF
Practical Receipts and Processes,

PRINTED ON FINE TONED PAPER.

CONTAINING 6,422 PRACTICAL RECEIPTS,

Written in a plain and popular manner, and illustrated with explanatory wood-cuts. Being a comprehensive Book of Reference for the Merchant, Manufacturer, Artisan, Amateur and Housekeeper, embracing valuable information in the Arts, Professions, Trades, Manufactures, including Medicine, Pharmacy and Domestic Economy. It is certainly the most useful book of reference for practical information pertaining to the wants of every-day life ever printed. THE SCIENTIFIC AMERICAN says: " It is worthy of a place in the library of any home, work-shop, factory or laboratory." Prominent among the immense mass of subjects treated of in the book, are the following :

The Art of Dyeing;	*Cements, etc.;*
Hard, Soft and Toilet Soaps;	*Soluble Glass;*
Tanning;	*Waterproofing;*
Distillation;	*Artificial Gems;*
Imitation Liquors;	*Inks and Writing Fluids;*
Wines, Cordials and Bitters;	*Aniline Colors;*
Cider;	*Liquid Colors;*
Brewing;	*Paints and Pigments;*
Perfumery;	*Drying Oils and Dryers;*
Cologne Water and Perfumed Spirits;	*Painting and Paper-hanging;*
Flavoring Essences, etc.;	*Kalsomine and Whitewash;*
Cosmetics;	*Oil and Spirit Varnishes;*
Hair Dyes and Washes;	*Varnishing and Polishing;*
Pomades and Perfumed Oils;	*Lubricators;*
Tooth Powders, etc.;	*Japanning and Lacquering;*
Syrups;	*Boot and Harness Blacking;*
Alcohol and Alcoholmetry;	*Photography;*
Petroleum and Kerosene;	*Metals and Alloys;*
Bleaching and Cleaning;	*Soldering and Welding;*
Scouring and Cleansing;	*Amalgams;*
Vinegar;	*Gilding, Silvering, etc.;*
Sauces, Catsups and Pickles;	*Electrotyping, Electroplating, etc.;*
Receipts for the Garden;	*Medicinal Preparations;*
To Remove Stains, Spots, etc.;	*Patent Medicines;*
The Extermination of Vermin;	*Medical Receipts;*
Pyrotechny and Explosives;	*Weights and Measures.*

607 pages, royal octavo, cloth..$5.00
Sheep.. 6.00

DICK & FITZGERALD, Publishers,
Box 2975.   **NEW YORK.**

Agents Wanted to Canvass for this Work.

Sent Free of Postage on Receipt of Price.

The Biblical Reason Why. A Hand-Book for

Biblical Students, and a guide to family Scripture reading. This work gives REASONS founded upon the Bible, and assigned by the most eminent Divines and Christian Philosophers, for the great and all-absorbing events recorded in the History of the Bible, the Life of our Saviour and the Acts of His Apostles.

EXAMPLE.

Why did the first patriarchs attain such extreme longevity?
Why was the term of life afterwards shortened?
Why are there several manifest variations in names, facts and dates, between the books of Kings and Chronicles?

Why is the book of the Prophecies of Isaiah a strong proof of the authenticity of the whole Bible?
Why did our Saviour receive the name of Jesus?
Why did John the Baptist hesitate to administer the rite of Baptism to Jesus?

This volume answers 1,493 similar questions. Beautifully illustrated. Large 12mo, cloth, gilt side and back...........$1.50

The Reason Why: General Science. A care-

ful collection of reasons for some thousands of things which, though generally known, are imperfectly understood. A book for the million. This work assigns reasons for the thousands of things that daily fall under the eye of the intelligent observer, and of which he seeks a simple and clear explanation.

EXAMPLE.

Why does silver tarnish when exposed to light?
Why do some colors fade, and others darken, when exposed to the sun?
Why is the sky blue?

What develops electricity in the clouds?
Why does dew form round drops upon the leaves of plants?

This volume answers 1,325 similar questions. 356 pages, bound in cloth, gilt, and embellished with a large number of wood-cuts, illustrating the various subjects treated of........$1.50

The Reason Why: Natural History. Giving

reasons for hundreds of interesting facts in connection with Zoology, and throwing a light upon the peculiar habits and instincts of the various orders of the Animal Kingdom.

EXAMPLE.

Why has the lion such a large mane?
Why does the otter, when hunting for fish, swim against the stream?
Why do dogs turn around two or three times before they lie down?
Why have flat fishes their upper sides dark, and their under sides white?

Why do sporting dogs make what is termed "a point"?
Why do birds often roost upon one leg?
Why do frogs keep their mouths closed while breathing?
Why does the wren build several nests, but occupy only one?

This volume answers about 1,500 similar questions.
Illustrated, cloth, gilt side and back...................$1.50

Frost's American Etiquette; or, Laws of Good Society.

A condensed but thorough treatise on Etiquette and its Usages in America. Containing plain and reliable directions for correct deportment in every situation and under all circumstances in life, including special directions and instructions on the following subjects:

Letters of Introduction.	*Etiquette in Church.*
Salutes and Salutations.	*Etiquette for Places of Amusement.*
Calls.	*Servants.*
Conversation.	*H. tel Etiquette.*
Invitations.	*Etiquette at Weddings.*
Dinner Company.	*Baptisms and Funerals.*
Balls.	*Etique te with Children and at the*
Morning and Evening Parties.	*Card Table.*
Visiting.	*Visiting Cards.*
Street Etiquette.	*Letter Writing.*
Riding and Driving	*The Lady's Toilet.*
Traveling.	*The Gentleman's Toilet.*

BESIDES ONE HUNDRED UNCLASSIFIED LAWS APPLICABLE TO ALL OCCASIONS.

Paper covers..30 cts.
Bound in boards, cloth back................................50 cts.

Live and Learn; or, One Thousand Mistakes of Daily

Occurrence in Speaking, Writing and Pronunciation, Corrected and Explained. There are hundreds of persons who are sensible of their deficiencies on many points connected with the Grammar of their own tongue, and who, by self tuition, may correct such deficiencies. For such persons this book has been written.

It Corrects and Explains 1,000 Mistakes of Daily Occurrence in Speaking, Writing and Pronunciation.
It Explains the many Perplexing points that occasion difficulty to the student,
It Explains most of the Latin and French words and phrases of frequent occurrence in newspapers, magazines and Books,
It shows how to punctuate and paragraph correctly.

It shows all the current improprieties of expression and gives rules for their correction.
It gives clear rules for the use of Capitals and Italics.
It gives plain, general rules for spelling.
It gives detailed instructions for writing for the Press in the various departments of newspaper and general literature.

213 pages, paper cover..30 cts.
Bound in boards, cloth back..50 cts.

Confectioner's Hand-Book.

Giving plain and practical directions for making Confectionery. Containing upwards of three hundred Recipes, consisting of directions for making all sorts of Candies, Jellies, Comfits, Preserves, Sugar Boiling, Iced Liquors, Waters, Gum, Paste and Candy Ornaments, Syrups, Marmalades, Essences, Fruit Pastes, Ice Creams, Icings, Meringues, Chocolates, etc., etc. A complete Hand-Book of the Confectioner's Art. Price................................25 cts.

Howard's Book of Love-Poetry.

A Curious and Beautiful Collection of Tenderly Delicate, Sweetly Pathetic, and Amusingly Quizzical Poetical Love-Addresses; containing a large number of the most admired selections from the leading Poets suitable for quotations in Love-Letters, and applicable to all phases and contingencies incident to the tender passion. 141 pages...25 cts.

"Trump's" American Hoyle; or, Gentleman's

Hand-Book of Games. This work contains an exhaustive treatise on Whist, by William Pole, F.R.S., and the rules for playing that game as laid down by the Hon. James Clay. It also contains clear descriptions of all the games played in the United States, with the American rules for playing them; including

Euchre, Bezique, Cribbage. Baccara, All Fours. Loo, Poker, Brag, Piquet, Pedro Sancho, Penuchle. Railroad Euchre. Jack Pots, Ecarté, Boston, | *California Jack, Cassino, Chess Checkers, Backgammon, Billiards, Dominoes, and a hundred other games.*

This work is designed as an American authority in all games of skill and chance, and will settle any disputed point. It has been prepared with great care, and is not a re-hash of English games, but a live American book, expressly prepared for American players. THE AMERICAN HOYLE contains 525 pages, is printed on fine white paper, bound in cloth, with extra gilt side and beveled boards, and is profusely illustrated........$2.00

Spayth's American Draught Player; or, The

Theory and Practice of the Scientific Game of Checkers. Simplified and Illustrated with Practical Diagrams. Containing upwards of 1,700 Games and Positions. By Henry Spayth. Fifth edition, with over two hundred Corrections and Improvements. Containing: The Standard Laws of the Game—Full Instructions—Draught Board Numbered—Names of the Games, and how formed—The "Theory of the Move and its Changes" practically explained and illustrated with Diagrams—Playing Tables for Draught Clubs—New Systems of Numbering the Board—Prefixing Signs to the Variations—List of Draught Treatises and Publications chronologically arranged. Bound in cloth, gilt side and back......................$3.00

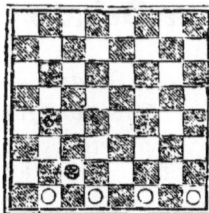

Sut Lovingood. Yarns spun by "A Nat'ral Born Durn'd Fool." Warped and Wove for Public Wear by George W. Harris. Illustrated with eight fine full page engravings

from designs by Howard. It would be difficult, we think, to cram a larger amount of pungent humor into 300 pages than will be found in this really funny book. The Preface and Dedication are models of sly simplicity, and the 24 Sketches which follow are among the best specimens of broad burlesque to which the genius of the ludicrous, for which the Southwest is so distinguished, has yet given birth. Cloth, gilt edges..........$1.50

How to Conduct a Debate. A Series of

Complete Debates,

Outlines of Debates, and

Questions for Discussion.

In the complete debates, the questions for discussion are defined, the debate formally opened, an array of brilliant arguments adduced on either side, and the debate closed according to parliamentary usages. The second part consists of questions for debate, with heads of arguments, for and against, given in a condensed form, for the speakers to enlarge upon to suit their own fancy. In addition to these are

A Large Collection of Debatable Questions.

The authorities to be referred to for information are given at the close of every debate. By Frederic Rowton.

232 pages, paper ....50 cts.
Bound in boards, cloth back.........................75 cts.

The Secret Out; or, 1,000 Tricks with Cards,

and Other Recreations. Illustrated with over 300 engravings. A book which explains all the Tricks and Deceptions with Playing Cards ever known, and gives, besides, a great many new ones. The whole being described so carefully, with engravings to illustrate them, that anybody can easily learn how to perform them. This work also contains 240 of the best Tricks of Legerdemain, in addition to the Card Tricks.

SYNOPSIS OF CONTENTS.

PART I.—*Tricks with Cards performed by skillful Manipulation and Sleight of Hand.*

PART II.—*Tricks performed by the aid of Memory, Mental Calculation and the Peculiar Arrangement of the Cards.*

PART III.—*Tricks with Cards performed by the aid of Confederacy and sheer Audacity.*

PART IV.—*Tricks performed by the aid of Ingenious Apparatus and Prepared Cards.*

PART V.—*Tricks of Legerdemain, Conjuring, Sleight of Hand and other Fancies, commonly called White Magic.*

PART VI.—*Tricks in White Magic, performed by the aid of Ingenious Contrivance and Simple Apparatus.*

PART VII.—*Natural Magic, or Recreations in Science, embracing Curious Amusements in Magnetism, Mechanics, Acoustics, Chemistry, Hydraulics and Optics.*

PART VIII.—*A Curious Collection of Entertaining Experiments, Amusing Puzzles, Queer Sleights, Including the Celebrated Science of Second Sight, Recreations in Arithmetic, and Fireside Games for Family Pastime, and other Astonishing Scientific Paradoxes and Attractive Amusements.*

THE SECRET OUT is, by all odds, the most curious book that has been published in many years, and lays bare the whole machinery of magic, and with a simplicity so perfect that nobody can fail to become a domestic magician in a week, with very little study and practice. Such is the unerring process of instruction adopted in this volume, that no reader can fail to succeed in executing every Trick, Experiment, Game, etc., set down, if he will at all devote his attention, in his leisure hours, to the subject; and, as every trick with cards known will be found in this collection, it may be considered the only complete work on the subject ever published. 400 pages, bound in cloth, gilt..............$1.50

GOOD BOOKS

Sent Free of Postage at the Prices Marked.

Barber's Book of American Ready-Made Speeches..............50 cts.
Dick's Quadrille Call-Book and Ball-Room Prompter..............50 "
The American Hoyle; or, Gentleman's Hand-Book of Games. By
  "Trumps,"..............2 00 "
The Art and Etiquette of Making Love..............50 "
How to Amuse an Evening Party..............30 "
Frost's Etiquette of American Society..............50 "
Frost's Original Letter-Writer..............50 "
North's Book of Love-Letters..............50 "
How to Shine in Society..............25 "
Dick's Recitations and Readings..............30 "
Frost's Humorous Dialogues..............30 "
The Banjo, and How to Play It..............50 "
Day's Bookkeeping without a Master..............50 "
Thimm's French Self-Taught..............25 "
Thimm's German Self-Taught..............25 "
Thimm's Spanish Self-Taught..............25 "
How to Learn the Sense of 3,000 French Words in One Hour...25 "
How to Speak in Public..............25 "
Jack Johnson's Jokes for the Jolly..............25 "
The Tramp and his Tricks..............25 "
The Modern Hoyle's Games..............50 "
How Gamblers Win..............50 "
Kavanaugh's Humorous Dramas for Private Theatricals..........50 "
100 Gamblers' Tricks with Cards..............30 "
Uncle Josh's Trunk-full of Fun..............15 "
Spayth's American Draught-Player..............3 00 "
Marasche's Manual of Chess..............50 "
The Amateur Trapper and Trapmaker's Guide..............50 "
How to Write a Composition..............50 "
The Young Debater and Chairman's Assistant..............50 "
The Young Reporter; or, How to Write Short-Hand..............50 "
"Look to the East," Masonic, (Webb Work)..............2 00 "
The Yankee Cook-Book..............50 "
How to Mix all Kinds of Fancy Drinks..............50 "
Parlor Tricks with Cards, 70 Engravings..............30 "
Book of 500 Puzzles..............30 "
Book of Fireside Games..............30 "
How to Conduct a Debate..............50 "
Howard's Book of 1,000 Conundrums..............30 "
The Parlor Magician, 121 Engravings..............30 "
Lander's Exposure of Odd-Fellowship..............25 "
Fontaine's Dream-Book and Fortune-Teller..............40 "
Day's Ready-Reckoner..............50 "
Book of Riddles, and 500 Amusements..............30 "
How to Make and Keep a Vegetable Garden..............50 "
Boxing Made Easy..............15 "
Brudder Bones' Book of Stump Speeches..............30 "

Send Cash Orders to   **DICK & FITZGERALD,**
P. O. Box 2975.   **Publishers, New York.**

www.ingramcontent.com/pod-product-compliance
Lightning Source LLC
Chambersburg PA
CBHW030840270326
41928CB00007B/1151